Stay with Me, I Want to Be Alone
A Chaplain's Search for Meaning

by
Keith W. Wakefield

PUNCHLINE
PUBLISHERS

First paperback edition October 2025

Cover design by Shuang Yu
Illustrations copyright © 2025 by Shuang Yu
Interior Design: Heather Seeger

Disclaimer: The events, places, and conversations in this book are the recollections of the author that have been recreated from memory and/or supplemented and/or condensed. It is acknowledged that some people may have memories of certain events that differ. Many names and identifying characteristics of both people and places as well as the order of some events have been changed. The hospital that is pictured throughout the present-tense portion of the narrative is an imaginative conglomeration of several different facilities across the United States. The patient visits and other interactions depicted throughout the book are all true, though they happened in various years and places throughout the author's career and all patients' names have been changed. The information provided within this book is for general informational and educational purposes only. The author's opinions, analysis, comments, and criticisms may not be universally applicable to all people in all circumstances. The information presented in this book is in no way intended as a substitute for spiritual, medical, psychological, or other professional counseling. The author makes no representations or warranties, express or implied, about the completeness, accuracy, reliability, suitability, or availability with respect to the information contained in this book for any purpose. The author of this book disclaims lia-bility for any loss or damage suffered by any person as a result of the contents in this book.

No generative artificial intelligence (AI) was used in the writing of this work. The author expressly prohibits any entity from using this publication to train AI technologies to generate text or for ML purposes, includ-ing, without limitation, technologies capable of generating textual or other works in the same style or genre as this publication.

978-1-955051-50-7 (paperback)
978-1-955051-51-4 (eBook)
Library of Congress Control Number: 2025911555

Published in association with Punchline Publishers
www.punchlineagency.com

www.keithwakefield.me

Instagram: @ChaplainKeith

Praise for STAY WITH ME, I WANT TO BE ALONE:

Wakefield has written a deep, textured description of the role of the hospital chaplain that courageously leverages his personal development to vividly portray the psychological and interpersonal aspects of this calling. This impassioned, culturally astute story mosaic made me laugh and cry. The book made me want to become a chaplain!

— Neil Wenger, MD, MPH
Chair, Ronald Reagan UCLA Ethics Committee

Stay with Me, I Want to Be Alone *brings humanity, humor, and reverence to the often misunderstood and complex world of clinical chaplaincy. Wakefield blends memoir with practical insight, offering a resource as valuable for teaching seminary and CPE students as it is engaging for the casual reader. With honesty and vulnerability, he invites us into moments of anxiety, joy, sorrow, and beauty—reminding us that spiritual care begins with shared humanity. Readable, relatable, and rich with wisdom, this book is both a compelling reflection and a practical tool. Chaplain educators will find it especially effective for CPE students and continuing education alike.* — Rev. Gina Harvey, ACPE CE, BCC
Sanford Health

Stay with Me, I Want to Be Alone is a disarmingly honest and captivating account of the work of a hospital chaplain. Written with heart, humour and humility, Keith Wakefield's direct and soul-searching insights into what is most important at the most critical moments of human life is a vindication of the whole work of spiritual care. I laughed, I cried, I cared deeply for all involved. A wonderful book for anyone asking the deeper questions about the value of a spiritual life and of the power of spiritual care.

— Vanessa Able
Founder and Editor of The Dewdrop
Author of Never Mind the Bullocks
Chaplain

Wakefield weaves pedagogy into compelling narratives that not only makes the art of chaplaincy come alive, but also his characters. He brings out both their light and shadow—the pathos, the beauty, the deep vulnerability—with such pain-staking honesty! He writes in such a way that you end up falling in love with them. Wakefield artfully—and with such uncomfortable honesty!—breaks open his own life as the character study of what chaplaincy entails. He doesn't merely explicate the process of being transformed, but takes us into the very heart. It's the kind of brilliant storytelling that takes us on a journey such that we see the various dimensions of his personality, humor, pride and pain that makes the writer so likable, relatable, and trustworthy.

Wakefield addresses the most poignant questions one could ask about chaplaincy—how we enter painful spaces; how we respond to tough questions; how to negotiate theology and personal pain; the ethics around life, and even the technical details that are assumed but never really explained or taught. He takes us into his thoughts as an educator, and imparts the wisdom— the goodies—collected from literature, plays, music, and esteemed intellectuals. It feels like a rich lecture through the medium of storytelling that both delights and instructs.

— Angela Song, BCC
Palliative Care Chaplain
Providence St. Joseph Hospital, Orange

Dedications

To my father, who taught me the quiet strength of presence, and to my mother, whose unwavering love shaped my path. Your sacrifices made this journey possible, even if you never fully saw where it would lead. I carry your lessons with me every day. To my sister, Lisa—who deserved a more patient older brother. Through all the chaos of growing up, you were always there, wanting to connect. I see that now, and I see you.

and

To Shuang, my partner in every sense—whose love, wisdom, and steady presence make all things possible. You radiate beauty and bring a creative spirit that transforms the ordinary into something extraordinary.

and

To TT, you are my greatest adventure. Being your dad is the best journey of all.

After thousands of hours at the bedside and thousands of hours in education with my students, one thing I've come to understand is that of all the contagious things in a hospital—measles and tuberculosis and Covid-19—nothing is easier to catch than anxiety. It spreads faster than you can say, "I'm nervous." And almost always, the most anxious person in the room is the last to be aware of it, even after they've infected everyone around them.

Chapter 1

Sometime before 6:45 a.m., Monday, August 22, 2022

"The man is dead," the nurse says.

She's standing next to me as we peer into the ICU room from the hallway. Next to the patient is a short, slim woman with long brown hair. She's wearing flip-flops and faded blue jeans cuffed high up on her shin, as if she's getting ready to wade into deep water.

"Who's she?" I ask.

"I don't know. She's been here all day."

"Does he have any family?"

"There's a daughter listed in the chart, but I don't think anyone's reached out to her."

"So the daughter might not even know he's dying?"

"Dead," the nurse says. "He's dead."

"Right. Right." We pause in an eternity of awkwardness.

"So. I wonder who that woman is," says the nurse.

"I'll go in and find out." But for a moment longer, I just keep watching. Emergencies happen all day and night in the hospital, but death is never one of them.

And I feel lost. My brain is foggy. What's the procedure again?

The woman in the room is now crying into her hands. I wonder if she's the dead man's significant other, though she looks at least fifteen years younger than him. She might be imagining a shared life suddenly altered: a conversation about what to make for dinner forever unfinished, the deafening quiet of a half-empty house.

I walk in slowly, on tip-toe. I speak to her in a loud whisper. "Hi. I'm Keith, the chaplain here tonight."

The woman turns to me and wipes her cheek. "Oh, hey," she says softly. "I'm Tasha. I don't know where I'm going to sleep tonight."

That's a new one. I draw back and cross my arms. "Wait. Is that why you're crying?"

"Yes. Don't judge me."

"I don't even know you." I recoil even further from her.

A man enters the room. "Frank," the woman says and dodges around me to embrace him.

"Is he...?" Frank stares at the dead man over the woman's head.

"He's gone." The woman's face is pressed into his chest, muffling her voice.

"Oh, Jesus, God, no!" Frank howls. "No, no, no! This cannot be real ... This isn't really happening ... What's happening isn't real ...."

I'm starting to think he's right. Or maybe I just hope he is. Everything about this visit feels off. Why did I talk to Tasha like that? What is wrong with me?

Shit—"off" is not a feeling. What am I feeling?

Frank's face reddens as the two of them squeeze each other more tightly. Tasha's hands travel lower on his back. Then she's murmuring things to him I can't hear. I don't want to hear them.

Unfortunately, one breaks through: "Maybe I could stay at your place tonight ...."

Frank asks, quiet and uneasy now, "Do his kids know he's here?"

Tasha pulls back and stares into his chest, now splotched with her tears. "They're my kids, too."

"No, they ain't. And they hate you. Did you call them?"

"I put in five years with this man. And you know what? Now they're just gonna take what's rightfully mine."

"Tasha, that's just—" Frank notices me. "Who are you?"

I clench a smile. "Chaplain."

"He ain't religious." Frank's tone wavers uncertainly between anger and apology.

I nod. "Well. I'm not here for him. And he's dead," I add unnecessarily.

A woman and a man in their twenties barge in, closely tailed by a young attending physician who was perhaps hoping to head them off.

"What the hell are you doing here, Uncle Frank?" the woman says. Then she sees Tasha. "And you," she snarls, "get out of here, now."

"I have every right to be here. I've been with him for five years. And his stuff is rightfully mine," Tasha says and lifts her pointy chin.

There is a charged moment as her implication zings around the room of the dead man. Then Tasha and the daughter lunge at each other. No fewer than two fistfuls of chestnut and golden hair have been gouged out at the root when a sudden motion in the one part of the room where all should be still makes the daughter scream.

The dead man rises in his bed. He opens his dry lips, but all that comes out is a sickening mechanical vibration. Everyone freezes and stares at him in horror ...

... and I feel a vibration close to my ear. I look through the glass towards the nurse in the hall, but her face is distorting, dissolving ....

I open my eyes. My phone alarm is vibrating near my pillow. It's 6:45 a.m.

For as long as I can remember, I've been a night person. I sigh and close my eyes again. Then I lie in bed for a while, getting down on myself for not having more internal motivation. I've learned to love being up early in the morning. But I still hate *getting* up early in the morning.

The other side of the bed is empty. Typically, my wife Shuang wakes up our son and gets him dressed before I take over with him.

I roll out of bed and stretch. I take a deep breath, realizing I have my on-call shift today. Once I get to the hospital this morning, I'll be there for twenty-four hours.

I make breakfast, grinding coffee beans and heating the water—I enjoy the flavor of a pour-over coffee better than drip. This is an intentionally spiritual time for me. I read something inspiring and thought-provoking while I drink. It's the quiet before the storm of my three-year-old. This morning, it's Dag Hammarskjöld's *Markings*:

> *The more faithfully you listen to the voice within you, the better you will hear what is sounding outside. And only the one who listens can speak.*[1]

I consider the words for a while, thinking about how they might apply to whatever I run into today. One word leads to another. Soon I'm musing about how it was rather clever of my unconscious to offer up the cautionary tale of a nightmare patient visit in the form of an actual nightmare.

*

In May of 2012, I started my first unit of CPE: Clinical Pastoral Education. I had never heard of it before and I had no idea what it was.

Where did I get the nerve to think I could work with people in a hospital? I'd never shown any interest in medicine, sickness, or cures. My first experiences visiting people in the hospital as a child were borderline traumatic.

Ignorance and desperation. That's where my nerve came from. A year after graduating from seminary, I had two degrees in theology and no desire to lead a church. I couldn't remember anyone in seminary ever mentioning CPE (which is not to say no one ever did). But a hospital system in Alabama wanted to hire my first wife to lead a physical therapy department at a brand-new Wellness Center they were building in a suburb of Mobile. They needed me to agree to move there.

"Our new branch needs a chaplain," a hospital administrator told me. "You need to complete a unit of CPE to qualify for the job." He made arrangements for me to join the upcoming CPE unit that ended a few weeks before the new hospital would open.

This administrator wasn't being transparent—or rather, he was stringing sentences together that didn't necessarily follow the rules of cause and effect. Probably he never had any intention of hiring me. In any case, before I even finished the unit, he hired someone else.

But I didn't know that before the unit began, when I started scrambling to learn more about CPE. I found a colleague, Greg, who had done "an intensive unit" the summer before. His responses to my questions about "what it was like" were at best indistinct and at worst alarming.

"Well"—He grimaced and lowered his voice—"I watched a lot of people die."

"You watched a lot of people die?" I was about to find out this was one of the key elements of the whole enterprise. It's a fundamental tool for being with people.

"Yeah."

"Okay, what else? What is CPE?"

"I ... I can't—you know, man, I don't want to talk about it." And he turned and walked away.

I looked behind me, wondering if something had spooked him. The more I asked this question, the more I started to resemble Michael Douglas' character Nicholas in the 1997 movie The Game, in which Nicholas, a successful investment banker, receives a voucher for a mysterious gift billed only as "an entertainment service, but more than that." No one will give Nicholas a clear description of what the game is, even when he overhears two men discussing it and asks them directly:

> BUSINESSMAN 1
> (to Businessman 2,
> knowingly)
> Ahh, what is it?
>
> BUSINESSMAN 2
> The eternal question.
>
> BUSINESSMAN 1
> (to Nicholas)
> I envy you. I wish I could go
> back and do it for the first time
> all over again...

He raises his glass. They toast.

> BUSINESSMAN 1
> Here's to... new experiences.
> (gulps drink)
> If you'll excuse me, I've got to
> be going. 'Night, Jon... Nicholas.
>
> [...]

```
                    BUSINESSMAN 2
          You want to know what it is?   What
          it's all about?
                    (off Nicholas' nod)
          John.   Chapter nine. Verse twen-
          ty-five.


                    NICHOLAS
          I, uh... haven't been to Sunday
          school in years...


                    BUSINESSMAN 2
          "Whereas once I was blind, now I
          can see."
                    (rises)
          Night, Nick.   Best of luck.
```

In the film, Nicholas accepts his gift despite its ambiguity. Soon after, the line between the game and his real life blurs and he descends into a surrealist nightmare.

As my friend Greg walked away, I wondered what the hell I was getting myself into. I read whatever I could find about hospital chaplaincy and did all I could to prepare for the "game" I was signing up for. But I had no clear grasp on the rules. "If they say this, then I say...?"

I was so nervous. "But what if they can't speak at all? Then what do I say?"

*

The Alabama weather didn't help. I grew up in a small town in Northern California. So I'm used to the heat—humidity not so much. Walking the streets of Mobile through a cloud of tropical steam and the heady riot of fragrant orange blossoms, my brain felt as boiled as a lobster in a pot.

On the first day of class, I met the man I mistakenly referred to as my "professor": Dr. Müller. He quickly corrected me: "Call me your educator. This is not a traditional classroom. Well—not in the modern sense, anyway. It's more akin to the classical way of learning before modern traditionalism."

Dr. Müller was a big guy, no more than five and a half feet tall and not quite wider than the table. A quiet Quaker man in his late seventies, he sat sideways at the head of the table with his thick fingers interlaced and resting on his belly, his eyeglasses balanced on the tip of his nose. One look into his eyes made me realize this guy saw through and into me in ways no one had before. Dr. Müller was made up of equal parts wisdom, depth, and cynicism. A deep exhaustion showed in his every movement, countered only by a drive to keep going until he was physically unable.

I was one of five students. Dr. Müller explained to us—sort of—what the unit of CPE would look like. "It's eleven weeks, from today to mid-August. By the time you know where the elevators and bathrooms are, the unit will be done."

I mustered a smile, but I still lacked context.

"Each of you will present ten verbatims. That's one per week. We'll have didactics and theological reflections. You'll each present once for the interfaith chapel service. Now, I don't mean to alarm you—or inspire you, for that matter—but by the end of this unit, your theology will probably change."

We all stared back at him. My reaction was half repulsion, half curiosity. I had had seven years of training to develop my theological understanding, or at least to thoroughly absorb my professors' theological understanding. How could all that change in such a short time?

"Okay," Dr. Müller announced, "go find your units, introduce yourself to people, and start visiting patients." Just as we were all about to rise, he raised a hand to stop us. "Oh, and one more thing."

In the room was an easel with a flimsy whiteboard balanced on it. In a dusty box, Dr. Müller found a black dry-erase pen. With a shaking hand, he drew a hash mark on the left side of the board and another on the right. He connected them with a line and labeled them:

Birth *Death*

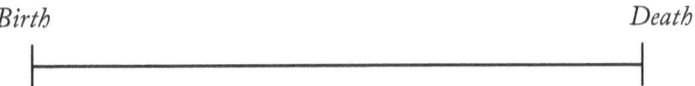

He dropped the pen back in the box and rummaged around some more. I shifted uneasily in my seat, feeling my shoulders tense. The sum of a human being's life from birth to death was laid out before me in three stark lines.

"Ah, there you are," Dr. Müller said to the red pen and uncapped it. He added one hash mark to the line:

Birth *Death*

"That red mark is 'the most traumatic moment of a person's life.' Chances are, you'll be there for it." Dr. Müller dropped the pen in the box and shuffled back towards his seat. But I wasn't watching him anymore; my eyes were fixed on the red mark.

"Okay," he said from behind me, "now you can go find your units."

I walked onto the neurological unit in a daze. The hospital still felt like an alien environment. But now I was part of it, one of the mechanisms that helped it function. I tried to familiarize myself with the place by introducing myself to the charge nurse (the nurse who manages the nursing operations of a given unit for a particular shift).

I had no idea how to gauge or assess who would and would not benefit from a visit; so maybe I could outsource that work.

"Is there anyone I should see?" I asked her, trying not to let my voice shake.

The charge nurse smiled and told me there was one woman who would be very sweet and would welcome a visit from me. As I forced myself to walk to her room, I really hoped she would say, "I don't want a visit right now," so I could run and hide somewhere.

I was sweating. I was wearing a suit and a tie, which I hated. The clothes were not only hot and uncomfortable but felt too formal for a hospital, given that patients wear hardly anything. At the time, this hospital was being taken over by a new system. The old system had a shoddy reputation and part of the plan for crafting a new image was sprucing up the attire of any personnel whose job didn't require scrubs. It only increased my disorientation.

I opened the door, then knocked on it. At the foot of the bed was a woman in her eighties, frail, her hands shaking. Bright red hair curled out from under the band of her neurological cap. No matter how many times you see it, this headpiece looks bizarre—both medieval and sci-fi. Made out of a material resembling cheesecloth, it's shaped like the close-fitting bonnets you see in 16th-century woodcuts, but fastened to the patient's head with little suction cups and plugged into a machine by a dozen or so wires.

The patient was eating lunch and my knock came in mid-bite. At the sound, she turned her head and half of her green peas fell off her spork. She smiled anyway.

I didn't know how to introduce myself. I said, "Hello. I'm Keith. A chaplain. I'm going room to room to see how patients are doing."

I couldn't have come up with anything more impersonal. She was just one of the patients in one of the rooms.

As she nodded, she lost the remaining peas on her spork. But she didn't seem to notice. She took a bite and I watched her chew on air for a few excruciating moments. Then she said, her voice crackling, "Oh … I've never met a female preacher before."

In seminary, my professors had taught me the theology and ethics of many complex ideas and situations, from the role of a pastor in a church to the concept of grace to the process of transubstantiation. But I couldn't draw up any lesson that helped guide me on the best way to handle the awkwardness and confusion of being misgendered by a geriatric neurological patient wearing a thin hospital gown while I was standing in front of her dressed like an insurance salesman.

I smiled and nodded, then backpedaled out of the room. I made it as far as the nursing desk, where the charge nurse watched me take a deep breath. "Did you see her?" she asked. "She ask you to read the commandments to her?"

"No, not exactly." I was still breathing heavily.

"Well, what did you do in there?" My discomfort under her gaze wasn't exactly subtle. I wondered if I would always be so closely monitored in the hospital.

"She called me a 'female preacher' and I didn't know what to say," I told her.

The charge nurse laughed. "Oh, isn't she sweet!"

Then her tone changed abruptly. "Go back in there," she said.

Without pausing to think, I turned around and walked back to the door. I opened it and knocked, stepped inside, saw the patient—still seated, still trembling, still eating peas.

"Hello. I'm Keith. A chaplain. I'm going room to room to see how patients are doing."

She had such a gentle smile. "It's nice to meet you, Keith," she said. "Please come in."

*

I'm not sure my theology changed, exactly, during my first unit of CPE, as Dr. Müller predicted. But it became embodied through the lives and deaths of others. Illness, disease, suffering, aging, the last moments before life fades away: I don't think anyone who looks these full in the face every day can help but search for meaning.

*

When I was in the third grade, I had a humiliating experience that ruined my enjoyment of school and learning for a long time.

At that age, I was smaller than most of the other kids, which made me an easy mark on the tetherball court. I also had a gap between my teeth big enough to plug with a popsicle stick and skin so pale my classmates liked to pretend to be blinded when I wore shorts. I was still laughing off teasing like that, but internally starting to feel ashamed. I'd always been excited about learning and worked hard on my homework, but my self-assurance there was about to crack too. Things at home were changing. This affected my attitude about almost everything.

Until that year, I was a straight-A student. Then one cold autumn day in the mid-1980s, my teacher asked us to take turns reading aloud from a science textbook. Usually, I would wait for my teacher to call on someone, then count the number of kids between them and me and match that number up to the corresponding paragraphs. This way, I could silently practice the paragraph I was likely to read before it was my turn to voice it out loud. I suspect I wasn't the only kid doing this.

Unfortunately, the teacher called on the student in front of me to read only a short sentence. Before I could even locate my paragraph, it was my turn.

Still, I started out with considerable bravado. At this point, I was confident in my academic prowess. Then I came to this sentence:

22

The process by which green plants and certain other organisms trans-form light into chemical energy is called photosynthesis (fōdō'sin-THəsəs).

I pronounced *photosynthesis* splendidly. The second word—hyphen-ated, odd-looking, filled with inexplicable parentheses—was not any English word I recognized. I paused. I tried to understand. I could not make sense of it. Why was "TH" capitalized? Why were the "e"s up-side-down?

I panicked. What was I going to do? At least thirty seconds had passed. Everyone was waiting for me.

Say something! I thought. *What's wrong with you? Maybe you're not as smart as you think you are....*

To make things worse, my teacher said, "Uh, Keith?"

"Yeah?" I mumbled, not looking up.

"The next word is 'the,'" he said.

The class started laughing. (Whether they really did laugh or not is immaterial. I *remember* they laughed).

I stopped trying. "Mr. B?" I whispered.

"Yes?"

"I don't want to read anymore." And he didn't make me.

The girl sitting behind me picked up at the spot in the text where I had stalled. The message I took away that day was transformative: my classmates are smart; I am dumb.

The disorientation was too great and I didn't seek anyone's help to walk me through it. Instead, for a long time, I simply worked hard to avoid any situation that might put me at risk of feeling that type of shame again.

Classrooms are dangerous, I told myself every time I walked into one. I didn't earn another "A" until my second year in university.

So when, in the second week of my CPE unit, my peers started calling me "Professor"—I had told them I'd taught a few college classes the year before I came to Alabama—I hated them for it. I was already feeling anxious and out of my element. The nickname made me feel like even more of an incompetent imposter. I was scared: scared to visit patients, scared to be in the hospital, scared my voice would fail and I'd be found out.

But it was in CPE that I began to connect my outsized resentment about a nickname to my childhood experience and to articulate that connection.

In the second week of the unit, I presented my visit with the red-haired woman as my first verbatim. This is a term used in CPE to refer to a clinical report of a visit. It includes facts about the patient and an assessment of their future needs. There's also a description, with as much detail as possible, of everything that happens between the chaplain and the patient, including not only words, but gestures and expressions: a blow-by-blow account of the inevitable rises and falls, the push and pull, the moments when a connection burns and when it fades. It's a kind of emotional topography of how the relationship changes from the first knock to the exit out the door.

I was the first one to present a verbatim and I wasn't sure how these sessions were supposed to go. I distributed a paper copy to each of my peers and my educator, as I was instructed to do. Then I waited for further instructions. Dr. Müller took the copy, put his glasses on his nose, swiveled his chair to face the wall, and reclined in it.

After a moment, he looked over his shoulder down the table. "You gonna read it?" he said.

"Out loud?" I asked.

He blinked a few times before turning back to the paper in his hands. "Well, it's your time."

I began reading. The familiar fear of being misunderstood rose, causing a pounding in my chest. I felt my blood pulsing in my fingers. I rocked back and forth in my chair a little and the words on the paper slid in and out of focus.

I filled the time with humor to make it pass more quickly, laughing at the patient calling me a female preacher. I felt very vulnerable.

We read aloud every word I wrote. In seminary, I'm pretty sure not even my professors read every research paper I turned in. Here, each word was not only said aloud, but deeply engaged: questioned and scrutinized.

Dr. Müller said very little. This made me even more afraid. I respected his wisdom and insights and I still didn't know him well. About fifty minutes into the fifty-five-minute session, he finally spoke.

"You're aware you use humor to protect yourself and to keep others from getting too close to you," he said.

"I—I'm not sure. I don't think so," I stammered.

"That wasn't a question," he said. "Just an observation you'd do well to explore."

He looked at his watch, sighed gustily, and said, "Well, I'm aware of time. See you all tomorrow." He rocked back in his chair, and using this momentum, shot forward and up onto his feet. Then he lumbered out the door.

None of us spoke for at least a minute. Dylan, my extroverted, Anglican, cigar-smoking peer who wanted CPE to be like the film *Fight Club*—mostly because the main rule of fight club is you never talk about fight club—broke the silence: "Wow, thanks for going first. Sure as heck am glad I didn't."

I looked at him. There was a huge smile in the center of his yellowing salt-and-pepper goatee. "Well, should we all go to lunch together?" he asked, standing and looking at the rest of us expectantly. My other four peers looked eagerly back. I was the only introvert in the group and my process for recharging after mind-bending sessions like this one almost always looked different from theirs.

"Sorry. I need some time to rest my brain," I said.

"Oh," Dylan said. "I thought that's what we've been doing all morning?"

*

Before the third grade, I loved school. Learning came easily to me and doing my homework was exciting. I would sit at the dining table my dad had made doing math problems, already looking forward to checking the answers to see how many I'd gotten right.

One afternoon in second grade, I was working on division problems and got stuck on one. I asked my mom for help. She came to look at it, frowning.

"Well," she said after a minute, "I think the answer should be four."

I looked at the problem more closely. Then I thought about it. "No, Mom," I said. "It should be three."

"No, I don't think so …." My mom tugged on a strand of her straight brown hair and nervously tucked it behind her ear.

When we checked in the back of the book, we saw that Mom was wrong and I was right. I was so thrilled I probably crowed with excitement. I have no doubt my mom, already insecure, self-conscious about everything from her plumpness—she was always ashamed that when I gave her a hug, I couldn't wrap my arms all the way around her waist—to the fact that her brother graduated from Berkeley before going on to law school while she never went to college, turned red and slumped a little in her chair.

If she did, I don't remember it. I was too busy gloating over my brilliance to notice.

It hurts me to think about that now; my mom had a rough childhood. I suspect she never received the interventions she needed to heal from some of the negative experiences she lived through.

But I also can't judge myself by adult standards. I was only a child. I was trying to grow and develop, trying to define who I was. Part of that process included seeing how I stacked up against others, and my ability to see how my triumphs might affect other people wasn't fully developed.

"You're so much smarter than I am," my mom told me. "I can't help you anymore."

At the time, I felt that at the tender age of seven, I had already licked school. I already knew as much as my mom, and she was doing all right in life.

But I also felt a flicker of worry. Who was going to help me now? After that day, I had to beg my mom to even look at my homework. It was already nearly impossible to get my dad—who was good at math—to answer my questions. He worked long hours every day and came home exhausted and needing to rest.

A class project that required some sort of building or assembly energized him, however. In those cases, he was often eager to help. He was so good at building things, and creative and skilled enough that he never wanted to follow the instructions. "No. I don't need those," he said, when I tried to show him the directions for the "Kite Kit" I brought home from school. Out in his shop, we cut pieces on the jigsaw, sanded and painted. It was great working with my dad and I can see now he was teaching me to think creatively, to see that to do great things, you sometimes have to break the rules and stand out.

I was proud of the spectacular results—until I showed my kite to my friends and they laughed. Their kites all looked the same and mine was different. It's hard to be proud of that as a little kid. I just felt outside the circle. *The tallest blade of grass is the first to be mowed down.* When we went outside as a class to fly our kites, I left mine in my desk.

After the math homework episode with my mom, I was full of pride—I felt now that I was different than my parents—but at the same time, I also felt isolated.

Then, the next year, the "*fŏdō 'sinTHəsəs*" episode happened and things got even worse. I was too ashamed to tell my parents what had happened, so they didn't have a clue what I was going through. I don't know how they could have helped me, but I know they would have tried. They loved me. I knew that and I never questioned it. But we were a family that didn't tell one another what we needed. We didn't work on finding the language to articulate those needs. I learned to hold it all in—then to blame myself and others when things didn't turn out the way I wanted.

My vertigo only intensified the following year when a seismic shift happened in our household. My parents took over the family business, a glass shop, from my father's parents. Before this, I had always counted on my mom being home to take care of and support me, educationally and otherwise. Every day, she brought me to school. Then she picked me up at the end of the day.

Now, she started working at the shop full-time. My sister Lisa and I—she was four years younger than me—were sent to daycare. I walked there every day after school through an alley and across a street and stayed there until my mom could pick us up after work. My days looked alien and strange. The change in my life happened so quickly I felt as if my head were spinning.

My parents' days must have been long and frantic as they figured out how to run a business by themselves while raising two small children. Often, my mom was late picking us up. When the clock started to tick close to the time the daycare closed, 5:30 p.m., I would start getting nervous, wondering if she would remember to come get us.

A few times we languished there until 7:30 p.m. We'd be sitting at the table eating dinner with our babysitters when she arrived. They'd tell us to stay put and finish eating while they went outside to yell at my mom.

Two years later, things changed again. I was switched to a school closer to home so no one had to deliver me to school or pick me up. I rode my bike, a steel-framed, royal-blue one-speed, three miles each way over back roads and through almond orchards. It was a dusty, windy route, a bit dangerous where Twin Creek Lane ran close to a creek, with cars whipping too fast around the blind corners. I was supposed to cut through a subdivision to limit the time I was on Twin Creek, but I often didn't. The danger and disobedience were fun. Who was going to stop me? Like many other kids of my generation, I was now officially a latchkey kid.

*

My parents never felt completely sure of themselves as business owners. After taking over the glass shop, this insecurity came out in complaints and belittling stories they told about the people they worked with. Everyone was a joke. No one could do anything right. As a child, I took my parents at their word. Around the dinner table in the evening, my sister and I became accustomed to asking for these mean-spirited stories about all the supposed buffoons who made my parents' lives so difficult.

Part of me must have known it was an act, overcompensation, an indication of vulnerability and fear; I absorbed their insecurity. I began to feel like an imposter myself, someone who only pretended to know what he was doing and at any moment would be uncovered as a fraud.

Later, I found out the women my mom hired to help with the administrative and accounting work gave her a fake account book to use because she made so many mistakes. They let her think she was doing the real accounts to protect her feelings, but in reality they were doing them in another book. My mom has always been a dreamer: creative and artistic, rather than a numbers person. She was out of her element there.

*

Even today, at moments when I feel insecure or inadequate, I whisper to myself before I walk into a CPE classroom to teach, "I'm not in third grade anymore."

I wish I could reach back in time and hold my third-grade self through that terrible moment. I'd tell him that it would be okay, that he wasn't doomed to failure.

But I'd also tell him that, eventually, he'd learn to lean into the pain. He'd confront it in pursuit of meaning and purpose, realizing that in avoiding it, he was sabotaging his own happiness. He'd come to see that his wounds were portals to vulnerability, through which the suffering of others would touch him and awaken him to a deeper connection with humanity.

Chapter 2

7:25 a.m., Monday, August 22, 2022

I hear my three-year-old before I see him. He rounds the corner of the kitchen already full of morning chatter, a Hot Wheels car in each hand and a winning smile on his face.

He looks like both Shuang and me, with my light-colored wavy hair and Shuang's dark brown eyes. There is one blue stripe in his left eye we call a birthmark. Everyone in my immediate family has blue eyes.

I give him breakfast and we talk about the vital issues of the day: *Paw Patrol*, the importance of not saying "poop" at the end of each sentence, why it's a problem when he opens the umbrella in my face.

At some point amidst the chaos, I get dressed. These days, I forgo the suit and tie for business casual: the type of comfortable dress slacks that are basically jeans but khaki-colored, a long-sleeve button-up. I've started to prefer black shirts to offset the reality of middle-age weight gain and in the summer, I wear short socks if my pants are long enough that I can get away with it.

Many of my colleagues dress similarly, though there's variety, too. Chaplains are encouraged to wear the traditional attire of their religious affiliation. Most Catholic priests wear a clerical collar, though some will experiment with taking it off to see if it makes a difference in how they are received by patients and hospital staff. Lutherans and other Protestants often wear a collar as well, even those whose traditions don't strictly authorize them to do so. There's an immediate level of respect the collar commands that's helpful for the insecure. I've tried wearing one myself. Though I wasn't entirely comfortable with the unearned respect—I'm a Seventh-day Adventist and we don't do collars—I did like the way it made me immediately recognizable as a chaplain.

Jewish people wear Yamakas, and my friend and colleague Yun, a Buddhist monk, wears a traditional robe that comes in different colors appropriate for various settings and occasions.

When my son's backpack and the small suitcase I take when I'm on call are packed, I send him back to Shuang, who brushes his teeth. Then we all meet at the door for a few moments before Shuang heads to her study. She's a landscape architect and works at home.

While we all say our hurried goodbyes, I gather my son's things and get his shoes on. "Bye-bye, Mama-poop," he says to Shuang.

"Buddy, don't keep saying that," I say.

'Sorry, Bàba-poop."

I could give this correction more teeth if his laugh afterward weren't so charming. It's the kind that goes silent near the end until he draws another breath. Then the cackle starts all over again.

I get him loaded in and buckled up. I have found tremendous joy introducing my son to the songs I used to sing when I was in my car seat. It's even better when he requests one.

"Bàba, I want 'Love Will Turn You Around.'"

And together we sing.

I first watched *Six Pack*, the film that features this song, at a young age. Kenny Rogers' character, race-car driver Brewster Baker, finds his heart opening to the six orphan children he inadvertently gets saddled with after they steal parts off his car. As a teenager, I had a very different experience watching the film, this time with a fixation on Diane Lane.

In the car with my son, I'm also thinking about my dad. I remember us listening to eight-tracks in his 1970s Dodge crew-cab pickup. It was two-tone, gold and white. I was old enough to bounce on the seat but too little to see over the dash. My dad sat behind the wheel in steel-toed boots; jeans always dusted with aluminum shavings, sawdust, silicone, or urethane; and a dark blue button-up work shirt with the name and logo of the family shop (Wakefield and Sons Glass, the "W" superimposed on a sun) above the pocket. A bigger version of the logo was stitched on the back.

I was looking up at a sliver of clear blue sky out of the top of the windshield the first time I ever cried in response to a piece of music. It was "I'll Be True to You" by The Oak Ridge Boys. In the song, a woman promises a man she'll be true to him when he leaves town. She's true, but he isn't. When he runs into her later, she's in a downward spiral. He walks away again even as she cries out to him to stay. Soon after, she drinks herself into oblivion, and dies alone in the early morning hours. He kneels by her grave, overwhelmed with regret. His tears fall as he whispers a promise to be true to her, understanding the weight of the pain he caused.

"What does that mean?" I asked my dad, tears streaming down my face, even as I couldn't put into words what I was feeling or why.

"Well," he said, "he found out too late he loved her."

*

This is a good time to confess: I am a chaplain because of Guns N' Roses.

When I was very little, I was exposed only to the music my parents listened to: Eddie Rabbit, Johnny Cash, Don Williams. Then, in the late 1980s and early 1990s, I started to hear something else. My friend and neighbor Chris listened to Sacramento radio station K-100 ("K-K-K-K-K 100!"), which played Huey Lewis and the News' "The Heart of Rock and Roll." Chris also loaned me his prized Huey Lewis tape. At the County Fair, my friends and I got our heads spun on the Zipper and the Kamikaze to the tune of "Pour Some Sugar on Me" or "Thunderstruck," because that's what the carnies were listening to. And starting in fifth grade, I was at home unsupervised for a few hours after school every day. MTV and the VCR became my babysitters.

This was music, too, I realized. It wasn't any "deeper" than The Oak Ridge Boys or Johnny Cash; but it was different.

Chris furthered my musical education when he gave me Bon Jovi's self-titled debut album for my birthday; my favorite song was "Runaway." I loved Bon Jovi, enough that at another friend's birthday party, while the other kids dove and dunked one another in the pool outside, I was kneeling in front of the stereo listening to *New Jersey*.

One of the kids came inside. "Aren't you going to come out and play?"

I stared at him, flabbergasted at the idea. "No," I said. "Why don't you guys come in and listen to this? It's awesome."

But the band that really broke me open was Guns N' Roses. In 1991, the record store in town held its first midnight opening to release the *Use Your Illusion* albums. This only added to my feeling that something monumental was happening.

I quickly became obsessed. It was the music, but more than anything, it was the words. What Axl did with lyrics blew my mind. While

I couldn't articulate it at the time, there was a philosophy here about the way people relate to one another, about the effort and energy required for true compassion.

The music took on significant meaning for me. I wanted to immerse myself in it, absorb it. I wanted to be wrapped in the experience of the music and learn from it how to live.

I set about memorizing the songs. Before I went to bed, I pressed "Play" and "Repeat One"; every night I listened to a different song from either *Use Your Illusion I* or *II*, over and over, the small desk speakers for my stereo resting on the pillow on either side of my head. I started to love mowing the lawn. I could plug my headphones into my yellow Sport Walkman and just be in my head with the music. The headphones inserted directly into my ears and hurt like hell, but I didn't care. I could never get it loud enough. That's likely why I have hearing problems now.

I have to learn all the words so I can sing it, I told myself. *If I sing it, I can understand it.*

By the end of a year of tenth-grade Spanish, I could say only "Qué? Oh, no sé." But I had written, by memory, every lyric to ever song on *Use Your Illusion I* in the back of my Spanish book, proudly culminating with the colossal "Coma" (which, incidentally, includes voiceovers contributed by doctors at one of the hospitals where I've worked).

Only later did I start to realize how much Guns N' Roses influenced my overall philosophy and outlook on life. In Axl I found a person who strove not only to express himself, but to truly know every part of himself as deeply as he could. Watching an interview with him in the backyard of his house in Malibu, I decided that while Guns N' Roses might indeed be "the most dangerous band in the world," they were also one of the most authentic.

"I have at least three voices," Axl said, "but they're all mine."

I was also drawn to Axl's bluntness and the way he didn't seem to care what anyone thought of him. Being immersed in my parents' insecurity and my mother's anxiety had left me in a kind of cloud. The brightest parts of the world were partly obscured, just out of reach. But Axl's clarity cut through, and in songs like "Don't Damn Me" and "Get in the Ring" I heard his invitation to speak my truth, even if it rattles people.

On one spot of my closet-door mirror, a piece of reflective backing had chipped off right at the height of my mouth. That spot became my microphone as I sang song after Guns N' Roses song. I would press my nose into the glass and stare directly into my eyes, wondering, "Is this who you really are?" Even as I fantasized about singing to millions the way Axl did, I knew deep down I never wanted to do that. I was too scared to be so vulnerable. Also, I knew I wasn't very good at music.

If I missed a lyric—or even a word—I'd start the song over so I could get it right. I wasn't searching for academic or even artistic perfection. It was unapologetic authenticity I was after, and I didn't tolerate mistakes.

*

I can't give Guns N' Roses all the credit for making me into the person I am today. There is also Jim Coons.

I was baptized and confirmed in the Catholic Church. But I wasn't exactly what you'd call a devotee. I never liked it, I never understood why I was going, and I was annoyed by my Sunday School teacher, who told me she was "grading [my] beliefs" with her big red pen.

"You don't believe that," she told me one day, when I voiced something I did, in fact, believe in.

I said, "I *do* believe that."

"You *don't* believe that, because the Church says it's wrong."

"Well, then, the Church is wrong," I said.

After that, a huge battle erupted in our home every week. My mom had to force me to go to church. She was mostly trying to please her father, my Grandpa Joe, who was Catholic. He told her she needed to raise Lisa and me "so they believe in something."

Grandpa Joe was domineering and often full of an inexplicable rage. My mom was afraid of him. So when I was about ten, she bribed me with a present to get baptized. After the ceremony, in which I was baptized with a boy named Brian, I found out the gift was a Bible and didn't even have any pictures in it.

"This is stupid," I said. "I don't want it."

Then, in the summer between seventh and eighth grade, I heard about a lock-in at the Presbyterian Church. Girls and boys would be allowed to spend the whole night in the church together. I thought with an event like this, church couldn't be all bad. And the girl I had a crush on, Andrea, was going to be there.

When I arrived, I witnessed something wonderful that made me fairly certain my feelings were reciprocated. Andrea caught sight of me as I walked down into the basement. Our eyes met. Flustered, she backed up into a card table with a big cake on it. The cake fell on her and she had to be taken home for a shower to get the frosting out of her hair.

I didn't sleep at all that night and at three or four in the morning, I walked to the 7-11 with one of the church's youth leaders, Jim Coons.

Only about ten years older than I was, Jim had long brown hair that fell to the middle of his back. He wore shorts and the same surfer-brand t-shirts we were all wearing at school, with white socks and Vans. He had a casual, easy way with kids and made us feel welcome in the church.

From that night on, Jim took an active interest in me. He was a stable adult in my life. I felt he genuinely liked me, which was something I didn't feel at home. There, I felt I was only tolerated.

I often complained to Jim, "My parents don't care about me at all." I described the way my mom was fully invested in my sister's cheerleading and had no time for me. I pointed out that though both my dad and Jim came to my soccer games, Dad was passive and remote. He rarely said, "Hey, good game," cheered me on, or talked with me about how I'd played, the way Jim did. And Jim didn't even like soccer.

Jim listened carefully. Then he corrected me.

"They don't care the way you want them to," he said. "They're very active and engaged with you, too. They just give you a lot of space."

Though it seemed as if Jim was defending my parents, I always felt he was on my side. He was adept at inviting me to see things in a different way.

I started growing my own blond, wavy hair long because of Jim. The more time I spent with him, the more I looked up to him. I also started to test him and a few times, he had to get tough with me. Once when we were walking along the boardwalk in Santa Cruz, I kept trying to trip him as he walked. I thought it was hilarious.

"One more time and I'm going to deck you," Jim said.

I grinned at him. *Yeah, right,* I was thinking. *A youth leader in the church is going to hit a kid?*

I did it again. As Jim started to fall, he managed to stabilize himself. Before I knew what was happening, he had landed a punch in my gut. Then he turned without a word and walked toward the ocean.

I definitely needed that.

*

Jim also knew how to play guitar. My feverish interest in Guns N' Roses had led to a desire for guitar lessons, but my parents balked.

"No," my mom said. "We got your sister piano lessons and she quit. We're not going through all that again."

Jim arranged for me to borrow a guitar from one of the other youth leaders. Then he gave me five or six lessons. The first song he taught me was the Guns N' Roses version of Bob Dylan's "Knockin' on Heaven's Door." Soon I was playing it on a Wednesday evening in the Presbyterian Church with other members of the youth group, strumming the chords G-D-A minor over and over.

That was in ninth grade. In tenth grade, the father of Brian, the boy I had been baptized with, died. I wrote a song for him called "Brian's Blues." A guy my mom knew had recording equipment and he set it up for me so I could record the song. Before I went to his house, I had to bring the guitar to Jim so he could tune it. I didn't know how to do it myself. I was careful not to bump the instrument on the way to the recording session.

I was not a musician; I was playing the guitar, not music. The song was pretty ridiculous, but it was sincere. Twenty years later, Brian told me he still had the recording. Recently, he had pulled it out and listened to it again.

*

Jim Coons gave me my first Bible (or, rather, the first Bible I was interested in cracking open). It was the New International Student Version.

"Where do I start?" I asked him.

He thought for a second. "Read Matthew. That's the first book of the New Testament."

"What's the New Testament?" Sure, I'd done my first communion and catechism in the Catholic Church, but the Bible didn't mean much to me there.

I read Matthew, Mark, Luke, and John. "Okay, now what?" I asked Jim.

"Read them again."

"What about all these other books? What about all these other pages? Why did you start me three-fourths of the way through? What's all this other stuff?"

"Nah, nah," said Jim, "just focus on Jesus."

"But what does that *mean?*" I asked him.

This was my favorite question, but Jim was never very interested in answering it. He was intelligent and thoughtful, but he just didn't share my appetite for philosophy.

Once I asked him, "What do you know about Revelation?"

Jim was adamant. "No. *Don't read Revelation.*"

"Why not? Why can't I read Revelation? It says right here it's 'the revelation of Jesus Christ.' So you want me to focus on Jesus, but not on his revelation? Why?"

"Because it's been misinterpreted so many times. It's just going to confuse you. Listen, there's all this crazy stuff in there. Beasts, prostitution, adultery...."

I was in ninth grade at the time. Did he think I wasn't going to read it after he told me *that?* When I did, I was, predictably, completely at sea.

I moved on to asking him, "What does the Bible say happens when you die?"

"Well, I believe—" Jim began.

"No, but what does it *say?*"

I think the message Jim was sending me was, *Figure it out on your own. Read it and come to your own conclusions.* When I was a kid, I could get angry and annoyed when I felt as if people weren't helping me enough. Getting help was easier than doing it myself.

But I was also genuinely interested in the question of why there were so many different interpretations, so many denominations. They could all agree on the same book, but it seemed as if that was all they could agree on.

*

This is a question I'm still curious about. What does the Bible say? Can I believe it when it seems to be clear, and can I still have faith when it's not?

*

Uncertainty is an important component of my faith. When I'm confronted with a given situation and all facts or evidence point to or away from the existence of God, I still can't be certain which is correct. Doubt and faith are opposing ways of resolving my uncertainty. I am uncertain if there is a God, but I have faith there is.

When I get to the point at which I just don't know anymore, I have to leap one way or the other. As a teenager, I said to myself, "There is either an intellectual higher being, or there isn't."

At some point, I leapt to, "There is." Once I leapt, I found that doubt could enhance my belief, because I'd had my doubts and worked through them. That's not to say my doubts no longer existed. But I knew now I'd had the confidence to leap despite them.

*

I played music for Jim's Wednesday youth nights several times. But he still hadn't gotten me into church on a Sunday. He eventually managed that by asking me to play with several other youth musicians at the 9 a.m. service. He said the organist would open the service, but we would play everybody out.

"What do we play?" I asked him.

"Anything you want. It just has to be instrumental," said poor unsuspecting Jim.

Unbeknownst to him, I had learned how to play Black Sabbath's "Iron Man." When I suggested it to the other kids, they looked uneasy.

"Dude, we can't do that," they said.

"It'll be fine. Don't worry. If there's any problem, I'll take the fall for it," I said.

"God be with you," the pastor said on Sunday morning. That was our cue.

We didn't sing it. But the riff is unmistakable. Jim was in the third row from the front, sitting up straight in the pew and looking proud he'd gotten me into church on a Sunday. When I started playing the opening lick, he leaned back, his arms crossed over his chest. Slowly, an anxious smirk grew on his face. It said, unmistakably, *I guess I should have been more specific;* and also, *You little son of a ....*

He had thought I would have more respect. Though I'm not sure I was being disrespectful. I think it was more of a complete and utter lack of awareness.

Jim wasn't a full pastor yet; he was just a youth leader without an M. Div. (Master of Divinity). After the service, the senior pastor, Jim's boss, came up to the band and said, "So. 'Iron Man,' huh?"

"Yeah," I said. "We just learned it."

"Why don't we choose a different song for the end of the next service?" he said. "What can we agree on?"

Despite the pastor's disapproval, I didn't get the boot—from him or Jim. Instead, I got the message that I could push the boundaries and still be accepted and educated.

*

Jim introduced me to the first Christian rock band I had ever heard, the 77s, which formed at a church in Sacramento. Then there was The Choir, Adam Again, Undercover, The Prayer Chain. I thought it was all pretty great. Jim also encouraged me to go to a Christian summer camp.

I didn't know exactly where I was, Christianity-wise; but I enjoyed the camp and I connected with people in that community.

Especially, of course, with Jim, who never made any secret of the fact he loathed Guns N' Roses. He thought they were cheesy. Once, when I was riding somewhere with Jim and his wife and a Guns N' Roses song came on the radio, they made me put my head out the window when I started singing.

Jim was obsessed with a band as well: U2. He loved U2 so much that at one point, some of us kids who hung out with him at the church started to hate U2 simply on principle. Jim was proud to own original t-shirts from the War and Unforgettable Fire tours. He kept them neatly folded, never worn, "in a box somewhere."

Preferring U2—and just about any other band—to Guns N' Roses didn't keep Jim from learning the opening lick of "Sweet Child of Mine," just so he could teach it to me.

"I'm only doing this because I care about you," he said.

But I think he must have secretly liked it at least a little. That lick isn't easy to play at all.

*

Whenever I need to process my emotions, I turn to music. It calms me, inspires me, charges me up. And for whatever reason, Guns N' Roses helps keep me feeling like I have my feet on the ground.

*

8:22 a.m., Monday, August 22, 2022

Singing in the car with my son, I am wholly focused on the present experience of our duet.

I start a line of "Love Will Turn You Around." Then I stop. He picks up right where I left off and sings the rest. These moments remind me

I'm truly happy in his presence: this magnificently adorable child.

At his school, I sign him into the classroom. He gives me a hug, takes his backpack, and turns to run toward the other kids. He looks back once and waves. Back at the car, I check how much time I have before the meeting. Thirty minutes. Just enough time. No need to rush.

Chapter 3

I turn into the hospital's multi-level parking structure and wind my way to the top. Each time I enter it, I use my badge to open the gate and think about how I am paying to go to work.

With my badge looped around my neck, I walk toward the building. It includes my first and last name, my department (Spiritual Care), and a washed-out photo. Just in case an enraged or frustrated patient or visitor decides to attack, staff badges are strung on breakaway lanyards to keep us from getting strangled. On the downside, the retractable portion breaks all the time from daily use. I go through a few every year.

I badge into the door and wave to the security guard, who waves back with a big smile. There are a few guards on rotation and I can never keep their schedules straight. Today it's Charles with his black curly hair straight from a photo of Bob Ross he must have shown to his stylist.

I know where the stairs are, but I usually take the elevator. I can't quite figure this out about myself. All day I visit patients who would give anything to sit up on their own. I'm physically able to trot up and down the stairs whenever I please, but I let the elevator do the work, almost in defiance of the freedom I'm afforded by my current state of good health.

I wind through the long, pastel-colored hallways to my desk. I set up my computer, unload my bag, put my lunch in the fridge.

I check the on-call log and listen to voice messages. Today there's a frantic and "urgent" call from Craig, the charge nurse in the ED (emergency department), asking that I get there "as soon as possible, Chap!" That was on Saturday. In the log, I see the chaplain who was on call that night made it there.

I check in with people around me—other chaplains, residents, interns, educators, staff. Then I take my place in the classroom to wait for the director of the Spiritual Care Department, Sofia, to guide us through the "Monday Report." We'll listen to each chaplain who worked over the weekend talk about what happened on their shifts. We also receive printed copies of each of their written reports, called referral notes. These are half-sheets of paper about those patients the chaplains met with whom they believe would benefit from another visit. The notes include information like the date the chaplain saw the patient, the patient's religion, any services the chaplain performed (prayer, sacrament, etc.), as well as a reason the chaplain is recommending a follow-up.

There's no formalized "prayer time" in the meeting. This is an inter-religious group. It's almost always like that, particularly in large city hospitals. While chaplaincy in the United States arose out of a primarily Christian tradition, and still tilts in that direction, there is a Buddhist here, a Muslim, a Hindu, a Mormon. Among chaplains you'll find Catholic priests as well as Catholic laypeople (who are authorized to perform many of the Church's ceremonies—basically, anything that doesn't involve oil); Orthodox and Reform rabbis; Universalists; Humanists; and Protestants of every stripe: Methodists, Baptists, Episcopalians, Lutherans, Friends (Quakers). Chaplains must be endorsed by an organization they are accountable to. The Humanist Society endorses chaplains, but other groups, like the atheists and the "spiritually independent," don't have an organization, so they often get lumped in with the Humanists.

The variety matches what we encounter in our work; there is no place in the world more diverse than a hospital. In the meeting room, however, the religious diversity poses a challenge when I'm trying to bring something of meaning in to share with everyone. I'm bound to offend someone by talking about something I believe in. But we work to bring purpose and value into an open and inviting place. We rely on a great deal of translation on the part of the listeners, rather than on each speaker.

Gina, one of the weekend chaplains, shares: "I got a request from an overzealous nurse for a patient who was getting dialysis. The nurse told me: 'She's sad, so she could use a prayer. Maybe you can sit with her and make her feel better. I'll get you a chair.'"

Some of us laugh.

"So I lean over the patient," Gina says, "who is falling asleep. She's struggling to keep her eyes open. I ask the nurse: 'Did this patient request to see me?' And the nurse says, 'Yeah, she should talk with you.' Again I say, 'I see. So she asked to talk with me?' 'Right,' the nurse says. 'I'll get you a chair.' I say, 'No, thanks, I'll stand—I'll be leaving in a minute.' I yell the patient's name, but she doesn't move. She's asleep! The nurse comes over and starts yelling her name, too. Some of the other patients wake up and look over, but not this patient. So I tell the nurse I'll follow up later when the patient is *actually* awake.

"And then," Gina finishes, "I ask the nurse, 'How are you doing?' to which she replies, 'I'm fine,' then takes off in the opposite direction."

"You wanted her to leave," I say.

"What do you mean?"

"You know asking a nurse how they're feeling is the best way to see how fast they can run."

All of us laugh then. We've all experienced the difficulty of attempting to care for the hospital staff. We try to make them aware that we're available to them as much as we are to the patients—maybe more so. Patients come and go, while staff are around much longer. Chaplains are trained to process the experiences we have in the hospital, but most other staff members aren't. Sometimes, this means they're not aware of the emotional history they bring into a room or how that history can affect how they do their jobs.

*

When I'm screening applicants for CPE, I give them a scenario about dealing with a staff member to see how well they'll deal with conflict.

Scenario: A patient is crying alone in his room. The nurse calls the chaplain and asks her to go in there.

"The patient is all alone," says the nurse. "He shouldn't be. I think he could use some support right now."

The chaplain goes in and introduces herself. The patient says he's fine and just wants to be alone with his tears.

"Is that okay?" he asks.

"Yes. Of course," says the chaplain. "I'm here and available if you want anything. Just let us know."

"Thank you," the patient says.

But when the chaplain emerges from the room, the nurse pounces on her.

"Why aren't you in there?" she demands.

Even when the chaplain explains, the nurse shakes her head. "No. That's the last thing he needs right now. You need to go back in there. He doesn't know what he needs. He was just told he has stage IV pancreatic cancer."

How do you respond? I ask the applicant. In their reply, I'll listen for an awareness of what the nurse might need and ideas about how to support her.

One of the goals of CPE training is to help students learn to see themselves when they look at patients: "The human condition of the patient is also *my* condition." But when staff members are struggling, the problem is often that the experience of a patient or a family member is coming disturbingly close to their own story. This can be disruptive.

I've found that while questions make staff members flee, statements about my own experience tend to open up dialogue. In our training, this is called the "use of self."

"This situation is really hard," I might say, or "I feel so sad for this man and his family."

If I get a like-minded response, I might venture to say, "Yeah? That's been your experience too?"

In the interview scenario, something about the situation has hit a nerve with this particular nurse. Maybe sometime in the past, she got some devastating news, too, or lost someone she loved. And when she felt the need to have people around her, she found herself alone.

I might say to that nurse, "You seem pretty close to this situation," and then give her some space to respond.

The goal is to help her realize her pain might be clouding her ability to see the patient's best interest and to respect his wish to cry in solitude. Ideally, along the way, she might start processing her own grief.

Anger can be an important part of grief: a person's way of showing they care. It can come out of a desire to connect, an invitation to step closer. "Can you meet me in my anger?"

*

In a way, I see the whole world now through the lens of grief. In every story, while there are gains and celebrations, there is also a loss in some capacity. When I'm at work, looking for that loss helps me formulate a context with which to meet people where they are.

The principle applies equally well outside of work. But I don't like to take it with me everywhere I go.

*

Sidenote on crying: there's a procedure for that, too.

More specifically, the procedure involves what to do about tissues. I teach my students crying is an effective way to express and release emotion. When patients and family members are vulnerable enough to cry in front of us, they give us a beautiful gift. Handing someone a box of tissues as soon as the tears start falling might feel helpful, but it can also send the message, "You're making me uncomfortable. Please stop crying."

If I immediately shove a tissue box in someone's face, the tears often stop. I've interrupted the flow of emotion. Instead, I just locate the tissue box in the room with my eyes. I don't push it away like some sadist if the patient reaches for it; but until they do, or until they let out a sigh and start looking around the room for the box, I just let them talk and cry. Let the tears soak their hands, their sleeves, their blankets, whatever is available—let it all pour out! When they're ready, their body language will let me know. Then I'll hand them the tissues.

*

9:29 a.m., Monday, August 22, 2022

Sofia ends the meeting: "I hope today is what it is supposed to be for you … for each of you."

It doesn't make much sense to wish each other a "nice" or a "good" day. Those words fall flat, feel strange or hollow. We know we'll be meeting with people dealing with illness and death—as Dr. Müller said, potentially the most traumatic moments of their lives.

In a similar way (though this one carries a heavy amount of superstition, too, a desire to avoid tempting the gods), we never wish anyone who's going on-call a "quiet shift."

Referrals in hand, I head back to my desk to organize and structure my morning. The CPE students will be in class for the next two hours, which means there are fewer people available should an emergency come in.

I've been in a lot of hospitals. They're all more or less the same, especially the ones built in the last ten years. It's common for new buildings to be connected to older ones with a bridge. Today, I walk across the bridge on the second floor of one building to enter the third floor of another without so much as an incline.

Of course, I've also been in hospitals that are moldy monstrosities, reminiscent of an old horror movie: dilapidated psych hospitals in dire need of a larger system revamping them or simply shutting their drafty doors for good.

I wind through the hallways and find my way to the elevators. There are staff elevators, public elevators, food-service elevators, code-blue elevators, and generally one specifically reserved for transport from the helicopter pad straight down to the emergency department. My badge works on all of them and on nearly every door in the hospital. In general, this level of responsibility makes me nervous.

I start on the medical intensive care unit, or MICU. A medical team is huddled outside a room on the end of the corridor, Room 42, discussing a patient. They acknowledge my presence with a "Hey there, Chaplain," then continue giving a debrief.

It's a common scene in an intensive-care unit in a university hospital. The longest white coat is in charge (the attending physician). The next-longest white coat is in the second position (fellow or chief resident), followed by the mid-thigh white coats (the residents). Then come the students, whose white coats are like short blazers barely covering their belts. This rank and hierarchy in uniforms matches the militaristic language of hospitals: "Disease is the *enemy*, which threatens to *invade* the body and overwhelm its *defenses*. Medicine *combats* disease with *batteries* of tests and *arsenals* of drugs."[2] We submit *orders* and give *shots* while *battling* illness. Patients often tell me, "I'm going to fight this."

Generally, in these team meetings outside patient rooms in ICUs, nurses "give report" on how the patient is doing, while the various physicians take turns sharing their knowledge about possible treatments and courses of action.

The nurse outside Room 42 says, "He came in as a code status, compressions in progress, until they stabilized him enough to get him up here. He's early twenties and in custody." Only then do I notice there's a police officer here. He's a big guy, strutting arrogantly back and forth in the hallway outside the room.

I watch him for a moment. In the hospital, everyone's anxiety level rises a little when the police are involved. The police don't really have jurisdiction in the hospital, but the law is gray. Technically, as I understand, their jurisdiction is the patient—and the patient's body if they die—because the patient is also "the crime scene." It's difficult to help families understand they can't touch their loved one, particularly if their loved one dies, because they "cannot disrupt a crime scene."

Hospital staff continue doing what they have to do when there's an officer around, but they feel as if they're being watched.

*

A few weeks prior to this visit, I met an officer outside the trauma room in the ED. Inside the room, a team was working on a patient. The officer was staring hard into the room through the glass. He kept shifting his weight back and forth. His left arm was hanging down, but his right hand was on his belt—not on his gun, but near it.

I approached him and asked, "How are you doing?"

He glanced at me. Then he said, in a quiet but sharp voice, "I'm trying not to kill this guy."

He was gritting his teeth. He wiped sweat off his brow. The fingers on his left hand began to twitch.

"This guy just killed my partner. I'm staying outside so I don't do something stupid. Can you pray with me, chaplain?" he said.

Maybe he was being dramatic, putting his feelings on display. Maybe he didn't care if he made anyone nervous. Maybe he even wanted to. But he was also overwhelmed with grief. He was the last person who should have been put in charge of guarding this patient. I admired how he was both honoring the difficulty of his task and maintaining his dignity and control.

A request had been sent to officers from a different county—the incident occurred just outside the hospital's county—to come relieve him, but they weren't showing up. I stayed with him for an hour, before running into the other officers standing in a hall nearby. They were laughing and chatting with one another, in no hurry to get to their babysitting gig.

"Are you here to relieve Officer Garcia?" I asked them.

A couple of the bastards in this group said, "Yeah, yeah. We'll go in in a minute."

I explained the situation. "I'm sure he'd appreciate some relief."

"Okay. Yeah," they said again. "We'll get to it."

Officer Garcia hadn't been able to name what, exactly, he wanted me to pray for, other than that he "didn't put a bullet through [the patient's] head." What he needed more than anything was to leave the hospital and process his grief. Maybe when he was finally out of there, he went to the firing range and blew off some steam.

*

Back outside MICU Room 42, the police officer has stopped pacing and is leaning against the wall with his eyes half closed.

The attending physician reports "the patient is currently brain dead, but the family just isn't able to accept this—they see his feet twitch and think he's doing the twitching." I look around and see the other white coats nod. But I get the sense they aren't all exactly sure what that means.

"What does that mean?" I ask. All the white coats look at me. The longer the coat, the longer the look. Slowly, they all return their gaze to the attending.

"It's like spasms in the muscles," the attending says, "but there's no activity in his brain. The family has asked for another opinion, but anyone else will conclude the same thing."

"Right." I pause. "I guess what I'm asking is: how are we going to help the family understand that?"

Most of them droop their heads. They press their lips together as they take in a deep breath. Their body language says, *I don't know*, but many physicians struggle with those words.

Even though I've never met a patient who demanded perfection from their physician. "It's the practice of medicine, after all," a patient once said to me.

The attending sighs as he turns toward the room. "Well, we'll have to think of something. Family meeting is later this afternoon."

My pager vibrates on my hip. The team moves to the next room to discuss another patient. I spot a phone on the desk outside the patient's room and gently nudge the officer out of my way.

"Pardon me," I say, as he grunts and lets out a small sigh.

I dial the number displayed on the pager. It's amazing how many advancements there have been in medicine in the last several decades and still I carry a clunky piece of technology invented a hundred years ago. When I'm on call, I carry three pagers. The first is my personal pager, which the five specific units I'm assigned to have the number for. The other two are the code pager, which goes off whenever there is a code blue or medical emergency, and the trauma pager, which alerts me when a trauma case comes into the emergency department.

This alert is on my personal pager. A nurse on the other end of the line informs me a patient in orthopedics "wants a Bible and a rosary. According to the patient," she says, "it's kind of urgent."

"Urgent? Really?"

"That's what she said."

"I'll be there in about ten minutes."

To date, no one has ever died because the chaplain was delayed. Almost nothing we do in chaplaincy is "urgent"—with exceptions such as summoning a priest to perform the Sacrament of the Sick when a Catholic patient is on the verge of death. Often, the sense of emergency in that situation arises when a family holds onto hope until the last minute and puts off the request longer than they should. Who can blame them?

I take the elevator to the first floor and walk toward the chapel, which is around the corner from the gift shop. It is dimly lit, with twenty chairs facing a marble altar. Behind the altar is a large stained-glass window: an image of clouds above a mountain river. An arrow printed out on a piece of paper and taped to the floor indicates which direction one should bow toward Mecca. (Not every hospital has something so janky—I once saw a compass incorporated into a mural on the chapel wall. It was clear, but subtle and beautiful). There are disposable prayer rugs in a wooden box at the back of the room and copies of the Bible, Quran, Bhagavad Gita, and other faith-specific and unspecific inspirational literature in a cabinet.

The contents of that box and cabinet can be just as helpful to me as they are to my patients. More than once I've given a Bible to a dying patient so I didn't get too emotional.

While I'm in the chapel, a thought comes to me: what most people call "faith" is really just a fear of death.

Where is this thought coming from? Why am I having it now? Something to do with the young man in the ICU whose body looks alive even though his brain isn't? Maybe this is where my faith is at the moment.

I unlock the cabinet with the key fastened to my ID badge, grab a Bible, and retrace my path to the elevator, heading to orthopedics.

I see the nurse I spoke with earlier. She's explaining something to some other nurses, so I just smile, hold up the Bible, and motion that I'm on my way to the patient's room.

I knock on the patient's door and wait until I hear a faint "Yeah?"

Inside is a frazzled-looking woman in her mid-fifties sitting up in bed. Her graying blond hair is sticking up and in knots, as if she's been out on the water all night on a speedboat. The television is too loud and the table by the bed is covered in wrappers, plates with scraps of food, and four or five open cans of ginger ale.

She's yelling into her cell phone: "I can't hear you. It's so noisy in here. Someone's here, I'll call you back." Abruptly she ends the call and says, "Oh, another doctor—now, do you have any answers for me?"

She looks so sad and bleak—it's as if she possesses a power that could darken the morning sun.

"I'm one of the chaplains. I understand you urgently need a Bible?" I hold it aloft, knowing I sound a bit snarky. I can't quite seem to hide it.

"Finally!" She sounds like a petulant teenager. "Yes, it *was* urgent! You bring the rosary too?"

Crap! I forgot it. "Oh, that's right … I can get one for you after we're done. Would that be okay?"

"I guess," she replies, far more air in her tone than necessary. I hand her the Bible. "It *was* urgent?" I let the question hang in the air.

She puts the Bible on the table next to her, then unwraps a saltine cracker. She fills her mouth with it before saying, "Yeah, *was*." Then she fixates on the television, even though there's nothing on but an ad for a non-stick pan.

"You sound frustrated," I say. She stops chewing but continues staring at the television. She sneaks a quick glance at me and notices I see her—I always watch a person's eyes.

"Are you upset I didn't get here in time?" Whatever "in time" means ….

She smacks on her cracker and fiddles with the wrapper, looking annoyed. "It's just that—no one takes me seriously. But, whatever. It's fine."

I am struck by this. Was I reading her body language wrong? Have I misjudged her? I know what it's like to feel neglected and misunderstood. *Only the one who listens can speak.*

"No one?" I say.

She shakes her head.

"I imagine that's incredibly isolating and lonely." This is a bigger risk. She turns and looks directly into my eyes. Hers are sharp and pale blue.

"Yeah, I'm all alone. All I've ever had is myself. My whole life, it's only ever been me." She holds the stare and smacks her lips. "So, I do what I gotta do and I get by. You can go now. And don't forget to bring me a rosary." She returns her gaze to the TV.

"I'm happy to give you privacy if that's what you'd like. I also want to say I think I'm hearing a lot of injustice has been done to you." She doesn't move. "Am I off in that assessment?"

"Nope," she barks. "I just can't explain myself to a complete stranger right now."

"Sure. I'll go get the rosary and come back." She's still motionless, but it's clear she's listening. "I can see there is strength within you, and you have good reason to be distrustful of others. I'm only here to see if I can help. Maybe my absence is what will be most helpful. So if that's what you need, I want to give you that."

Still no response. But I've learned to be comfortable with silence.

"Thanks for opening your room to me," I say. "I'll be back with a rosary."

"Thanks." And with that, she's done. I head out the door.

I'm often curious, when being rejected, to hear if the person can tell me what minimum thing I could do to satisfy them. Sometimes it is simply leaving. But even when they ask for that, I don't think it's always what they really want.

She definitely wants a rosary. I can do that.

I knock on her door again. The television is still blaring. When I step inside, she says immediately, "Just put it on the Bible there. Thanks for coming back."

Then she rolls over, her back toward me, and pulls the blanket over her head.

"Will do." I lay the rosary down. "You take care and let us know if you need anything else."

She doesn't move or make a sound.

Outside of her room, I check my phone. It's only 10:30 a.m.

I find a computer and open up the census: a list of every patient who's currently admitted to the hospital. I don't have any calls pending right now, so I check to see if there are any consults for patients on my units. Consults are chaplain requests submitted through the electronic records system. These come second on our priority list of patients to see. Here's the breakdown:

1. *Direct page/call*
2. *Consult orders*
3. *Verbal request from someone on a unit (charge nurse, bedside nurse, social worker, etc.)*
4. *Self-initiated visit*

Consults include the name of the person who submitted the request and the reason it was made, but information on the latter is often woefully inadequate. Many times, I've seen "Reason for request: Crying." Or "Emotional." Sometimes it's "Praying" or "Christian." Less often, we get great information that helps us prepare: "Patient just given difficult diagnosis. Not taking it well. Have seen him praying and believe he could benefit from a chaplain visit."

Currently, I don't have any consults. So I sort my patient list by age, youngest to oldest, and start with the youngest. I can't remember exactly why I started doing it this way, but now it's a habit. Maybe it's because younger patients are less likely to talk for extended periods of time. If I start with the young ones, I can get to more patients and feel more productive. Whatever the reason for my process, it's most certainly about me.

An eighteen-year-old came in over the weekend with a gunshot wound. I find his H&P note—the first note submitted after patients arrive. It's an overview of the patient's inpatient "*H*istory" and "*P*hysical" condition. I read he was "at a party, heard shots, and went to see what was happening. Was struck in left upper arm by stray bullet. Endorses mild alcohol use."

There's also a nineteen-year-old with "autism and developmental delay." The social worker's note states "Parents are at bedside most of the time." I'm thinking I'll stop by there and see if they're in.

Then I see the name of my nineteen-year-old patient Shawn. After tapping my badge on the badge-reader to log me out of the computer, I make my way to the general medicine unit.

The story about how Shawn ended up on the unit is rather odd. He was transferred from the children's hospital to ours because although patients can stay there until they're twenty-five, the doctors were at a loss for what to do with him.

His medical records were complicated and extensive, stretching back to when he was a toddler. An ethics meeting was called to discuss his bewildering case, and as the unit chaplain, I was a part of that committee. At the meeting, as everyone was studying and discussing his records, someone noticed a pattern: the patient would be in the care of one doctor for a given amount of time until the doctor and the boy's mother disagreed on a plan of care. Then there would be a sudden shift to another doctor. The care started over and the boy got sicker and sicker.

This pattern repeated itself year after year until two months ago, when he arrived at our hospital on a ventilator. His care team was considering hospice care for him. The ethics committee met because nobody could quite understand what the problem was: "What is his underlying cause of disease or illness?" No one had an answer.

Finally, in this meeting, in which four of Shawn's previous pediatricians were in the same room together, there was a startling moment of clarity. One of the doctors said, "Might this be a Munchausen by proxy case?"

At this point, I knew only "Munchausen by Proxy" was the name of Zooey Deschanel's character's band in the film *Yes Man*. The name took on new meaning for me.

Munchausen syndrome by proxy, or factitious disorder by proxy, as the DSM (*Diagnostic and Statistical Manual of Mental Disorders*) refers to it now, is a psychological disorder in a child's primary caregiver. The caregiver "induces or simulates the illness or disease process in the victim and then presents the victim for medical care while disclaiming any knowledge about the actual etiology of the problem."[3] Sometimes, Shawn's mother would claim Shawn was having symptoms when he wasn't. At other times, she intentionally harmed him so he would. Basically, a caregiver doesn't act this way for any external incentive—like making money—but out of a deep psychological need for attention; they "assume the sick role by proxy."[4] Sometimes, caregivers are motivated by the praise they get for being so devoted to the care of their child. The DSM reports "Cases are often characterized by an atypical clinical course in the victim and inconsistent laboratory test results that are at variance with the seeming health of the victim."[5]

This was the case with Shawn's strange medical history. The hospital moved rapidly, calling CPS (Child Protective Services) to get his mother away from him. Within days he was doing much better.

That was about six weeks ago. Today, I find him walking around on the unit. His coke-bottle glasses, patchy facial hair, and hospital tube socks pulled up tight to his mid-calf remind me of Richard Dreyfuss in *Jaws*. But that isn't the only reason I like him. His whole demeanor suggests he understands the seriousness of life at a deep level and is determined to make the most of the rest of his time. Unlike other patients on the unit, Shawn doesn't just mechanically put one foot in front of the other. He strolls. He's alert. He's free-spirited, attentive to everything around him, as if he's not in a hospital corridor but a park, whistling and noticing the birds after just being released from jail.

I walk up next to him. "Hey, Shawn."

"Oh, hey! I got one for you," he continues as I keep stride with him. "What did one toilet say to the other?" He looks at me with a huge smile, his feet still moving forward but veering left toward the wall. He can't wait to get to the punchline.

"I don't know, Shawn. What?" We turn left at the back of the unit and come back toward the main desk.

"You look a little flushed!" His laugh is infectious and his heart is so innocent. He is loved by everyone on this unit. And everyone knows by now there was nothing wrong with him except for how his mother's psychological issues manifested in his body. With her gone, he is getting healthier each day.

"That's a good one," I say. "But what a crappy conversation."

Shawn stops in mid-step. Dramatically, he takes a deep breath before bursting out laughing so loud I'm sure they hear him at the other end of the unit.

I come by to see Shawn every day or at least every other day. I check in on how he's doing and we just hang out. Sometimes, we watch cartoons or sports or play board games. He really likes "Chutes and Ladders." Recently, someone brought in a video-game console and hooked it up to his TV.

We near the front desk. Nina, the charge nurse for the day, asks, "What was so funny back there, Shawn?"

"Do you know what one toilet said to the other toilet?"

Nina smiles and tilts her head, her eyes rolled up to the ceiling. She taps her lips. "Hmm. I don't know."

"I don't know, either, but it was a crappy conversation that left one of them flushed." He laughs so hard he snorts, which makes him laugh even more.

"Shawn, you changed the punchline!" I say in surprise.

"You are such a clever young man." Nina sniffles and quickly glances away; she's holding back tears.

Shawn continues laughing.

"Okay, I'm going to keep walking around. It feels so good to be out of bed!"

Nina and I shake our heads at each other. I feel so many things: relieved, angry, resentful, excited, concerned, full of wonder, apprehensive—a myriad of emotions best summarized as "overwhelmed."

What's next for Shawn? He's getting better and he's legally an adult. Where does this boy who's been sick and helpless his entire life go when it's time for him to be released?

My pager beeps, Nina returns to her work, and Shawn starts another lap around the unit.

The text message on my pager tells me a patient died on the neuro ICU and "a few family members are wanting to know what the next steps are."

I take the stairs up two levels. I feel good about it until I remember the staircase is closer to the unit than the elevator is. So maybe I'm still just lazy.

Chapter 4

When I was about Shawn's age, I graduated from high school, class of 1996, with a 1.6 GPA. I don't know why they even passed me.

In high school, I was diagnosed with test anxiety because of my struggles with algebra. I got to take many of my tests at home—Guns N' Roses blasting on my stereo—but it didn't help much. The only thing I did well on at school was book reports. That was ironic, because after my paralyzing incident with "*(fōdō 'sinTHəsəs)*" in the third grade, I hardly ever opened a book. I didn't even read the books I wrote reports on. Instead, I opened randomly to a page and read a few paragraphs until I found a point I could strongly affirm or disagree with. I'd fluff it up with my own thoughts and perspective and find some way to pull it all together. Then I'd repeat this process four or five times, working my way through higher and higher page numbers. Near the end of the book, I'd find a passage I could connect to a point I'd referenced from the beginning.

It wasn't hard, but why in the world didn't I just read the book? It would have been easier and way more enjoyable.

When I was thirteen, I started working at my parents' shop, Wakefield and Sons Glass, during the summer. My dad's father had opened the business in 1936. My parents loved to tell me how fortunate I was that someday I would inherit the business they were building for me.

I was equally forthright about my lack of interest in that prospect. I built window screens upstairs in 115-degree heat, a few fans blowing my sweaty hair around. Wearing jeans and heavy boots, I worked outside on houses and storefronts, the wicked heat of the California sun radiating off the glass. For me, my physical discomfort was sufficient motivation to aspire to a desk job, even if I hadn't slashed my thumb open on broken glass on my first "outside job." I lost so much blood I dripped it all over the house my dad and I were working in and soaked the shop floor when I got back. I wrapped up my thumb, put my head down on the desk, and passed out. My parents wouldn't take me to the hospital—something about not wanting to deal with workers' comp. I still have a scar.

*

My dad enjoyed the work at the shop and was good at it. I was not. I knew education would be my way out. But given the circumstances of my academic performance, how I would make that happen remained a mystery.

*

My mom had always wanted to go to school, too. But she was held back by many things. As a child, she was abused and she carried her trauma for the rest of her life. And after her parents' divorce when she was a teenager, my mother was left largely on her own.

When I was in fifth grade, I found myself in the same boat. That same year, my mom tried going to night school. But she didn't do well and it didn't last long.

Then, in ninth grade, I was put in charge of my younger sister Lisa for a few hours every day after school. I resented taking on that responsibility. I started being drawn to kids at school who were also largely left to their own devices. I wasn't any better of an influence on them than they were on me.

Like a lot of teenagers, I was pretty self-absorbed. Lisa remembers me not wanting to go to work, which frustrated her, because it made it seem as if I didn't care about the family business. I did care. I was just struggling to see my place in it.

I feel bad when Lisa remembers me being angry much of the time. All she wanted when I was watching her after school was to hang out and connect with her older brother; I'm sure my resentments got in the way of that.

Lisa and I used to race each other to get into the shower every morning. If I got there first, I'd often relax so deeply under the hot water that I'd fall asleep leaning against the wall. I wouldn't wake up until the hot water ran out. By the time Lisa jumped in to take her freezing cold shower, she was already so behind in getting ready that she was often late for school.

*

One of the earliest lessons I got from my mom was to "always tell the truth." Once in the third grade, I was caught in a lie. I don't remember what I lied about, but I distinctly recall my mom telling me to never lie again.

Not long after that, I was home with her one day when the phone rang. I picked it up and a woman asked for my mom. I went into my parents' bedroom to tell her.

She was pulling a dusty cardboard box of Christmas decorations down from the highest shelf in the closet. It was about a month before

Christmas, her favorite time of the year. Every year, my mom spent every moment of her free time between Thanksgiving and Christmas hanging garland and snowflakes, arranging ornaments and decorations on every available surface, making fudge and baking our special family walnut rolls from a recipe that had been passed down from her grandparents. She made real hot chocolate, not from a packet like everyone else but with real melted chocolate. She hung hundreds of ornaments on the silver-tip tree we went out as a family to cut down in the Sierra Nevadas. My friends loved coming over to our house because it looked like a Christmas store.

Christmas made my mom so happy—it made the rest of the family happy, too. We loved seeing her that way.

My mom grunted as she heaved the box down. A dust bunny had settled on her bangs and she blew upward to chase it away. She laid her hand longingly on one of the cardboard flaps of the box.

"Tell them I'm not at home," she said.

I stared at her for a long moment. I didn't know how to reconcile her instruction to lie with her typical rule, which I had taken to be sacred and everlasting. She was my mom. I was still young enough I thought both of my parents could do no wrong. It was a long walk back to the phone.

I told the woman on the other end of the line, "She told me to tell you she's not at home."

I thought it was a genius answer. I was both confused and hurt when my mom blew up at me and sent me to my room for an hour or two.

After that, I knew I could never be certain if I was going to be right or wrong when it came to lying or telling the truth. It all depended on my mom's mood, which was fickle and unstable. I just had to guess, with a fifty-fifty chance of being right. If I chose the wrong answer, I'd have to either beg for forgiveness or stand my ground and try to justify my decision.

One minute, my mom was hardly paying attention to my participation on a traveling soccer team. Then she was going on an embarrassing rampage to the soccer board complaining I was being treated unfairly by the coach. Maybe it affected my prospects and maybe it didn't. But in the next season, I did well in the try-outs but didn't make the team. A friend with knowledge of the matter insinuated the board didn't want to "deal with your bitch of a mother."

No matter what my mom did, I began to feel, I was going to get hurt.

After the soccer incident, I told her to leave me alone. She began to focus on Lisa's cheerleading instead—so fully that I think Lisa struggled, after a point, to feel her life was truly her own.

*

When I was in the second grade, my teacher, Mrs. Cooper, hired my parents to put new windows in her house. She was the first teacher I saw out of school. It was a strange experience, like seeing the school building in the slanting evening light on Back to School Night in the late summer. Before I saw Mrs. Cooper in the house where she lived with her family, I knew, as everyone did, teachers lived at the school. That's why they were always already there when us kids arrived in the morning.

Now, she became real to me as a person. I realized this is where she lived, and teaching was what she did when she wasn't at home.

That meant "being a teacher" was a thing you could do, a profession. And maybe I could be a teacher someday, too.

My dream of being a teacher never wavered, though when I started to do badly in school, it did go through a few adjustments. In junior high, I was getting to know Jim Coons and the other youth leaders and pastors at the Presbyterian Church. I reflected that pastors were basically teachers as well. I started to think, *Well, the qualifications to become a pastor seem to be lower than they are for teachers. Maybe I can do that instead.*

It also seemed that their lives were easier and more flexible than Mrs. Cooper's. The senior pastor taught only once a week, and that was pretty much just a monologue in front of a docile crowd of adults who handled the discipline of the youngest members of the congregation for you. The pastors I knew didn't seem to do much on weekdays. I imagined they worked only a couple of hours a week.

I didn't realize that whenever I ran into them in the church, part of their job was to stop what they were doing and make time for me. I would learn the folly of my assessment the hard way.

*

After I graduated, Jim Coons and I played in a worship band together with a girl who came to my high school as a foreign-exchange student the year after I left. Her name was Marianne and she played bass. She was originally from Norway and Jim used to call her "Viking."

My relationship with Jim was changing. We were becoming friends, though I never quite stopped seeing him as a mentor. For years after I met him, I always called him whenever I needed guidance or advice.

After Marianne graduated she invited me to play guitar in the worship band at her church. I had first seen Marianne at a high school soccer game. She wore baggy clothes and had shaved her dark-blond hair all the way around her head an inch above her ears. On top, her hair was long. She wore it in little braids, each of them no thicker than a pencil. She'd pull two of the braids out through a hole she'd cut out of the beanie cap she always wore. The braids hung by her eyes, which were bright blue and shone against her very tan skin.

I was talking to some of my old soccer friends at the game, starting to wonder why in the world I'd even come. Didn't I want to forget high school had ever happened? Then this odd and arresting girl passed by.

Whoa, I thought. *Who's that?*

Soon, I found out that Marianne's host sister was a friend of mine. That same year, my sister Lisa's cheerleading squad was invited to a competition in Disneyland. My parents and I were planning to go. I wanted to support my sister, but I was trying to dig up a friend to go with me. I didn't love the prospect of hanging out in Disneyland with only my parents and a bunch of high-school cheerleaders.

So I called Marianne's host sister. The first few times I tried to reach her, I didn't catch her at home. I talked for a while with Marianne instead. She had a Norwegian accent that made her even more exotic and attractive. She was also full of energy and a lot of fun. I liked her more every time.

Marianne was a Seventh-day Adventist. She introduced me to Paul, the youth pastor at her church. Paul was not much like Jim Coons—or like me, for that matter. From the South, he was very conservative and awkward as hell. He nodded with an exaggerated motion—front to back, rather than up and down like everybody else. He also made loud "hmm hmm" sounds to show his care and concern for whomever he was talking to. When he got excited about something he'd learned and was passionate about sharing it, he would point and wag his finger as if he were preaching.

Tall with black hair, thick black eyebrows, and a pleasant smile, Paul looked like a typical straight, clean-cut guy from a snobby boy's school. But he was simply very sheltered. Once at a Bible study at his house, a sorority girl started talking about pledging. Paul said, "Hmm, yes. Now, what's a sorority?"

Even his wife Bethany—who had way more modest flower-print dresses than jeans and with a prayer cap could have been mistaken for a Mennonite—laughed.

"Oh, Paul, no," she said.

Paul shrugged and smiled. "I just don't know these things," he said.

Then he waited for an answer, totally unembarrassed. His purity and confidence appealed to me. Also, I sensed something likeminded in him. I had given up on reading Scripture after my frustrations with Jim. But quickly after meeting Paul, I asked him, "So, what do you know about Revelation?"

"Actually, not very much," Paul said. "You want to learn? Why don't we study it together?"

From the beginning, that's all I had ever wanted: someone who was as interested as I was in figuring out what the book said. What could we agree on when it came to interpreting it? What could we not, and why? And how could we apply this knowledge to what we believed?

Once, I was upstairs in my parents' shop working on screens when my mom came up to tell me I had a phone call. It was Paul.

"I hope it's okay I'm calling you at work," he said. "If it's not, this can wait. But I just wanted to share this with you."

He told me he'd been reading in search of answers to some of my questions. One was about the body and the soul. Can one survive without the other—and if so, how? Paul had found something in Genesis 2 about the spirit and the breath of God and how that breath is returned to God. When the breath is returned, Paul wondered, does that mean the soul is, too? I vividly remember standing in the front office in my dirty jeans and work boots, dripping sweat and talking about theology. My mind was as far away from my present circumstances as it could be. Paul's enthusiasm matched mine and I was touched that he cared enough about me to work so hard at finding answers.

I went to Jim Coons, full of oblivious excitement—and maybe a little condescension—to try to teach him what I had learned. He was uninterested and we drifted apart a little. A year after I graduated, he moved away to go to seminary.

I didn't apply the same level of exegetical rigor to my studies at the community college, which I was attending while still working at my parents' glass business. I was diligent about attending parties; the same could not be said of my classes.

I *was* trying harder than I had in high school. But some days I just wouldn't go to class, for no good reason at all. In the evening, I might talk to another student about what we did that day. He'd list not only going to class, but starting an assignment, reading in the library, attending a study group.

"How about you?" he'd say.

I'd think about it before saying slowly, "I put gas in my car."

I knew I was wasting my life, but I didn't know what to do about it. It didn't help that when it came to college, my parents were trying to thwart me at every turn. They would schedule me for installation jobs when they knew I had class.

"Well, I guess you'll have to decide what's more important: your family or yourself," my mother would say.

Soon, I was on academic probation. I felt frustrated being in my hometown and I was floundering in college. Only on the 20-mile commute between them with the radio on, belting out songs at the top of my lungs, did I feel free, happy, safe.

Marianne was along on some of those trips. She was going to the same community college as well and I sometimes gave her a ride. A natural student and a hard worker, she was doing much better there than I was.

On the road with me, she seemed to feel the same thrill of escape. Back in Norway, her home life hadn't been great. Her parents were separated, she was largely estranged from her father, and her mother wasn't well.

In the States, Marianne was experiencing a level of emotional freedom she'd never had before. After graduating from high school, she didn't want to go back to Norway. She was a great athlete and she convinced the volleyball coach at the college that he needed her on his team. I was with her the day we found the coach in the gym and he signed a letter certifying the reason that allowed Marianne to extend her student visa.

I was drawn to how driven Marianne was. If people—or institutions like the INS—got in her way, she would do what she had to do to get around them. I felt as if Marianne was everything I wasn't, everything I wanted to be. I felt cowardly, aimless. I didn't know how to think of something that I wanted and go after it.

When I hit the gas and turned up the volume on the stereo on our way home that day, Marianne closed her brilliant blue eyes and grinned as if she couldn't believe her luck.

*

On that drive home, we listened to Dave Matthews Band. Music was a big part of our friendship; it brought us closer together. But for a while, Marianne didn't want to give up her freedom. She didn't want to be in any kind of romantic relationship.

I made no secret of how I felt about her. In 1999, Marianne got another scholarship, this one to attend a more reputable university. Something about being on the cusp of leaving made her admit she was feeling the same way about me. She wanted us to start dating.

"Well, that sucks, because now you're leaving," I said.

Her new school was three-and-a-half hours away. I drove there almost every other weekend and Marianne and I went on our first official dates: mostly concerts. I remember standing with her in a beautiful theater, watching Alien Fashion Show open for the Brian Setzer Orchestra.

After a semester, we started to spend even more time together.

Marianne injured her shoulder and couldn't play volleyball anymore. So she transferred to be closer to me.

*

Then things started to get serious. In 2000, I found myself in a foreign country making two significant life decisions.

On June 25, I got baptized as a Seventh-day Adventist in a pond in Norway. The church believes in full-immersion baptism for adult believers. It rained all day and I walked down the gravel road between the church and the pond, then down the muddy shore, holding up the edges of my billowing baptismal robe to keep it out of the muck, even though the whole thing was about to get dunked. It sounds too cheesy to be true, but at the last minute, the rain stopped and the clouds broke. The photographer got some great shots of me and the pastor, me in all white, him in all black, with the sun sparkling on the water.

The water was freezing but I came up happy and laughing because I had managed to keep water from going up my nose. Also, earlier in the church, a girl had come up to tell me my testimonial about why I wanted to be baptized had moved her deeply. It had made her realize she wanted to make the same decision.

This was a revelation to me. I had never thought of myself as someone whose words could reach someone like that, influence someone else's life decisions. It was an amazing feeling.

While we were in Norway, Marianne and I also got engaged.

*

My parents were happy I was happy. They're incredibly indirect and phlegmatic. If they were put off at all by the way Marianne burst onto a scene, by how direct and driven she was, they kept their complaints and criticisms to themselves.

Marianne and I didn't live together right away. As conservative Christians, we believed marriage had to come before sex. When we got back to Northern California, I moved into a house with five other guys.

One of these roommates, Brandon Vedder, became a close friend. Brandon was an aspiring filmmaker living on a tight budget. His dedication to putting as much time and as many resources as he could into his artistic work was inspiring to me. While the other five of us rented bedrooms in the house, Brandon paid a smaller amount to rent the pantry in the kitchen. The pantry was big enough for a twin bed and a folding chair, though he couldn't open the door unless the chair was folded up.

As a creative type, Brandon didn't want to waste time on menial tasks like laundry; he didn't wash his clothes, only dried them. He figured if there was anything alive on his laundry, the heat would kill it.

"Warm clothes equal clean clothes," he would say, with a benevolent nod and the light of wisdom shining in his grin, as if he were a sagacious guru and I a mere neophyte benefitting from his insight and expertise.

*

I wasn't in that house long. In July of 2001, Marianne and I returned to Norway to get married. In a serendipitous turn of events, we arrived in time to attend the baptism of the same girl who had spoken to me at my baptism. When she saw me, she ran up and gave me a hug.

"I knew there wasn't any way you were going to be here," she said, "but I prayed you would be."

The story had come full circle. The pieces were coming together for me: the relationships I had with Jim Coons and Paul, people I looked up to and respected, and their influence on my life, and now this—it felt like validation. I was starting to articulate something I wanted: to be in the ministry.

Marianne and I got married a few days later. Jim and Paul led the service; it was the first time they met each other. My childhood friend Chris came, as did my parents, my sister, and Marianne's mother. Brandon missed the wedding, though he made the bachelor party.

Marianne was only twenty-one; I was a ripe old twenty-two.

*

Paul hadn't stopped at studying Revelation with me. He'd also entertained all my questions about faith, religion, God, theology, and Seventh-day Adventism.

Seventh-day Adventism came out of the Second Great Awakening, a Protestant religious revival in the United States in the late 1700s and early 1800s. It was propelled by revival meetings and led to a big increase in church membership around the country and the establishment of many colleges and seminaries. The focus in Seventh-day Adventism on a strong church-based educational system finds its roots here; there are thirteen Adventist colleges and universities in North America. Adventists are also known for promoting vegetarianism and healthy living. Advent Health is one of the largest faith-based hospital systems in the world.

Out of the Second Great Awakening came the Millerite Movement in the 1830s. Before William Miller, most people had interpreted the books of Daniel and Revelation in the same way: they understood the events described in Revelation happened in the past. William Miller, however, felt they hadn't happened yet. Miller believed the "cleansing of the sanctuary" referred to in Daniel 8:14 ("Until two thousand and three hundred days; then shall the sanctuary be cleansed") referred to the Second Coming of Christ, an event he called the Advent. The Advent would spur into motion the events described in Revelation.

Unlike most Christian denominations, Adventists honor the Sabbath on Saturday instead of Sunday. Also, the concept of Advent leads to an understanding of a "nothing period," a "sleep" after death, rather than immediate ascension to heaven. This period of rest is followed, eventually, by a resurrection.

The Adventist doctrine on this point in particular made sense to me; it felt logical. What's the point of a resurrection if you're already somewhere else?

*

Marianne knew I had it in me to be a good student. I started to believe it, too.

I knew if I were ever going to succeed in school, I needed to get away from my parents' interference. So I could start somewhere else in the fall, Marianne pulled an insane schedule—forty-two credits in two semesters—and graduated early. A month after we got married, we moved to Tacoma Park, Maryland, where I started classes at Columbia Union College.

On my last day of work at my parents' shop, my dad brought in a carrot cake decorated with the words, "Don't Let the Door Hit You on the Ass on Your Way Out." Both of my parents seemed to be full of mixed feelings. They were sorely disappointed; they'd always hoped I'd change my mind about the shop. And the fact I'd been failing so abysmally at school must have raised their hopes. The mid-summer sun blazed through the office windows as we ate cake. I can still remember the sticky melted icing dripping from a fork onto my tongue. How could I have known that disappointment can sometimes taste like cream-cheese frosting?

I think my parents were proud, too. The message on the cake was probably my dad's weird way of saying he loved me. It's hard to know. He's only ever said he loves me three times—yes, I'm counting—and then only in response to me saying it first.

Of course, this means I've only said "I love you" to my dad three times as well. I can't be too hard on him without also being hard on myself.

I know some people aren't good at putting their feelings into words. I know this very well when I see another family in a similar situation. It's just difficult for me to reconcile the universal truths I've come to objectively understand with my personal experience of love, embedded as it is in my own memories and my own pain.

I can be strangely protective of my dad. In theory, I know working long hours at the shop to build up the business was his way of loving me. It was also about fulfilling his own dream. Just because he imagined a specific place for me in that dream doesn't mean it wasn't still about him. Trying to force a "gift" on someone when they don't want it is not a very loving thing to do.

When he came home from work when I was a child, I just wanted him to show he wanted to spend time with me. Not just someday in the future, when I was a man, too, working beside him in the shop, but now. I had to beg him to throw the football around with me.

*

Recently, I asked my dad how he and my mom came up with my name. I've never liked "Keith" very much. I don't love the sound of it and it's hard for foreign speakers of English to say. My name comes out as a lisp.

My dad thought about it for a minute. "Well," he said, "your mom liked Brian Keith. You know, the actor. But there were an awful lot of Brians around. So one day your mom says to me, 'Well, what about 'Keith'? And I said sure. That's fine. I don't care."

"You didn't *care*?" I was astounded. My wife Shuang and I put a lot of effort into deciding what to call our son. It took us countless hours to choose a meaningful name we both agreed on.

"Well," my dad said, looking a little surprised.

"My name is Keith because you just didn't *care?*" I said.

*

In Maryland, I began to learn how to do better in school. Marianne helped me a lot. She coached me on study habits in the evening while she worked a few part-time jobs during the day. She also taught evening classes at a few local colleges.

The first class I took was called Interpersonal Ministry. I still got frustrated when I was taking notes and studying for tests. I had trouble figuring out what information was important and what wasn't. I still struggle with that.

I managed to pull a 2.33 GPA. I was proud of myself. I had done it all without my mother's intervention.

My parents did come to my graduation. I could tell they felt ill at ease in that white-collar world, but when my professors said to them, "You must be so proud," they beamed.

"Oh, yes," they said.

I'm sure I managed a smile for my professors. But I thought it was pretty rich my parents were taking credit for my accomplishment. They hadn't exactly encouraged me to be a scholar and they certainly didn't offer me any financial assistance.

"You're married now. Pay for it yourself," they'd said.

*

While we were in Maryland, my friend Brandon got hired to film each show of Pearl Jam's 2003 Riot Act tour for what would eventually become *Pearl Jam: Live at the Garden.* When the band played in Philadelphia, Marianne and I drove up and hung out backstage.

At the bottom of the totem pole, Brandon was also in charge of the band's laundry. When we were watching Eddie Vedder on stage singing "Evenflow," I remembered Brandon's laundry habits when we were living together.

I pointed to Eddie's t-shirt and asked, "Did you wash that?" Brandon just gave me a sly smile.

*

I graduated from college in 2004. In the fall of that year, I was hired by an Adventist Conference in the Pacific Union. They placed me at a church in California where I began a two-year internship as an associate pastor.

While we were there, Marianne started working on a master's degree. To save money while she went to school, we moved in with my childhood friend and neighbor Chris. It was great to spend time with him again and I was happy that he and Marianne could get to know each other better, two people who were so important to me.

There were seven hundred members in the church. I was eight months in when, even though this was only my first job as a pastor and I didn't have a seminary degree, I was suddenly responsible for all of them. The senior pastor there left and the church didn't find a replacement right away.

Until that point, my position had been mainly about learning the ins and outs of the job under the tutelage of the senior pastor. In my free time, I'd also been doing some learning on my own. I was starting to read some of the books I'd been assigned in high school and community college but hadn't gotten through at the time. *Brave New World*, *1984*, *David Copperfield*. *A Tale of Two Cities*, now one of my all-time favorites. Howard Zinn's *A People's History of the United States*. I even went back further to *A Wrinkle in Time* and *Where the Red Fern Grows*.

One of my other favorites was Raymond Chandler. *The Big Sleep*, *The Long Goodbye*, *Farewell My Lovely*. Chandler's Philip Marlowe appealed to me in particular: his snappy one-liners, his hardboiled observations of every imaginable layer of southern California humanity, from the rich and powerful to the guys parking the cars and running the rackets and sweeping the streets. Marlowe, who cared but hated that he cared—because it was always so damn inconvenient.

He was sharp and clever. He was also poetic and his metaphors brought both people and places to life.

I'd have to get my head off Chandler's characters—stalking his noirish world "soundless as shadows on the grass,"[6] "as calm as an adobe wall in the moonlight"[7]—and into the pulpit.

I had to figure out how to be a leader. To lead an entire church! What did that mean? What would that look like for me?

I decided it was not my role to do everything—and I knew I couldn't do everything. I needed help.

But like my parents, I'm incredibly indirect. I couldn't get myself to ask outright, or to say what I was thinking: *You're an elder in the church. With that role comes responsibilities, and I need you to rise up to them.*

So I often took a card from my mom's book: subtly putting myself down, playing up the "young and inexperienced pastor in over his head" thing the way my mom would say, "You're so much smarter than I was at your age."

I would ask a congregant, "Can you lead the prayer this weekend? Or visit this or that sick congregant in the hospital?"

(More than any other task, I was always trying to pass off hospital visits. I knew my aversion to hospitals was connected to some sad and frightening experiences I'd had as a child, but I hadn't fully faced or processed those memories yet.)

Sometimes, I got resistance. I'd say, "Okay, well, what do you want to do?" My underlying message was, *How are you going to help make this work? Without all of us, this ministry doesn't function.*

*

One Saturday, I sat in the back of the church during the main worship time and realized I had no responsibilities that day. I'd found other people in the congregation to cover all the components of the service.

I wondered, was this because I was passive and lazy? Well, maybe—but maybe not.

The service went well. That was not only because everyone had stepped up and worked hard. I'd put in many hours during the week showing them what to do and encouraging them when they felt nervous or uncertain.

I found myself feeling so grateful to them—and proud. There was something about watching them work and knowing it "wasn't about me" that was very satisfying. I knew that behind the scenes, I had played a part in my congregants' success. I loved the feeling of seeing them rise up to do what they could do—of seeing them shine.

Even more importantly, I played a part in changing who they were. After the service, those congregants came up and thanked me for putting my trust in them. Taking on those responsibilities and following them through had made them more confident. They were proud of themselves.

One week, I gave handwritten thank-you cards to everyone who took part in the service. One of these congregants, a nearly ninety-year-old man, waited for me in his car after church. When I walked out into the parking lot, he waved me over.

"I've been in this church my entire life," he said, "and I've never gotten a thank-you card for anything. It meant so much to me." He thanked me for making him feel seen. He began to cry and it moved me. I began writing notes every week.

*

Leading a Christmas Eve service at the church that year was particularly meaningful. I was old enough to be feeling nostalgic about my childhood Christmases and grateful to be back in California spending the holidays with my family.

Many things had stayed the same. Between Thanksgiving and Christmas, my parents' house was still covered in dozens of boxes of ornaments my mom gradually sorted through and hung around the house. She still stayed up so late every night decorating and baking that she wore herself out and spent the holiday sneezing and coughing with a virus. Today, my sister Lisa carries on that tradition. She turns the house she lives in with her husband into a Christmas wonderland complete with a Christmas village Christmas tree: a seven-foot-tall structure with flat wooden "branches" on which she places dozens of miniature ceramic replicas of houses, churches, candy stores, carolers, children sledding, and the like.

That Christmas morning in 2004, we still ate cinnamon rolls my dad picked up at a bakery called Granny Ann's. And we followed the same ritual in opening presents I'd always liked: someone "played Santa," handing out presents one by one. I always appreciated the special attention we gave one another.

Every year when we were kids, after all the presents were unwrapped, Lisa and I would watch our mom. She'd start looking under the tree with an expression of growing puzzlement.

Lisa and I would grin at each other. "Did you forget one, Mom?"

She always forgot at least one. One year, I didn't get my forgotten gift until the next year. Unfortunately, it was a model of Castle Grayskull from the *He-Man* cartoon. By then, I had outgrown my interest in it.

When Marianne and I joined my family for Christmas that year, my dad got his usual gift of a few new pairs of Lee jeans. He made the same joke he did every year: "Well, these aren't mine. It's says they're 'Lee's.' But I'll wear them, anyway. Thank you."

*

After six months, the church found a replacement for the senior pastor. This guy was a one-man show. He set about changing the community model of leading worship I'd been cultivating; he wanted to be in charge and make his mark.

He also micromanaged everything I did. "You didn't pick your phone up after the first ring," he'd say, or, "The desk in your office is too close to the door."

Then, a week later: "Your desk is too far away from the door." One day my office was too dim, and the next it was too bright.

I found myself thinking, *This will be a good learning experience to look back on. Unfortunately, I have to go through it first.*

*

My two-year commitment to the church was coming to a close. The church wanted to help send me to seminary so I could get my degree and become a full pastor.

However, the most important thing I had learned while in the position was I had no desire to lead a church. I wasn't even sure I wanted to go to seminary.

Then Marianne's mother Inger, who lived in Norway, got sick. She was hurting and lived alone. The time that had passed since high-school graduation had softened Marianne's feelings about her family. She decided she wanted to be near her mother to support her.

We discussed it. "It's not bad timing," I said. "You're done with your master's program. I don't want to be a pastor anymore and the two years are up. I don't owe the church anything and they don't owe me. So I can leave on good terms."

That settled it. We were going to Europe.

Chapter 5

11:20 a.m., Monday, August 22, 2022

I ascend the gray and pictureless, fire-proofed stairwell alone, with each step making the mental transition from nineteen-year-old Shawn's toilet jokes to a death in the ICU.

In the unit, I show myself to Seth, the bedside nurse. He's a hefty guy in his late thirties with a big personality, a long gray beard, and bright shining blue eyes. His height and bulk are belied by a grace that allows him to float around the room in his neon orange and aqua-green Hoka sneakers.

"Oh, they went to the solarium," Seth says, busily moistening the deceased man's eyes.

"Gotcha … Is he a donor?"

"Yeah, but waiting to hear if he's eligible. I'm doing eye-care just in case."

I thank him for what he does and walk to the solarium.

Through the glass door, I see two women seated with their backs to me, staring out one of the glass walls. The wall overlooks the parking lot and surrounding neighborhood. In the distance is the city skyline. The sky is deep blue and very clear. I knock softly, enter, and introduce myself.

I learn one woman is the patient's wife and the other is a friend. They are an odd pair. The wife is thin and frail, elegantly dressed, with long white gloves and a cloth handkerchief. Her friend is in jeans and a hoodie, a woman you wouldn't be surprised to find out rides a motorcycle. I bet she has a tattoo. And I bet that tattoo has flames in it.

"So, we just have to figure out what to do with his body?" the wife asks.

"That's correct. Once you select a funeral home."

There is silence, stillness. The air seems pressurized, like the solarium took in a deep breath and has yet to exhale.

The friend glances up at me, then smiles at the wife. "Well, good thing we brought the truck. We can just … throw him in there."

They both laugh. The pressure releases.

"Sorry," the friend says to me. "I'm a nurse in a burn unit. Our humor is a bit dark—or charcoaled."

"That's the sort of joke he would have loved," the wife says.

I wish I knew them in a different context; they seem fun.

*

The burn-unit nurse's comment might be less of a joke than the wife thinks it is. I once saw an employee from a funeral home show up at the hospital in a 1980s green Toyota crew cab. He rolled a body out of the hospital on a cart, then unceremoniously flipped it off into the truck bed, where it landed with a big thud. He threw a tarp over it and drove away.

*

While not everyone involved in a situation can always agree on the appropriateness of the where and when, humor is an important part of coping in the hospital. Joining in on the humor is also often a way for me to connect with staff. The same goes for swearing.

A case in point: once when I was on call, I got a page from ACE (the acute care for elders unit). Someone had dropped off an elderly man at the front door and left. Informally, we call this "granny-dumping." I know there are reasons, circumstances I can't imagine. But how can one have faith in society when people do things like that?

I arrived and checked in with the unit director who had paged me.

"Thanks for coming," she said. "I don't think there's anything specific to do. But could you check on my staff? The bedside nurse isn't taking this well."

"Yeah, it's a horrible thing to do," I said, the understatement of the year.

I appreciated the unit director's attention to the well-being of her team. I told her so and went to find the bedside nurse.

She was getting the patient settled in his room. Most moments in a nurse's shift are busy, but the moments following a patient's arrival are some of the busiest. Nurses must get things done in the new arrival's room while they keep half of their mind on the other patients who need attention once they're done.

The timing wasn't great for a conversation about the bedside nurse's emotions. I knew a direct question about how she was feeling was likely to elicit a response along the lines of, "I don't have time for feelings."

Still, I was open for surprises. So I stepped into the room. The nurse looked at my badge and said, "Oh, hey."

She was in her late twenties, with shoulder-length black hair she wore tucked behind her ears. Her voice was quiet and so were her feet when she moved gracefully around the room. She unfurled the sheet into the air above the bed with a soft snap. We both watched it drift slowly down to the mattress.

I looked at the patient. He was slumped over in a hospital wheelchair, a dusting of dandruff and a line of drool on his food-stained brown t-shirt. His face drooped and his deeply sunken eyes were nearly hidden in a cave of shadows and brow hair. He didn't turn toward me or show any sign that he was seeing or engaging with anything around him.

I said, "This is messed up."

The nurse eyed me. "It's fucked up is what it is," she said. "Sorry, Chaplain."

"You don't need to apologize to me—that's an astute observation."

She laughed a little. Then she let out a deep sigh.

"The only intelligent tactical response to life's horror is to laugh defiantly at it." This is a quote often attributed to Søren Kierkegaard (even though there's no evidence he actually said it).No matter who first uttered this statement, the bedside nurse's laugh embodied it. What else could she do? She could tuck the sheet under the mattress, make the bed comfortable, speak kindly to him even if he didn't seem to notice. She had to compartmentalize the manner in which he had arrived and care for him as she would any other patient.

*

This compartmentalization helps; it's necessary. It can also have disastrous effects on one's health and well-being.

A physician once told me a story about doing chest compressions on an infant in the NICU (Neonatal ICU) when she was a resident. The procedure is to press down with both thumbs at the same time on the baby's chest.

The baby died. The physician moved on, accepting the sad outcome as part of the job. Then one day ten years later, she was washing her hands in the bathroom and the soap dispenser jammed. When she put both thumbs on it to work the spring mechanism, she instantly collapsed to the floor in tears. She had never processed the infant's death. She'd just tried to forget it.

"But that's not really possible. We can put it out of our memory," this physician told me, "but the body remembers."

*

In the room with the elderly man who had been abandoned, I said to the bedside nurse, "Thank you for what you do for him." She was rushing from corner to corner of the bed in a methodical way. It was clear she'd done this many times.

"Of course. It's what we have to do." The pace of her movement didn't slow.

"No," I said, "you don't have to. But you do. And he's fortunate to have you caring for him."

She stopped and squared her shoulders and looked at me. Then she dropped her gaze to the floor.

"Thank you," she said.

I smiled. "Let me know if you need to vent."

"I will. Thanks, Chaplain."

*

In a situation like this one, I can validate the use of swear words— strong language to reflect strong feelings—without using it myself. Early in my career, I would use the actual words at work, but I tend not to anymore, or at least not as much (as opposed to how much I use them internally or in my personal life). At work, I started to feel as if the language cheapened what I represented as a chaplain: the spiritual, supernatural authority other people need me to embody in those moments.

I know chaplains who disagree. They cuss freely in the hospital, perhaps feeling it makes them seem more down-to-earth and approachable. But I'm not sure it works. I find it cringeworthy.

"A family in the Neonatal ICU is requesting some support," says a nurse.

"Well, let's fucking get down there and get them some fucking support," I've heard one of these punk-rock chaplains reply.

Am I being judgmental? Maybe. I think I'm just trying to figure out what my role is and what works.

Jerry Seinfeld tells a story about delivering a joke early in his career.[8] The joke had the F bomb in it and it got a huge laugh. The second time he told the joke, he took out that word and no one thought it was funny.

The experience made him realize *he* wasn't funny yet; it was only the word that the audience found funny, maybe the shock of hearing the word. He knew to succeed as a comic, he had to figure out a way of telling a story so it was funny on its own, without relying on a cheap language trick.

In my work, I need to look for the words that allow me to be authentic but also a spiritual presence. This means not relying on swear words as a shortcut to show I'm invested, that I understand the gravity or enormity of a situation.

There are exceptions, of course. Sometimes, only the strongest words will cut it.

*

11:47 a.m., Monday, August 22, 2022

I go back to one of my regular unit floors and walk around to see if any of the patients need or want a visit. In all the rooms, I'm politely dismissed. That's just fine. Sometimes, what people need from me is my absence.

I check in with the nurse for the nineteen-year-old patient with autism and developmental delay. She says she hasn't seen his parents this morning and doesn't think she will—they said they would be back in a day or two.

"Okay, sounds good. If they show up, just page me," I say.

"Will do," she says.

It's nearly noon. I make my way back to the break room to get my lunch—stir-fry and rice—and heat it up. Hopefully I won't get paged. I coordinate with my friend Megan to meet outside on the patio between the back of the hospital and the administration offices. Many of the staff come out here to eat. The day is hot, already ninety degrees, so I find a table in the shadow of the bridge that links the two buildings together. Lining the sidewalk in front of me are a sandwich shop, a coffee shop, a pizza place, an Indian restaurant, and, for some reason, a bank. I wave at Megan with my chopsticks when she arrives.

Megan is a staff chaplain at the hospital. She has short brown hair and black-framed glasses and would never dream of being caught in a dress. Today, she's wearing a button-up shirt and blue slacks. We met when she was a first-year resident and I was beginning my Certified Educator training. As we got to know each other, we discovered how much we had in common: she was a married lesbian woman and I was a divorced straight man who had to google the correct spelling of "lesbian."

As we eat, I tell Megan about the dream I had last night. I explain how my befuddlement in the contentious room was probably similar to those dreams overachievers have about sitting down to take a test and realizing it's for a class they forgot to show up for all semester. Megan nods knowingly and takes a big bite of her sandwich. When I tell her about the macabre Poe-like scene of the dead man sitting up and bleating like an alarm clock, she laughs so hard she almost chokes, her mouth full of lettuce and sourdough.

"See," she sputters, "if you hadn't sucked so much at de-escalation, the poor guy might not have had to come back from the dead to do it for you."

"If I remember right," I say, trying hard to recall the hazy ending, "we had to call security, anyway. So the dead guy sucked at it, too."

As we joke, we try to keep the level of our voices contained to the perimeter of our table; there could be family members and even staff out here who wouldn't appreciate our word choice and tone. But the laughs we let out. There has to be somewhere we can do that. At the dining table feels the most appropriate.

We start debating who the dead man favored in his will and end up trading "last wishes" stories. I tell Megan about a woman I met when I was helping her fill out her DNR (do-not-resuscitate order). She was originally from Maine and loved lobster more than any other food in the world. She insisted it be documented that when she was on her way out, she would get to experience eating lobster one last time, even if it had to be puréed and jammed through a feeding tube.

"That's awesome," says Megan.

"She was cool. I remember thinking, *You are a person I would like to get to know.*"

I tell another one about a man who wanted a Modelo before he lost the ability to swallow. Hospital staff looked the other way while his Mexican-American family drank a six-pack with him in the room. The patient got down about half a bottle. The remainder of it was on the tray in front of him when he died.

Last wishes run the gamut of the senses—taste, sound, sight, touch, smell—the very substance of life. Sometimes it's a certain song or piece of music someone wants to hear, or they want to see someone's face. We often hear, "I want to feel the sunshine; I want the fresh air to come over me." This is hard in the hospital, as the windows don't open. Sometimes it's impossible. Once, one of my students performed a wedding ceremony for a dying patient and his partner. The plan was to do it in the hospital's rose garden so the patient could breathe in the blooms' heavy fragrance. But his condition took a turn for the worse and he had to be hooked up to life-saving machines. So my student performed the ceremony at the patient's bedside. It wasn't legally binding, but it was a beautiful thing.

"I got a good one," Megan says. "Listen to this." She tells me a dying patient once beckoned her close and spoke to her in a low voice. She had a final wish and she needed Megan's help.

"I want to feel my boyfriend inside me before I die," she said.

"Oh," Megan said to her. "You mean …."

Yes, the patient said, that was exactly what she meant. She asked Megan if she could stand guard at the door so they could have some privacy. She wouldn't want the nurses to know "what was going on inside."

"Inside is right," I say. "I wonder if they worried about getting pregnant?"

We both guffaw with laughter then. In the middle of it, my trauma pager beeps. This alert comes from the emergency department. It notifies the trauma team a trauma patient is arriving. In this hospital, these patients always arrive in one of seven rooms, all next to each other and opposite the charge nurse's station in the emergency department.

"It was nice to have this uninterrupted time," says Megan.

We don't have to explain what happens next; we all carry this pager when on call. I get up and throw my rubbish in the bin.

Before I go back inside, I breathe in the smoky scent of freshly roasted beans from the coffee shop, rich tomato-and-oregano from the pizza place, the spicy-sweet aromas of the Indian restaurant. I follow a path that passes by a few big cement flowerpots, too.

*

Scent is powerful, perhaps particularly in a hospital, where a medicinal, antiseptic aroma pervades—except when it's pierced by the corporeal reality of everything that happens here.

*

In 2013, when I was still at the very beginning of my career as a chaplain, I had a breakthrough, a moment of self-discovery: the kind of "Aha!" moment I'd heard other CPE students talk about. Until it happens, you never know if it's going to come for you or not.

I'd been visiting a sepsis patient. I was walking down a hallway in an Alabama hospital when the scent of a visitor's strong cologne hit me. I don't often smell perfume in the hospital because staff aren't supposed to wear it, due to scent allergies. (Deodorant is allowed, thank goodness). So when I do smell perfume or cologne, I always notice it.

This scent I *really* noticed. Immediately, I was brought back to a childhood memory. I was in the hospital then, too, and this was the same scent my dad's friend Tweed used to wear.

For a long time—particularly when I was dreading and avoiding hospital visits as a pastor, even though I knew how important this ministry was—I had been wondering where my fear of hospitals had come from. Now, the formative memory of visiting Tweed with my parents when I was about ten came rushing back to me in full color.

Tweed was an odd guy whose oddness was also a familiar part of my childhood. He had a very bushy salt-and-pepper moustache and a high, nasal voice like Slim Pickens. And when I say he wore the same cologne as the man I passed in the Alabama hospital, it would be more accurate to say he bathed in it. You could smell it from across the room. Tweed never married and he lived with his mother his entire life. He was afraid of her and didn't want her to know he smoked, hence all the cologne. It was the same brand my grandfather used, which is how I know it was from Avon and came in a green glass bottle shaped like a vintage car.

The overwhelming cologne may have been part of why my mother never liked Tweed much—that and the fact he never took his black cowboy boots off when he came into our house. To go with the boots, he favored blue Wrangler shirts with pearl-snap buttons, tucked into light blue work jeans cinched with a big belt buckle. But he was into vehicles, not horses; he built cars with my father that they raced at the local speedway.

The same year I visited him in the hospital, Tweed gave me a sky-blue radio-controlled toy car for my birthday. It was fun for the first few minutes, when I was getting it out of the box and searching for the spot where the batteries went in. Then I realized it was on a cord. Whenever I played with that car, I felt as if I were taking it for a walk.

Even worse, my mom made me give Tweed a hug to show my thanks. I smelled like his cologne for the rest of the day.

The next time I saw him, a brain aneurysm had left Tweed unable to speak and slow to comprehend what people were saying. When we came into his room, he looked right at us; it seemed that he recognized us, but he couldn't do anything about it. He just grunted and groaned.

The features on one side of his face seemed to be sliding off like food oozing dangerously near the lip of a plate. His big body looked so strange in a hospital gown instead of his usual cowboy clothes and a plastic cover rustled disconcertedly whenever he shifted on the bed. My dad carried on a one-sided conversation with him while I hung silently back with my mom and six-year-old Lisa, who was clutching my mom's leg.

Did anyone warn me it was going to be like this? I don't remember that they did. I kept looking to my mom for guidance, but she looked as uncomfortable and unhappy to be there as I was. That only made me feel worse. After thousands of hours at the bedside and thousands of hours in education with my students, one thing I've come to understand is that of all the contagious things in a hospital—measles and tuberculosis and Covid-19—nothing is easier to catch than anxiety. It spreads faster than you can say, "I'm nervous." And almost always, the most anxious person in the room is the last to be aware of it, even after they've infected everyone around them.

Looking in horror at Tweed, I had trouble believing this was the same mustached man who had given me my race car. He certainly resembled him; but this man was more of a zombie than a person. How could it be him?

But maybe it *was* him. And if Tweed's appearance and presence could so terribly, so drastically change, could the same thing happen to anyone? To my mom or dad? Even to *me*?

Tweed began to groan louder and he started to rock back and forth. The collective anxiety level in the room shot up even higher. My dad kept trying weakly to translate Tweed's grunts, but he looked stunned when with a tremendous effort, Tweed managed to swing one hairy bare leg over the guard rail on his bed.

My mom's voice was panicked. She pressed her hands to her cheeks so hard they left white finger marks when she pulled them away.

"Oh, God, he's trying to get out!" she said.

Hearing her talk about Tweed as if he were a mad gorilla rattling the bars of its cage freaked me out. Keeping my eyes on the wildly erratic man thrashing in his bed, I backed all the way into a corner of the room. I eyed the door. Tweed began rocking more fervently. He was trying to raise his other leg.

Then Tweed locked eyes with me. Or, rather, only one of his brown eyes was able to focus on me. It was wide open in an expression I can see only now must have been pure desperation. His other eye sagged into the sunburnt skin of his face.

I thought Tweed was going to attack me. He moaned one more time. Then I smelled and saw a dark stain spread on his gown.

"Oh, no. He's peeing. He's peeing," my mom whimpered.

After a second, Tweed stopped struggling. He sank back onto his bed with a sigh.

"I'll go get a nurse," my dad said.

*

Tweed's unpredictable appearance meant his behavior, too, was hard for me to predict. Tweed had always been a little strange, but it was a strangeness I could count on.

What could I count on now? I had the strong feeling even Tweed himself might not know what he was doing or what was happening to him. That was terrifying. So much of who we are depends on remembering who we are.

Research has shown that "there are two primary domains of uncertainty … uncertainty about perception and uncertainty about action."[9] I was unclear about what I was seeing. Therefore, I was unclear about what would happen and what I should do.

*

When I remembered this story in 2013, I was able to see it in a new way. I can only imagine how humiliated Tweed must have felt. He knew he had to use the bathroom, but he couldn't communicate it.

Finally understanding this moment, and feeling a rush of compassion for Tweed, was the greatest discovery of my adult life. My new understanding of where my fear of hospitals had come from settled like a soothing balm on that fear. I felt as if I had been set free.

*

Every time I go into a hospital room, I enter an ambiguous space.

The prefix "ambi" has two distinct definitions: "bothness" (ambidextrous) and "aroundness" (ambiance).

Merriam-Webster gives two definitions for "ambiguous": "doubtful or uncertain especially from obscurity or indistinctness" and "capable of being understood in two or more possible senses or ways."[10] My childhood visit with Tweed fits both of those descriptions.

Unresolved ambiguity can be painful, even hurtful if it's intentional. Sometimes people carefully cultivate ambiguity for some nasty reason. They might intentionally create chaos simply for the pleasure of watching someone else struggle through it or withhold affection or approval to maintain power in a relationship.

As a chaplain, I must be ready for uncertainty every time I'm poised at the edge of a doorway. Once I step in, I'll use all the information about the patient I have at my disposal and all my previous experience to attempt to comprehend what I'm seeing and hearing. At the same time, I must be wary of letting that information or experience color or cloud my vision too much. Just as easily as it can illuminate, it can also keep me from seeing what's there. Everything might look familiar, but that familiarity could be cloaking a secret or a surprise.

Likewise, I can't predict what my own emotional reaction will be to whatever I find in there. You can never take it for granted that you know who you are.

And who knows what my interaction with the patient and the family will be like? That often depends on what they'll need most at the time, another thing I can't know for sure until we make contact.

Will we discuss practical matters or an emotional issue? Or maybe a thorny philosophical one? Will I be in there for a minute or an hour?

Will I leave feeling I want to laugh or cry?

*

1:15 p.m., Monday, August 22, 2022

The trauma alert that interrupted my meal with Megan has led to a "hurry up and wait" situation. The patient has arrived, but the family isn't here yet.

After a while, I step away and go up a few floors to check on the family I learned about this morning in the MICU (code status, a lack of brain activity, a police officer waiting in the hall). There's a different officer guarding the room now, this one short and slim with a blond buzz cut.

I find the charge nurse standing at the station desk. It's Tiffany, who has been on this unit for many years. She has long brown hair, skin that's almost orange from a tanning bed, and bright white teeth. She's courageous and strong and often takes me aside to tell me about her struggles. I think the fact that she's willing to share and process is part of what keeps her so grounded and resilient.

She's signing a form—discharge, maybe? I can't see. "Did the team meet with the family of the patient in 42?" I ask her.

"No." She finishes her signature, drops the pen, and looks up, not at me, but at my badge. "Oh, Chaplain. Hi. No, so"—she inserts a laugh—"they decided not to come back to the hospital today. They'll be meeting with their lawyers instead."

"Shit," I say, very quietly, so only Tiffany can hear. This is one of those moments that necessitates an exception to my swearing "rule."

As long as the family doesn't come back to the hospital, the team can't take action. It's a way for the family to buy time. I exhale and cross my arms across my chest. Am I unconsciously protecting myself? I feel the pain of the impossibility of their situation. Families and patients have an uncanny ability to make others feel what they are feeling: this family is feeling pressured to make a decision about life support, but they are feeling stuck—they don't know what the right decision is. In turn, the patient's care team is stuck because they need an answer from the family before they can proceed.

"Yeah. They are really pissed."

"Well, yeah. I understand that. It's them against everyone."

"Right. It's such a shame they have to do this to protect themselves and their son, at the same time they're trying to wrestle with the reality that he's dead and the police are involved."

"He's in custody, right? That's why the cops are here?"

"That's my understanding."

"How are the officers behaving?"

"For the most part, okay. We've had to clarify a few times that their jurisdiction is only the patient—not the hallway, the room, or even the bed. They're just kinda in the way."

"Yeah."

"There's no brain activity."

"Are you still talking about the patient?" I give her a smirk.

"Well—" She doesn't finish what she was trying to say. She's laughing too hard.

Chapter 6

The secluded hamlet of Øye in southwest Norway sits nestled at the head of a deep fjord, surrounded by towering mountains draped in green during the summer. The narrow streets are lined with wooden houses painted in hues of red, yellow, and white, their roofs often covered in grass. There's a timeless, almost mythical quality to the place; Ibsen's *Peer Gynt* comes to mind ("Up to the highest mountain-tops; I'll see the sun rise once again, and gaze upon the promised land"[11]).

At the heart of this fairy-tale setting stands the historic Union Øye. Built in 1891, it is a charming hotel with red timber beams and intricate carvings on its walls. Inside, the cozy dining hall—"The Conservatory"—is lit by wrought-iron lanterns, smells of freshly baked pastries, strong coffee, and the caramelized aroma of *brunost* melting into thick slices of bread. The rooms are warm and inviting, with woolen blankets, hand-carved furnishings, and windows that frame postcard-perfect views of the fjord below.

It was perhaps the best and worst place for two starry-eyed virgins to have sex for the first time on their wedding night. At the beginning of my marriage to Marianne, I simply didn't have the mental capacity to real-ize how unprepared we were for marriage and sex. My parents never gave me any talk about the birds and the bees and Marianne and I were in-credibly naïve about how the world works. We'd both developed a simple technique for dealing with complicated situations: running away. As a high-school student, Marianne had run away from the difficult situation with her parents. I'd run away from my parents' business and their plans for my life. I took for granted that the stable job and home my parents had built would always be there if I needed them.

Neither Marianne nor I knew that eventually, we'd have to stop running. If we didn't confront our problems, they'd confront us.

Now, in 2007, I had run away from the church in California. We were back in Europe to be close to Marianne's ill mother, Inger, who looks like Marianne with her short blond hair, tan skin, and blue eyes. Like her daughter, she is also a dynamo of energy who is always on the go; this woman irons clothes to decompress. When we visited Inger in Nor-way, the three of us would go on epic shopping trips in which Inger refused to buy all her items at one place when she knew she could get the same item ten cents cheaper at another store. We'd travel to four or five shops burning up the extra change on gas. Whenever I pointed this out, Inger would get angry at the disruption and Marianne would hiss at me to leave it alone.

I admire Inger, though. She's a strong woman who has survived a lot and still continues to smile and have hope in the goodness of others. She also makes amazing cloudberry jam and peerless lefse (a traditional Norwegian flatbread made from potatoes).

With Marianne's Norwegian residency, and because Norway is a member of the European Economic Area, we could live and work anywhere in the European Union. We settled in Munich as it had a lot of employment opportunities and it wasn't too far from Norway—by

American standards anyway. It was also a beautiful city. I reveled in the food there: heavenly chocolate croissants, the crusty bread I bought at a bakery that had been founded in the 1300s. The city successfully merges old-world German culture with modernity as well. Every brewery had a non-alcoholic beer I could drink.

We lived in the Moosach district near Olympic Stadium. I was very aware that Guns N' Roses had filmed their "Estranged" video there. Marianne didn't like to hear me talk about it. She disapproved of Guns N' Roses and thought they were a bad influence on me: they weren't a Christian band, their lyrics were raunchy, etc., etc. Marianne tended to see the world in black and white. Things were either bad or good. She wasn't interested in hearing about Axl's authenticity or the call for empathy I heard in "Breakdown."

"Who's this?" she'd say if she came home and "Right Next Door to Hell" was playing on the stereo. "Oh. I see. And you think you're getting closer to God by listening to that?"

The easiest job for foreigners to get in Germany was teaching languages for a private language school. I taught English. Marianne taught a few Norwegian classes. I was excited but nervous; I had never been an "official" teacher before.

Soon, I found the work deeply satisfying. I was still catching up on all the reading I'd missed the first twenty-some years of my life, and I enjoyed integrating these books into my classes. I found that the "how-to" method—listing parts of speech on the board, surprising my students with pop quizzes—didn't work as well for my adult students as a conversational style did. Often, we simply talked about interesting things. My students expressed their thoughts and opinions while I gently corrected their grammar.

One of the books I incorporated was Elie Wiesel's *Night*. I'd ask if anyone had been to Birkenau, Auschwitz, or Dachau, the closest concentration camp to Munich. I'd ask what it was like to carry this history. I found most of my students were open to talking about it—and they all felt shame.

One class included high-level administrators in Munich. We were talking about East Germany versus West and one student said, "The East was so far behind. The West was so much better."

"Hang on," another student said. Then she turned to me. "Is that right?" she asked. "'Hang on'?" When I nodded, she smiled and turned back to her fellow student. "I never know homeless or hungry until I come to West Germany," she told him.

The man looked stunned. "You're from East Germany?" She said she was. "But you have no accent," he said.

"I know. I want to get a high position, so I lose my accent."

The other students began asking her questions about what it was like to grow up in East Germany. She had never revealed it to any of them before.

My students liked learning English while also being seen in the classroom and discussing deep issues in a complex way. They praised the method in their feedback and evaluations. I began to feel I might be pretty good at this.

*

Later—as both a student and a CPE educator—I would find out that soliciting and being open to feedback is also an integral part of CPE.

When students start CPE, they enter into a performance and learning covenant. They understand they're committing to the program for a set period. Once that period begins, they must fully participate in both CPE learning and their place in the clinical rotation (visits to patients). They agree to abide by certain policies and procedures.

One of those procedures is to always respond to a page. I once had a CPE student named Dorothy. She was in her early sixties and completing her second unit of CPE. Toward the end of the twenty-two-week unit, she started to exhibit behaviors that made me wonder if she was trying to get me to kick her out of the program. One day, she didn't have her pager on her for hours and no one could get a hold of her. Another time, she showed up to work without her pager and had to go back out to her car to get it—not a simple task. The parking lot was a half-mile from the hospital and she needed to take a shuttle. The whole process took an hour.

The incidents kept happening. Other chaplains had to cover for her.

I reminded Dorothy of the policy. I was frustrated, but I tried to respond with curiosity rather than rejection, to offer her a corrective emotional experience. I tried to show her what impact her behavior was having on others. As her educator, I was responsible for her. I invited her to take responsibility for her actions.

To be honest, her actions annoyed the hell out of me. At the same time, I also had compassion for her. Her home life was spinning out of control—her husband's health was failing but he was bad at communicating with her about it. She felt disoriented much of the time.

Dorothy managed to squeak through the rest of the unit. Now, it was time for me to write her evaluation. I wrote two versions. The first said exactly what I wanted to say, with the exact level of exasperation I needed to express. That felt good.

I set that report aside. When writing the second version, I asked myself, *How can I say things in a way that Dorothy will be able to hear them?*

About six weeks after she received it, she contacted me.

"I'm just calling to say I'm sorry," she said.

It had taken her a lot to get to this point. When she first received my evaluation, she was furious. She was so upset, she brought it to her therapist.

"Look at this," she said. "It's so unfair. He ripped me apart."

The therapist saw the evaluation as mostly affirmative, however. She invited Dorothy to highlight all the positive things I'd said. She was left with a document that was glowing with praise.

For a while, this made Dorothy even angrier. She wanted to blame me for the bad taste in her mouth she got whenever she thought about how the unit had gone.

But eventually, she was able to take responsibility for it. She saw she was the author of her own story.

"I made things very difficult for you at the end," she said. "Thank you for helping me get through the unit."

*

Speaking of annoying—some of the students I taught in Germany were enrolled in Arbeitsamt courses. Arbeitsamt is the equivalent of the unemployment agency in the U.S. One requirement of receiving benefits from Germany's social programs is that participants enroll in continuing education when they're unemployed to prove they're actively trying to improve themselves and society.

Most of the English teachers I knew there dreaded these classes. A high percentage of the students tend to be people who try to milk the benefits of the social system as long as possible without contributing to it.

Such as: the mother-and-daughter team I taught once. They sat in class with brand-name clothes and bags and talked about how they wanted to marry rich. They were lazy about learning and had a bad attitude. When I asked the daughter what jobs she had had in the past, she said, "Work? I don't work. I don't need to. I'm pretty."

But they're not all like that. There was, for example, my student

Aslam.

Originally from Iraq, Aslam grew up within walking distance of his entire family: not only parents and siblings but grandparents, cousins, aunts, uncles, dozens and dozens of people in a tight network. At some point, he was forced to leave Iraq. He ended up in the Czech Republic with his wife and two children. They were trying to establish a life there, but at some point, it made more sense for Aslam to come to Germany, where he could earn higher wages and send money back. He worked hard and traveled to see his family only a few times a year.

I taught Aslam English a few days a week. He was in his mid-50s. He always carried a dark blue backpack and one of his black shoes—the old-style Reeboks marked with the British flag—was often untied. His English wasn't great, but he was a diligent student and I liked him.

After class, Aslam and I sometimes rode the same train. His stop was one before mine, so often his English lesson would continue after class, which I didn't necessarily appreciate. I was often rushing to teach a class at another location and this was my only time to rest.

But one day on the train, Aslam opened up to me about his past. He told me his move from Iraq had been prompted by the killing of half of his family by Saddam Hussein's regime. Those left alive scattered to various places. Since then, some members of his family had moved back and reunited. Only Aslam and his wife and children had not returned.

"Sad" is a woefully inadequate way to describe how I felt. I also felt very young, inexperienced, and incompetent. I didn't know what to say.

"I'm sorry, Aslam," I said.

"Thank you." He smiled. "I like you. You are good teacher." Then he hesitated. I looked out the window of the train and realized he had stayed past his stop; the buildings of the city had given way to large agricultural fields. I stood and threw my bag over my shoulder and got ready to get off. I wondered why Aslam was lingering. Maybe to ask more English questions? Maybe he just wasn't paying attention? My mind was focused on getting to my next class and mentally preparing for it, so I wasn't fully present to Aslam. If I had been, I think I would have sensed that it was something else.

Aslam stood as well. He squared his shoulders and looked directly up at me with his big brown eyes. He was only a few inches over five feet, and at not-quite-5'11", I towered over him. Still, Aslam seemed bigger than me, larger than life. Maybe a loss as great as his does that to a person.

He seemed fidgety. He was rocking back and forth a little, partly due to the train, partly because he was struggling to put his thoughts into English. He said, "For one month, a U.S. bomb. All my family is no more breathe."

I shivered and felt a heavy wash of guilt. I didn't want to confirm what I was pretty sure he meant, but I did.

"Aslam, you mean a U.S. bomb killed the rest of your family?" I said. "Your family is all dead?"

"Ah, yes. 'Dead'! That is the word. Yes," Aslam said. "Yes."

*

For the first time in my life, I felt a real connection to a place: my country. And it didn't feel great. I didn't feel responsible, exactly, but I was ashamed.

When I returned to the United States, I told many friends and family members this story. I was a little shocked by their reaction. While almost universally they expressed sadness that Aslam had lost the first half of his family, only one person I spoke with did not, when hearing about the death of the second half, move quickly to justify the U.S. for "what we are doing there to liberate the people."

"We are helping people like Aslam," one man said.

"People like Aslam," I said, "but not specifically Aslam."

"There will always be tragedies."

"Like the first half of his family?"

"Exactly. He will thank us later."

*

Aslam was right. "Dead" is the word he was looking for.

Inevitably, at the beginning of every CPE unit I teach, a student will use the word "passed" to describe a death.

The student might end a story with, "And then she passed."

"Passed what?" I say.

I'll see a flicker of confusion and fear in the student's eyes. They're uncertain how to use the "D" word.

"Gas?" I'll suggest. "A kidney stone? A test? A basketball?"

"No," the student says slowly. "She passed away."

"Oh, you mean she died? She's dead?"

"Yes."

"All right. Then say that." One problem with "passed" is that it leaves room for hope and confusion. I've seen physicians sit down with families and say, "I'm sorry. She passed." Then a family member is forced to seek clarification: "You mean my Charlie is dead?" Don't make a family do this work, I tell my students. While every family and every situation is different, in my experience, cloaking the truth in misty language tends to compound the pain rather than soften it. When physicians use the "D" word, the vast majority of families I've seen in this situation were better able to receive the news and enter their grief.

*

When I talked to Aslam, I didn't have the training and experience I have now. I'm glad, at least, that somehow I had enough instinct not to say, "I'm sorry for your loss," "It's part of God's plan," or "God needed more angels." There are a lot of euphemisms and platitudes commonly used in response to death.

I know people struggle to figure out what to say in the face of another's devastating tragedy. These kinds of phrases can provide a comfortable shorthand to fill a silence many find uncomfortable.

To me, however, many of them are problematic. Some create a barrier between the aggrieved and the comforter. The "your" in "your loss" holds the aggrieved an arm's distance away—it's my loss, not yours, and you're not interested in coming close enough that you might have to share a glimmer of that pain with me.

Others impose a particular theology on the listener. If God needed another angel, or this death was part of the plan, does that mean God took my loved one from me? This phrase presumes that any of us can know what the hell God needs or wants. And presumptions about angels and heaven can feel like meaningless fluff, or worse, if the person who died was not particularly angelic. We might say with just as much confidence, "The Devil needed another demon."

"Everything is going to be okay." No. In fact, for a while, things will be awful. And as bad as they are right now, at some point they'll likely get worse. The rolling on of the days and weeks following the death will establish what life is really like now that my loved one is gone.

Related to this one is "Just give it to God." The implicit message in this one feels to me like "Just get over it already. Move on from your grieving. And if you can't, it's because your faith isn't strong enough." Neither of these phrases honor the depth of the mourner's feelings. And like the condolence about "your loss," there's a coldness and a distance to them—they don't offer an invitation for closeness and emotional availability.

"God is in control." Really? Of what? How can you possibly presume to know what God is and is not in control of? So if God is in control, that means God gave me cancer? Or gave my brother a heart attack? Or directed the bomb that destroyed Aslam's family? If God is so in control, why does everything around me feel so out of control? Is God in control of me? So is it ever worth it for me to do or feel anything?

"I know how you feel." Since every person is different, and every relationship is different, you don't. You may have had a lovely, close relationship with your aunt or grandfather and talked with them every day. But I ask you to consider the possibility that I may have been estranged from or abused by my relative. Or maybe I'm feeling an immense amount of guilt because I never returned their last call.

If a patient says, "Why is God doing this to me?", I've learned not to take the bait. Once, I made the mistake of engaging a patient when he uttered this Job-like lament. As I was going on about banishment from the Garden of Eden and Romans 3:5 ("But if our injustice serves to confirm the justice of God, what should we say? That God is unjust to inflict wrath on us?"), he interrupted me.

"You have no idea why this is happening to me," he said, "so don't pretend you do by offering me an answer."

Point taken. Now I say, "I wish I could answer that question" or "I don't know. If I knew that answer, I would tell you."

In general, I also try to steer away from telling someone what they should or shouldn't do or say. I once heard a mother whose child had just died say, "I wish God would have taken me instead."

In a corner of the room, the woman's sister shook her head and covered her face with her hands.

"You shouldn't say things like that," she wailed.

It's excruciating to hear someone you love wishing for death. And in a situation like this one, a grieving mother's words spring from her bottomless grief. A statement like this aptly expresses the depths of her fear, her sense of isolation and abandonment. She just needs to say it out loud. Having been admonished, she might now feel that she must censor herself—just another thing she has to worry about amidst the turmoil her life has become.

*

Things I do say: "I don't have the words," or "I wish I knew what to say that would make things better."

My wife Shuang jokes that all I do is show up every day and say, "I wish I knew how to help you," and get paid for it. It's kind of true. But it also takes a hell of a lot of courage to enter into people's pain.

"I wish I could take it away" goes far with people because it's so raw. Every time, it's genuine. When we say it, and follow it up by staying near, we're proving we mean what we say. We allow people to be by themselves, but in our presence. We can't underestimate the power that our presence has; it probably goes further than any words we can say.

My dad once told me he had heard his friend's wife had died. "But …" he said and trailed off.

"You haven't called him?"

"I don't know what to say."

"Well," I said, "call him and say that."

If a patient or family member of a patient asks me to pray, I ask, "What would you like me to pray for?" I don't want to assume I know the answer, and the question gets them to express and explain what they're feeling. "What's most important to you right now?" is another way to put it. Their answer can help me assess where they're at emotionally and what they need.

I sometimes hear, "Pray for members of my family—they're having trouble accepting this." This might be a sign that they're trying to distance themselves from their own pain.

If someone asks me to pray for healing, I ask, "What would healing look like for you?"

I've had several patients respond, "I fall asleep and don't wake up." One added, "That would be a miracle." So much for assuming I know what a miracle looks like. Not everyone prays to be cured.

"Okay. Let's pray for that." I take zero responsibility if it happens—or doesn't. Like the mother who wished out loud she could replace her child in death, my goal is to get the patient to voice their suffering and despair. A patient might also need to talk about how they are trying to move forward but are getting resistance from family members. They might have trouble talking freely about wanting to die when their family is around.

I want to meet people at the emotional level of where they are, to give space for that. I am trying to be a presence that invites them, that gives them permission to be and do whatever they want to be in those moments (within reason—I don't stand by with my hands folded beatifically if they start breaking things or become a threat to themselves or others). I fill that space with words if that's what they want. Sometimes they don't want that, but they still want me there. They need to be alone. At the same time, that aloneness is only bearable if someone is with them.

It doesn't matter what's going on with the patient. They might have a terminal disease or just a broken arm. Even a broken arm can make someone feel alone, remind them of the fragility of life, confront them with the human condition. I try to communicate that I'm not here to judge them or anything they need to say, however dark or melodramatic their words might sound.

"My brother doesn't care about me," a patient once said. "If he did, he'd be here."

"I don't know if this is true for you," I responded, "but people often tell me how alone they feel in their illness."

"Yeah … I miss him so much and I'm so scared." He paused to wipe his tears. Then he said, "He's probably scared too."

*

I'm glad I didn't say to Aslam, "You're going to get through this." There's no way through. I know this from personal experience. You'll get through the intensity of your grief, but you'll always grieve. The loss will always be present in you.

I got a beautiful piece of feedback once after losing someone I loved. It's always stayed with me. I talked about my loss in a paper I wrote when I was in CET (Certified Educator Training). When he read it, one of my committee members wrote, "This reads like he still lives in grief—he needs to learn how to let the grief live in him."

As chaplains, we must acknowledge that the people we work with are often living through the deepest throes of fresh grief, and hope one day the grief will instead become part of what makes them who they are.

*

About a year after we had been in Munich, both Marianne and I woke up one morning with a revelation. We were talking in the back of a tram, passing by a cemetery. We discovered that both of us had had a dream the night before that left us with a sort of mystical certainty that I should go to seminary.

"It's a sign!" we said.

We laughed at ourselves. We didn't believe, exactly, that the coincidence was part of a divine plan. At the same time …

It did show us we'd been thinking the same thing. We took that seriously. I knew after my stint as an associate pastor in California that I didn't want to lead a church. But after a year of teaching students like Aslam, I felt I did want to be in the ministry in some capacity. I had no idea what that would look like. However, getting my Master of Divinity would open the door to—something.

*

It must have been incredibly difficult for Aslam to sit through my class and get to know someone from the country responsible for the death of so many of the people he loved.

I'm grateful to him for having the emotional capacity, the openness, that allowed him to do so. My encounter with Aslam brought me closer to the road that led me to chaplaincy. I learned from him that despite everything that could have stood in the way, I was able to hold a safe space in which he felt comfortable enough to reveal his grief to me.

A few weeks after our conversation, I told Aslam's class I would be returning to the United States. On the last day of class, he gave me a card and some chocolates. He cried a little and gave me a hug.

He never thanked me for what my country did to his family. He thanked me for what I had done for him.

Chapter 7

I applied and was accepted at the Seventh-day Adventist Theological Seminary at Andrews University in Berrien Springs, Michigan. We left Europe in 2008.

In seminary, I read deeply in theology, philosophy, poetry, and church history: Bonhoeffer, Goethe, Alasdair MacIntyre, Cyprian and Tertullian. Studying the English Reformation led me to Thomas More's *Utopia*, which bridged fiction and religion and showed me how novels could explore moral truths.

I also kept studying lyrics to songs. More than ever, I mined complex moral and religious meaning from popular music that directly or indirectly asked theological questions. Like Tom Waits' cry about God's absence, even neglect, in "Georgia Lee."

I began to understand what Leonard Cohen meant when he said, "Music is the emotional life of most people." I found the emotion of theology and religion through music, especially when I discovered classical music near the end of my final year.

I started with Bach, Haydn, Mozart, Tchaikovsky, and Elgar. Then, through the deeply personal reviews of Tony Duggan, I found Gustav Mahler's ninth symphony. Regarding Leonard Bernstein's recording of the ninth with the Berlin Philharmonic, Duggan describes the meeting of two great artists, composer and conductor. He explains how Bernstein elicited a specific performance from the orchestra by not only making extraordinary artistic decisions but expressing his reactions to the music out loud. Duggan writes that the strings were

> ... *especially encouraged to greater and greater levels of emotion by Bernstein grunting and humming occasionally: Mahler with all the stops pulled out. At the assault of the final climax it sounds as though Bernstein has fallen off the podium but even this could not explain what happens between bars 118 and 122. Here, at the climax of the whole work, where maximum power is needed from everyone, the trombones simply stop playing. The whole trombone section should play right through that passage, underpinning everything, but they are nowhere to be heard ... Just one of those things that makes this recording memorable, I suppose.*[12]

Encountering Mahler's music was strange. I was startled when I experienced feelings I couldn't have imagined before. The transition between the first movement of the ninth and the second provoked a swell of something more than joy: a new ecstatic exuberance.

Then the high, sharp notes of the violins brought razorblades of pain—but only for a second. The pain was released, only to return. Then there was relief again. Mahler is comforting the dying—comforting himself. In middle age, Mahler was diagnosed with an abnormal heartbeat. The symphony begins with an irregular rhythm that Bernstein believed was a documentation of the beat of Mahler's damaged heart.[13]

And the last page of Mahler's ninth, according to Bernstein,

... is the closest we have ever come in any work of art to experiencing the very act of dying—of giving it all up. The slowness of this page is terrifying. Adagissimo, he writes, the slowest possible musical direction. And then, if that weren't enough, he then writes langsam.[14]

"Langsam": a German term for "slow," a metronome marking that indicates a pace slower than the lowest number in the normal average range of a person's beating heart.[15]

In his lecture series "The Unanswered Question," Bernstein talks about how Alma Mahler, Mahler's wife, attended his rehearsals at the 1960 Mahler Festival in New York. Her presence made him feel he was directly linked to Mahler and his message. When telling this story, Bernstein rubs his forehead; his eyes are pained and full of sorrow. Bernstein seems to be channeling Mahler's understanding of the world through his understanding of Mahler's piece. He says of Mahler's ninth, written only a few years before the start of World War I, that it was this work "that spread the news, but it was bad news and the world did not care to hear it. That's the real reason for the fifty years of neglect that Mahler's music suffered after his death ... it was simply too true. Telling something too dreadful to hear."[16]

*

Bernstein's quote puts me in mind of the design of modern hospitals. Today, hospitals can feel more like hotels or museums than places for the sick and dying. Hang original artwork on the walls, fill spaces with bright colors and open areas to give people a sense of calm and awe—hell, maybe people will make a special trip to the hospital gardens for a pleasant stroll. "Stop by for a visit! We've got great farm-fresh food and a sculpture by a rising star you must see. Just keep your eyes averted from the patients' rooms—unless you want to be reminded that we're all going to die."

It's not hard to keep from looking. The architectural plans for these buildings are designed to keep the sick away from the non-sick. Obviously, this is a good choice for practical reasons like the prevention of the spread of infectious diseases; but from a "learning from life" perspective, it feels problematic. As Bernstein says, the finale of Mahler's ninth symphony "is a sonic presentation of death itself ... which paradoxically reanimates us every time we hear it."[17]

*

I started my training to become a CPE educator in 2017. That year I was introduced to American psychiatrist Irvin D. Yalom's book *Existential Psychotherapy*, which changed my perspective about how I live and see the world.

In that book, Yalom outlines the four ultimate concerns of life: freedom, death, meaninglessness, and isolation. He describes how engaging deeply with each of these concerns helps people live more authentically and recognize when they are deceiving themselves.

I had been reading Buber, Kierkegaard, and Nietzsche. Yalom brought all their philosophies together in a practical theory. When I was with patients, I started to listen for these ultimate concerns in what they said. I found that responding according to which "concern" I heard created a deeper connection between us. They welcomed the questions I asked. And answering those questions helped them better understand themselves and what they were going through.

Categorizing life experiences helped ground me. It gave me a useful lens through which I could more clearly see and hear the world. As a CPE educator, I try to help my students learn how to do this, too.

For example: in *Existential Psychotherapy*, Irvin Yalom describes death as a "boundary situation," which is "an event, an urgent experience, that propels one into a confrontation with one's existential 'situation' in the world." Such a confrontation is meant to "provide a massive shift in the way one lives in the world."[18]

Meaning: death is important to the living. It can show us how to live.

One of my CPE students, Janelle, wrote about responding to her first trauma page in her final evaluation. Final evaluations are statements students write at the end of a unit in which they discuss how they believe they've met the outcomes and standards for the unit.

Janelle was young and intense. After I gave her feedback on her first verbatim, she told me she was disappointed that I wasn't harsher on her.

"I expected CPE to rip me apart," she said.

It was only a matter of time. One hot summer day, she was on one of her units when she got the page. It contained the limited information that there was a trauma patient coming in and she should come to the emergency department. Janelle crossed the bridge that connected the two parts of the hospital, loud, anxious thoughts running through her head. She didn't know what to anticipate; her imagination was vivid, exploratory, envisioning worst-case scenarios. Her temperature rose from the walk and the heat of the day. She was sweating a little by the time she got there and her heart was beating fast.

She reminded herself that this was the intensity she'd been looking for. But now, she was terrified to find it.

When Janelle arrived at the trauma room, the first thing she saw was blood dripping from a gurney. Then she saw the patient—a 90-year-old man who had fallen off a ladder—convulse and die.

Immediately, Janelle felt a wave of dizziness. She backed out of the trauma room and into the counter outside of it.

Where did her dizziness come from? As Kierkegaard writes, "Anxiety is the dizziness of freedom."[19] To illustrate, he describes the anxiety he feels while standing on the edge of a cliff. His anxiety is disturbing, even unbearable, until he understands it.

Is he afraid of falling? Not exactly.

He's scared of his compulsion to jump—which stems not from a desire to jump, much less a desire to die, but simply from his awareness that he has the freedom to do so.

*

Reading Yalom also changed the way I listened to music, another resource to share with my students.

I realized I could categorize songs by their primary ultimate concern. I made an "Ultimate Concerns" playlist (one playlist in four parts) and shared it with my CPE students. They all loved music and were excited about it; they started adding songs and sharing them with me.

*ULTIMATE CONCERNS: THE PLAYLIST**
Ultimate Concern #1: Freedom
Top Ten:
    1. Ballad of Big Nothing—Elliott Smith
    2. You Can't Always Get What You Want—The Rolling Stones
    3. The Word—The Beatles
    4. Time—Pink Floyd
    5. Redemption Song—Bob Marley and the Wailers
    6. I Know There's an Answer—The Beach Boys
    7. Down in the Flood—Bob Dylan
    8. Glory—John Legend and Common
    9. Keep Your Eye on the Prize--Unknown
    10. Hope—R.E.M.

---

*See page 283 for a link to all playlists.

The Beatles thought a lot about the connection between freedom and responsibility. The lyrics of "The Word," encourage listeners to embrace their responsibility to take action and by doing so they will find their true freedom.

*

Until Janelle saw the moment of death's arrival—the first time she'd ever seen it—her anxiety had no place to go. She was walking into the unknown. Her anxiety was spinning out wildly, ethereally, yearning for something solid to attach to. She needed a structure, a system, to hang it on so she could transform her anxiety into a plan of action. But not knowing what she would find, she didn't know what she would do.

Then she saw something to be afraid of: death. Non-existence. She was able to displace her anxiety onto an actual thing and work through that fear.

Leaning over the counter outside the trauma room, blinking hard to regain her focus and trying to catch her breath, Janelle saw the family of the patient approaching. She straightened up. She remembered she not only had the freedom to act, but the responsibility to. She walked over and introduced herself.

*

In the trauma room, the chaplain's primary job is to stand and watch, keeping a space of calm and stillness amidst the chaos. The chaplain is a visual reminder that it's okay to slow down.

A trauma room is a big space with very bright fluorescent lights. There's room for as many as a couple dozen people to work in there. During an emergency, it's filled with doctors, nurses, techs, a transcriber, social worker. It's loud and chaotic. While everyone is working on the patient, someone from imaging will arrive, rolling in a machine to take

X-rays. This technician has to force and wedge their way in. Before they take images, everyone clears out. At a computer against the wall, a nurse charts everything that's happening. So much relies on the job each person is doing that for the most part, no one has the capacity to worry about anyone else.

The moment when the work room changes into a viewing room is full of weight. There's a momentous and grave but brief pause, the bridge between one action and another. Then doctors, nurses, and techs begin filing out. Movement and life go on even though death is only a few feet away. Witnessing this moment was probably jarring for Janelle, too.

There is often a family waiting outside to see their loved one. Before they're ushered in, a nurse might pull the curtain to hide the space until it can be cleaned up a little. It's usually a mess. There might be speckles or even pools of blood on the floor. Plastic wrappers that held new instruments are scattered everywhere, as are discarded paper gowns and the orange plastic caps from syringes.

The nurse also does some cleaning on the body. Doctors may have put in a central line from the femoral artery to the heart to administer fluids and medications. Central lines tend to bleed all over the patient's legs and groin. When blood and fluids are wiped away, a nurse will place the patient's arms down at their sides and cover them with a sheet up to the neck. If the arms look all right, they leave them out, so family members can hold the patient's hand. If the arms are very damaged, they get tucked in.

Any tubes running into the patient's mouth are removed—if it can be done easily. If it can't be done easily, the trauma team might call someone from respiratory to come do it. But since death isn't an emergency, it might be a while before anyone comes. And the tubes are only removed right away if the patient has been in the hospital for a long time. If they died within a short time of coming in, only the coroner is authorized to allow staff to remove them.

On the unsettling day of her first trauma page, the trauma just kept coming for Janelle. The staff chaplain invited her to help with body clean-up of the elderly man who had fallen off a ladder. When Janelle raised his arm, it was broken in so many places that it completely collapsed. It snapped in half at the midpoint of his forearm. She watched his fingers fold back to his elbow.

*

Anxiety is not always something to "get over." It's a condition for living. As a CPE educator, I accompany students on their search for philosophical meaning in the midst of their anxiety. A first unit of CPE is basically four hundred hours of helping students become aware of their anxiety. Once they develop some awareness, they can learn what to do with it.

Meaning: before we act, we need to pay attention to our desire to act. We can ask ourselves: "Why do I feel a need to act right now? Am I anxious? If so, what am I anxious about?" Many students find themselves looking for something to do. Anxiety doesn't really give you something to do; it just motivates you to move restlessly around. This can make anxiety worse.

*

After Janelle's experience, I helped her realize that death gave her a way to understand her anxiety. It helped her come to a place where she could say, "I've never been this close to a dead person and it's made me realize I'm afraid to die."

One of Janelle's peers said in her final verbatim of the unit, "That patient who's dying—she's me." Then she turned to her peers and added, "She's each of us."

It's my hope that by the end of their first unit, every CPE student can experience that transfer, can see the reality of their own mortality through the mortality they're seeing every day.

*

ULTIMATE CONCERNS: THE PLAYLIST
Ultimate Concern #2: Death
Top Ten:
1. *There Is a Light That Never Goes Out—The Smiths*
2. *The Crossroads—Bone Thugs-n-Harmony*
3. *If Tomorrow Never Comes—Garth Brooks*
4. *He Stopped Loving Her Today—George Jones*
5. *Dirt in the Ground—Tom Waits*
6. *Lost One—Jay-Z*
7. *Prayer for the Dying—Seal*
8. *If You Were Here—Poe*
9. *The One I Love—David Gray*
10. *Golden Gate Jumpers—Cold War Kids*

George Jones' song "He Stopped Loving Her Today" tells the story of a man who swears his love for a woman will last a lifetime. The "she" who responds assures him he'll get over her, but the speaker in the song uses a clever conceit to show us just how wrong she is. Sure, the "he" stops loving the "her"—but not before he's been dressed for burial and flowers hang on the wall in his memory.

*

I worked hard while I was at seminary. For the first time in my life, I succeeded in school.

I was hired as a graduate assistant and helped my professor finish his dissertation on Theophilus of Antioch and his view of Creation. I graduated in 2011. The kid who had given up on learning out of humiliation and terror in the third grade now had a master's degree. I was proud of that.

I had spent much of my time at seminary steeped in the creativity of great artists like More and Mahler. The desire to create was stirring in me, too.

The first time I listened to Mahler, I had a sudden, irrefutable thought: *I must make meaning of my experience, my life.*

Chapter 8

I excuse myself from Tiffany, the nurse, and take my leave from the MICU. I'm relieved I won't have to be involved in the contentious case with the patient in police custody any longer—at least not today. It's been an emotional shift and I'm not yet halfway through it. I need some time to collect my thoughts, to examine where I'm at right now.

I exit the elevator on the ground floor and walk out to the garden. A narrow brick trail leads to a rickety arch woven through with vines, then circles a stone birdbath that doesn't have any water in it. The space still attracts birds, though; they're chirping quietly in the heat.

I'm just about to sit when I decide my experience will be more enlivening with a drink in my hand. Back inside at the coffee cart, I order a red-eye espresso before finding a seat in the garden on a white steel bench that's too big for one person but too small for two. When I came out here five minutes ago, the garden was blissfully empty. Now, there's a woman pacing under the magnolias, talking quietly on her phone.

My coffee is an homage to Kierkegaard's cigar. He puffs ruminatively in the Fredericksburg Garden in *Concluding Unscientific Postscript to Philosophical Fragments*:

> *It is now about four years ago that I got the notion of wanting to try my luck as an author .... I had been a student for half a score of years. Although never lazy, all my activity nevertheless was like a glittering inactivity, a kind of occupation for which I still have a great partiality, and for which perhaps I even have a little genius. I read much, spent the remainder of the day idling and thinking, but that was all it came to. So there I sat and smoked my cigar until I lapsed into thought. Among other thoughts I remember these: "You are going on," I said to myself, "to become an old man, without being anything, and without really undertaking to do anything. On the other hand, wherever you look about you, in literature and in life, you see the celebrated names and figures, the precious and much heralded men who are coming into prominence and are much talked about, the many benefactors of the age who know how to benefit mankind by making life easier and easier ....*[20]

I can relate ... why not?

I drift into thought as I sip my stimulant. I ponder my proclivity for idleness.

When I work, I think, *I work hard; but I, too, have a genius for wasting time. I start many books and finish only a few. This intellectual flakiness carries over into my artistic endeavors. Oh, the number of unfinished manuscripts that clog the digital memory of my devices—books, articles, volumes of poetry! Ah, yes ... and for every film I've finished, there are a dozen that are still nothing but vaporous images in my head ....*

Will I ever, just to name one example, light upon a darkly humorous storyline worthy of the rakish main character of my fragmentary screenplay Bad Chaplain, *who licks an ice-cream cone during a trauma call and makes a pass at the deceased's comely wife—or, maybe, like hardboiled Philip Marlowe, struts around the hospital rattling a rocks glass and marking his exits from the rooms of wheezing elderly ladies with "Goodnight, sweetheart, don't think it wasn't nice"? (A useful character, this, whom I initially dreamed up after I fell on my face at a patient visit—figuratively. Afterwards, steeped in gloom, I asked myself, "Well, what's the worst thing you could have said or done?" to find some consolation in the knowledge that at least I didn't do that).*

You have become, I preach, *aged and tired without having done much worthwhile or contributed to society. Look around you. See the nurses, physicians, and other healthcare workers who have done much and been esteemed for it—quite rightly so. They've had an impact. They've made a significant difference in other people's lives. Some of the people who have been fortunate enough to cross their paths are still walking the earth only because of their efforts. Who's still alive only because of you?*

I tilt my head to the sky. A fat gray-brown mourning dove skitters past on an overhead wire, cooing and beating its wings. I swirl my coffee as I would a glass of wine.

You must find something to do that will reverberate beyond your life, I go on. *Forget your limited capacities. Find a meaningful, ambitious goal and set forth to accomplish it. But what is "it"? Ah, yes ... You must commit to wrestle with what it means to be a human being.*

The volume of the woman talking on her phone is rising. While in most areas of society today, people stare at or scroll on their phones in isolated silence, in the hospital, people tend to use their phones in the old way. I think those whose families or friends are in crisis feel the need to talk and to hear familiar voices. It's therapeutic. It helps them process what's happening. Everywhere you look, in the halls, in the cafeteria, under the sweet pink blossoms of a magnolia tree, someone's talking on their phone, broadcasting to every ear within range the patient information the staff works so tirelessly to keep confidential.

"A secondary infection. Yes. I think that's what it's called. I think that's what she said," the woman says.

This woman is younger than me and of a different race. Her black-and-white patterned hijab indicates a different religious affiliation, too. But the depths of our humanity go beyond race, color, gender, religion, politics … Internally, we all wrestle (to widely varying degrees) with hatred, discrimination, and self-doubt.

You must gaze beneath the surface, I tell myself, *and meet people in the depth of their being. Listen to people. They will tell you who they are. In this process, you will discover yourself.*

The idea pleases me tremendously. Listen to people, and thus find your way to self-discovery—counsel to satisfy both the empath and the narcissist in all of us!

*

Probably most people worry, at one time or another, that the work they're doing isn't important, or that it pales in comparison to the impact other people have on the world.

In 1876, physicians gathered in New York for the second annual meeting of the American Neurological Association. One of the most novel and discussed presentations was physician George M. Beard's "The Influence of the Mind in the Causation and Cure of Disease and the Potency of Definite Expectation." In his paper, Beard observes that disease sometimes appears and disappears not because of any discernible physical factor or treatment, but only because of an emotion. After his presentation, according to David A. Steere in his book *The Supervision of Pastoral Care,* one physician "remarked that if the doctrine advanced by Beard were to be accepted, he would feel like throwing away his diploma from medical school and joining the theologians."[21]

I don't know if any physicians discarded their diplomas. But Beard's ideas heralded a major change in the way people were cared for in American institutions. In the early part of the 20th century, several movements toward cooperation and collaboration between the "healing professions"—fields like ministry, medicine, and social work—took root in cities like Boston and Cincinnati. In particular, momentum grew to require clinical experience of seminary students as part of their theological training. They were brought into social service agencies, prisons, mental institutions, and hospitals, where they could, as physician Richard C. Cabot wrote in 1925, "practice theology where it was most needed."[22]

That same year, Cabot worked to have a chaplain officially appointed at Worcester State Hospital, a mental hospital in Worcester, Massachusetts. The chaplain brought four theological students into the hospital as chaplain interns and organized what many call the first modern CPE program. The interns visited patients and recorded their observations. They routinely attended meetings with medical staff, as chaplains do today, and presented on the ways in which religion and spirituality might help illuminate and bring relief to those suffering from mental illness.

*

In 2012, I began to find my way in CPE in Alabama. I also started thinking more seriously about engaging with my creativity. I contacted my friend and former roommate Brandon, who was making his dream of becoming a filmmaker happen. Filming the Pearl Jam tour had helped him pay for film school. Now, he was working on La Source, a film about the Haitian activist Josue Lajeunesse.[23]

I asked Brandon what he thought about making a film about chaplaincy. I told him how so many patients were eager to open up and connect. I thought that having cameras in the room wouldn't bother some of them at all. They might even welcome the chance to share their stories in a bigger way.

*

In September of 2012, Marianne told me she was unhappy at her job in Mobile. She wanted to quit and look for work in California so we could move back there. I begged her to change her mind. I was only a week into a hospice residency at the time and I wanted to stay in Alabama long enough to finish out my three-unit residency. Then I'd have four CPE units under my belt and be eligible for board certification.

Marianne went ahead and interviewed for—and was offered—a job in Southern California. Luckily for me, they couldn't hire her until the following fall semester. Unluckily for me, Marianne disliked her job so much that she agreed to stay in Alabama only until the beginning of the summer. That was her compromise. I quit my residency one CPE unit short of the four I needed.

In Southern California, Marianne began teaching in her new position while I scrambled to find a job. I settled into a PRN position (this stands for the Latin term "pro re nata," which means "as the situation demands; it's basically a fancy term for working on-call or "as needed" instead of full-time) in hospice care.

As Marianne got further in her field, it increasingly became a major part of how she defined herself. Once during this time, we were at a faculty banquet sitting at a table with a well-known and controversial theologian. When he reached for dessert—a small plate with a piece of baklava on it that looked amazing—Marianne pointed at it.

She said loudly to me, "How many calories do you think are in that?"

The theologian dropped his plate on the table in front of him so hard the baklava bounced. I looked longingly at a tender flake of phyllo that had landed on the white tablecloth. I was pissed, too. How could I take a piece now?

The theologian snarled, "Do you try to ruin people's experiences, or does it just come naturally to you?"

Marianne shrugged. She seemed completely unbothered. "What? I'm a physical therapist. I have a responsibility to draw people's attention to the choices they make."

*

In the fall, I started teaching some classes at Loma Linda University through the School of Religion. There, at a Christmas party, I met Wilber "Wil" Alexander, a man who would become one of my most influential mentors in chaplaincy.

I called Brandon. "I think I found the subject of our first film," I said.

*

Where does creativity come from? The premise of Rollo May's *The Courage to Create* is that anxiety is a source from which to create. Reading this book not only inspired me to create; it changed my whole theology. Or, rather, it altered my perception that my theology was flawed.

In college and seminary, I often got the message from professors and classmates that from a religious perspective, the fact that I struggled with anxiety was a problem. I shouldn't be anxious about the future because God knew what was coming. God had a plan.

That sentiment never meant much to me. But when I expressed this, I felt shunned. When I reported still being anxious, I was told to pray. I'd also get the patronizing promise that I'd be prayed for to make my faith stronger.

Okay, I would think, *I'm just not praying enough. I'll pray more and God will take care of my anxiety.* That just made me more anxious. When the anxiety didn't go away, I wondered why not. Was I doing it wrong? Did God hate me for some reason? Thinking about God in this way didn't feel right to me.

I've accepted that I'll never be free from anxiety. But I can channel or harness that nervous energy into a different focus. For me, that focus is creating.

When I'm working on a film, I'll come home from a day at the hospital and start editing. It's become a spiritual act that's meaningful in multiple ways. I make meaning of the world through the film I'm working on, and the act of working on the film helps me make meaning of my work as a chaplain.

While I'm editing, I'm also processing all the events that took place throughout the day. So many of these events are big: death, life-changing accidents, excruciating pain, old family wounds. I need a small task to conceive of and achieve, like the slow, tedious, and minute process of editing twenty-four frames per second.

*

ULTIMATE CONCERNS: THE PLAYLIST
Ultimate Concern #3: Meaning/Meaninglessness
Top Ten:
  1. *The Dance—Garth Brooks*
  2. *Both Sides Now—Joni Mitchell*
  3. *While My Guitar Gently Weeps—The Beatles*
  4. *For What It's Worth—Buffalo Springfield*
  5. *I Still Haven't Found What I'm Looking For—U2*
  6. *Round Here—Counting Crows*
  7. *Dead Horse—Guns N' Roses*
  8. *Whirlpool—The Prayer Chain*
  9. *Double—L.S. Underground*

10. Us and Them—Pink Floyd

It's easier to find "meaning" in songs than "meaninglessness." Garth Brooks in "The Dance," for example, shows how a simple moment in time becomes far more significant and meaningful.

Pink Floyd could do meaninglessness, though. "Us and Them" is filled with phrases that create a sense of uncertainty and aimlessness, like a marble shooting randomly around on the floor as if we're all caught in a revolving cycle with no clear way forward.

*

Yalom's concept of the ultimate concern of "meaninglessness" directs me to "the principle of engagement." Finding meaning to strive for in my life fortifies me against potential catastrophes.

It also orients me in the world. When I see what I value, I can find a purpose that emphasizes those values. Then I find specific things to do that help me fulfill that purpose—for me, the more specific the better. I think of it as drawing lines or boundaries around my actions so my purpose doesn't feel too big, too bottomless.

I draw those lines by playing games. While I was in Seminary, I got interested in the concept of gamification and how it is used to motivate human behavior. I read some of the emerging research on the topic and brought the concept into chaplaincy.

*

Seeing the world in this way was a natural fit for me. When I was a kid and my family visited my volatile Grandpa Joe, I'd often play games with myself to see if I could shape the way the visit went.

I bet I can get him to laugh in five minutes, I would think. I often achieved it, too. I wasn't being malicious. I wanted to be playful with him in a way that other people were scared to do.

"Don't set him off," my mother would beg. When Grandpa Joe went into a rage, it ruined the whole night.

I'd play another kind of game to try to get him to say what he really wanted.

"Can I take your hat?" he'd say in his deep voice when he opened the door. He felt it was disrespectful to wear hats inside.

I'd look back at him, tall and thin with a thick head of orange-blond hair. I kept a neutral look on my face that didn't betray my intentions. "No, no, that's okay …."

After a few minutes, the tension beginning to rise in his voice: "You going to take that hat off?"

"Oh, is that what you want?" I'd say and smile. "Sure. I'll take it off."

Most of the time, he let me get away with it. Maybe Grandpa Joe sensed I was trying to see beyond his anger—to uncover who he was other than just a cantankerous old man.

Once, I brought my new girlfriend over to meet him: "This is Marianne. She's from Norway."

Grandpa Joe looked at her for a moment. Then he said, "Well, at least you're not Japanese … all right, come on in." He turned around and started to limp back into his house; both of his knees were bad.

Marianne and I exchanged a look. I said, "No, no … we'll come back when you're in a better mood."

Today, I rely heavily on the skills I developed when trying to navigate the moods and prejudices of my Grandpa Joe. Many patients are grumpy and angry. Sometimes, I can break through by toying and playing with them in a similar way.

*

In chaplaincy training, there is a heavy emphasis on leading with your emotions. I've heard phrases like "You need to develop more emotional availability" and "Get out of your head and into your heart" many, many, many, many times.

But I understand the importance of the theory. Early on in my education as a chaplain, I realized that leading with my emotions would be a difficult part of the job for me. I found myself trying to connect with patients in a particularly "heady" way. I'd listen to a story someone was telling and try to engage by commenting on the content. The problem was that if I got a detail wrong, the patient would often get flustered and correct me. This created distance between us.

A patient might describe going fishing with their grandfather. I'd be listening hard and struggling to recall the details of a drive Marianne and I had taken over to Orange Beach to try to spot some dolphins and eat divine tiramisu at an Italian restaurant we suspected was run by the mob.

"Oh, that must have been at The Wharf," I'd say, my face most likely screwed up into a squint.

"No. No! It was on Dauphin Island. You're not listening," the patient might complain.

So I tried a different approach. I knew I was lacking when it came to having a fully developed emotional language. I started asking myself, *Can I tell the difference between sadness, anger, and fear? Do I know what "irked" looks like? How can I recognize it?*

I found a list of "feeling" words in Marshall Rosenberg's book *Nonviolent Communication*. I printed out that list and carried it with me throughout my workday for a few years.

I made a game out of it. *When I go into this visit, I'm going to name three feelings I hear in this patient's story. I can't predict what these feelings will be or if I'll be right or not. But three named emotions equals three points.* I was motivated by counting how many points I could get by the end of the day. The next day, I'd try to beat that number.

I discovered a fascinating pattern. When I tried to name emotions rather than content details, and got it wrong, I'd still be corrected, but in a different way. I'd be invited further into the patient's story.

"That must have been frustrating," I'd say.

The patient might pause, considering this—then say thoughtfully, "No, I wasn't frustrated. But I was definitely disturbed by it." At that point, they'd continue, go deeper.

This method helped me get closer to people. The content of a patient's story is important, but not as important as the place it gets to emotionally. If I search for that place, I'll find them.

*

Soon, I found it easier to identify other people's emotions. I also got better at figuring out where I was emotionally before I went into a room. I felt progressively more aware and in control of my breathing, my body, my actions. It might sound counterintuitive, but the boundaries and rules made me feel freer and less anxious about walking into a room. Feeling calmer helped me channel my anxiety in ever more creative ways. In a sense, I tricked myself into thinking I was creating something.

*

This practice also affected the spiritual dimension of my life. I read Scripture more deeply, went to church with more intention. I understood all the foundational doctrines better. This helped me see more clearly which ones were important to me and which weren't.

What drives me in chaplaincy is the spiritual aspect of things. When I say "spiritual"—versus "religious"—I'm referring to inner meaning, where a person finds strength. When someone says at bedside, "I'm not spiritual," I don't believe them. I ask, "Well, where do you find your strength?" Or "Where do you find meaning?"

I'll meet people's religious needs if I can. Sometimes the answer to the question *Where does this person derive or find meaning?* is *In religious rites and rituals or in doctrine.*

In that case, I'll say, "Okay. Let's do that." Performing a ritual together can be incredibly meaningful for certain patients.

It bugs me when people say, "I'm spiritual but not religious."

Okay, so what the hell do you mean by that? (I think but don't say). The person is probably simply saying they don't like religion. Fine. But what special thing are they claiming for themselves, then?

Out loud, I push them a little. "What does that mean?"

I try not to show my annoyance. Maybe the patient lacks self-awareness or they don't see themselves as special at all. And their statement most likely stems from pain. They may have had a negative experience with a religious person or organization. In the words of one patient: "I feel bad enough. I don't need religious people around making me feel worse."

Most people don't leave religion because of the doctrines or beliefs. They leave because of other people. And actually, that's the source of my annoyance.

The prayer that always gets the most laughs—and generates further conversation—is the one that acknowledges this type of pain: "God, please save me from some of your followers." I first saw this sentiment expressed on a bumper sticker—without the "some"; we added that—when Jim Coons and I were riding in his VW Rabbit one day when I was in high school. The sentiment made us howl with laughter. Then we delved into some serious theological and sociological reflection.

"Yes!" a patient often crows when I turn that bumper sticker into a prayer. "Yes! Why do people have to get in the way?"

The late Wil Alexander was ninety-three years old when I met him at Loma Linda. He'd been a professor of religion there for more than forty years. I can think of two ways to best explain what kind of person he was and what I learned from him.

The first is to talk about where the word "chaplain" comes from. To me, Wil exemplified the gentleness and generosity demonstrated by Saint Martin of Tours in his legendary story.

Around 300 A.D., Martin of Tours was a young soldier in the Roman army. The story goes that once when he was stationed in Gaul (now France), Martin saw a beggar shivering in the cold. The man did not have warm clothes and no one was taking care of him.

Martin had only his military cloak. He cut it in half to share with the man. That night, he had a dream in which Jesus was wearing the half-cloak.

In the dream, Jesus said to his angels, "Martin clothed me with this robe."

Martin's faith was bolstered by this experience. He was baptized as a Christian and refused to fight in the army any longer as a matter of conscience. He was thrown in jail for his insubordination but was eventually released and lived a life of service to the poor and the sick.[24]

The half of the cloak that he kept became a carefully preserved relic in the church. The priest in charge of taking care of it was called in medieval Latin a *cappellanu*—the custodian or keeper of the cloak—from which the Old French *chapelain* is derived.

*

Wil was a "keeper of the cloak" if I ever knew one. He was drawn to those who were suffering and never lost his desire to search out the best ways to alleviate it in each individual case.

To prove it, I'll show you him in action. One sequence of the film I produced with Brandon about Wil, *A Certain Kind of Light*, opens with a shot of a wide-open Western sky. It's sunrise. The sky is very clear. Near the horizon is a layer of orange-pink and a jagged line of dark-blue mountains. Soft ambient music plays. Someone is narrating lines from Mary Jean Irion's *Yes, World: A Mosaic of Meditation*. It's Wil's unhurried tenor voice:

> *Normal day, let me be aware of the treasure you are. Let me learn from you, love you, savor you, bless you before you depart. Let me not pass you by in quest of some rare and perfect tomorrow. Let me hold you while I may, for it will not always be so.*[25]

We follow Wil as he gets ready for the day. He splashes his face with water. He gets in his car and drives. He wears black-framed glasses and has a short white beard, neatly trimmed. He wears an argyle cardigan over a red turtleneck. When he walks through the hospital, his back is bent over a little, but not much. He looks at least ten years younger than he is. Maybe even fifteen or twenty.

When Wil gets in a room with a patient and ten or so physicians, medical students, and the patient's wife (as well as Brandon, who is doing the filming, and me), the first thing he does is sit close to the patient and ask about his children.

"So. Three boys?" he says.

The patient is forty-eight and has colon cancer, stage four. He's been in the hospital for months with one infection after another. But now, he says, he's feeling positive. He's got an IV in his arm and is propped up halfway between reclining and sitting up in his bed. His arms are crossed, his blanket pulled up over his chest. He's small and slender with a highish voice. It goes up even higher when he tells Wil after he was diagnosed, the doctors told his wife to "Let him die. Send him to hospice and let him die!"

He shakes his head. One arm crooks back on the pillow.

"I refused," he says.

At one point, Wil asks my favorite question, one I've used many times since I first heard Wil utter it. While he was alive, I shadowed him as often as I could.

"What are you famous for?" Wil asks.

"I'm not famous for anything."

"No. I heard three boys. I heard a wife of twenty-six years."

Later, Wil moves on to the heart of the matter:

```
                 WIL
      So. What's the spiritual part of
      all of this?


                 PATIENT
            (shaking his head)
      Uh, I'm not a very religious per-
      son.


                 WIL
      No, I didn't ask if you were reli-
      gious. "Spiritual."


                 PATIENT
      Spiritual?
            (eyes flickering back
            and forth between
            two points on the
            ceiling)
      Hmm.
```

                    WIL
All this tells me you are a beautiful man.

                  PATIENT
I try to be.

                    WIL
You love beauty and you love life
and that's pretty spiritual.

                  PATIENT
I love getting out on the road and
riding a motorcycle.

                    WIL
Whoa.
          (to patient's wife)
You let him ride a motorcycle?

                PATIENT'S WIFE
          (laughs)
Yes. Not anymore. Not while he's
here.

                  PATIENT
When they told me, they basically put a death sentence on me—I
sold my motorcycle last week. But
we put the money in the bank. And
when I get better, my goal is to
get a new motorcycle and head out
on the road again. I love getting
out there and not listening to my
cell phone ring.

Wil's intuition working is visible on his face. In his mind, he's now seeing a man alone on a road. The atmosphere in the room changes. Everyone present can feel it.

                        WIL
        One of the things we run into with
        illness is that people feel they are
        all alone in this. Even though you
        express it the best you can, nobody
        can really understand. That's when
        I think your talk with whoever you
        talk with "up there" is so import-
        ant.

                        PATIENT
        Right.
                (voice breaking, eyes
                filling with tears)
        Because there are times when I've
        had
                (gesturing to his
                wife)
        some major breakdowns.

And a minute later:

                        WIL
                (leaning closer to
                the patient and ges-
                turing to his upper
                arm)
        Tell me about the tattoo. You got
        it way up there so you try to hide
        it. What's it say?
                (to the patient's
                wife)

Is your name on there?

                    PATIENT
It says "Harley Davidson."

                    WIL
Oh, I knew it—I shouldn't have
asked.

Laughter all around the room.

                    WIL
          (to Patient's Wife)
And what's it been like for you,
doll?

                PATIENT'S WIFE
Being the caregiver of it all,
you feel like you have to hold
your peace a little more and be a
lot stronger in order to help him
through the downtimes.

                    WIL
And so who takes care of you?

The room goes still. It's almost silent save for
the distant mumble of voices in the hall.

                PATIENT'S WIFE
          (looking up and
          around the room,
          searching for an
          answer)
Myself. Family. My dad has been a
huge help.

                    WIL
              (to Patient)
Would you mind if any of my troops
here asked you a question? I've
asked all the good ones, I think.

                  PATIENT
I'm open to all questions.

          ATTENDING PHYSICIAN #1
I had one question. In spite of
everything bad that's happened
these past couple of months ...
can you think of one good thing
that's come out of it?

                  PATIENT
              (crying, his fingers
              fluttering on his
              chest)
I got to see my two-year-old
granddaughter.

                    WIL
              (patting the Pa-
              tient's leg)
Ah! Yes ...

                  PATIENT
It was only the second time.

                    WIL
And that gives you a reason to go
on?

                  PATIENT
Absolutely!

```
                    WIL
    All of those things kind of add up
    and affect you overall. So how does
    the future look?

                    PATIENT
    The future looks good.

                    WIL
    Yes.

                    PATIENT
    Because I have proven that I can
    beat this cancer.

                    WIL
    Yes. You're a blessed man.
```

*

Wil's question to the patient's wife invites her to go beyond her previous answer. She'd kept her feelings at a distance: "*You* feel like you have to hold your peace" rather than "*I* feel like I have to …."

The patient hasn't expressed much concern for his wife in the visit. Wil's picked up on that. His question provokes everyone in the room to shift their attention to her.

After the encounter with the patient, Wil discusses it in another room with the medical staff who were there. He brings up the way the patient repeatedly expressed his belief that he would beat his illness and get his life back.

"Did I give him false hope?" Wil asks the room. "It made me nervous to do it."

One of the physicians admits that though this patient is in remission, the survival rate of his condition is bleak. Most patients with his condition die of it.

"But not all," says Wil.

*

At that time, I had a personal reason to hope Wil was right about miraculous recoveries.

While I was in seminary, I had reconnected with the other great mentor of my life, Jim Coons. By this time, he had three children. He was back working as the youth pastor at the Presbyterian church where I'd met him. But he'd been diagnosed with colon cancer at only thirty-eight. He was treated for four years before going into remission.

Just when he was starting to feel like himself again, his father died. Jim's father, a highly respected presbyter in the church, was Jim's hero, his mentor. The loss broke him. He got sick again.

During the time I began filming Wil, I was teaching classes to medical students: topics like Death and Dying, Crisis Intervention, and The Art and Science of Whole Person Care. One of the major things I was trying to teach them was to listen to their patients.

I called Jim with an idea. Could I interview him and film it? I thought that recording patients on film and asking physicians to watch the footage might be a good way to teach this lesson. The film would capture a one-sided conversation. Doctors couldn't talk back and consequently forget what the patient was saying as they got absorbed in their own questions and requests for information.

Jim agreed to it. Marianne and I drove up to Northern California for Christmas and I went to see Jim at his mother-in-law's house in nearby Auburn.

He wasn't feeling well that day. He was in bed, halfway propped up with a pillow behind his head and one under his knees. He wore a t-shirt and flannel pants. A gray Volkswagen cap covered up his now-short hair.

I set up two cameras and sat on the bed. Jim smiled and we both felt better after laughing over some satisfyingly tasteless jokes about him being a creepy youth pastor asking me to climb into bed with him.

Jim's eyes were the same as I remembered them: hazel and turned down at the corners. That gave him a wise and soulful look. When his fourteen-year-old son came to lie with him on the bed, looking at his phone while Jim spoke, his head resting in the crook between Jim's arm and his chest, I was conscious of the fact that I'd been the same age as this boy when I'd met his father.

Jim talked honestly and deeply about illness and death. "I'm no closer to death than you are right now," he said to me. "You could walk out and get hit by a bus." His son snickered. As his father went on, his smile faded. "The only difference is that I can see the bus," Jim said. "I can see the license plate on the bus, I can see the person driving, I can see the passengers. It's very vivid, very clear. So it's taken some of the mystery out of death."

I edited a few clips together and played the footage at a conference at Loma Linda. A lot of people heard and learned from his story. I told him so when I talked to him on the phone afterwards, but that day in Auburn was the last time I saw him.

Jim died on April 4, a date with poetic resonance for him, as it's mentioned in the U2 song "Pride (In the Name of Love)." At his funeral, a flower arrangement filled with mementos of his life included a card with "U2" written on it alongside a wedding photo and a "World's Greatest Dad" rosette.

That was in 2015. A few years later, I would make some drastic decisions that changed my life completely. The way I executed these changes left me in utter isolation and despair.

At that point, I couldn't consult Jim anymore. I wonder now what would have happened if I had been able to talk to him. I wonder what he would have said and if I would have listened to him. His was the voice I always listened to the most.

*

After Jim died, I wrote a song for him:

Life Sure Ain't Fair

Electric trees and neon wood
It feels good to be understood
Flying high in the Pasadena sky
Too soon, we said goodbye
"I love you," you told me
You always knew who I could be
With your long hair and your 90's clothes
I always thought we'd grow old
But now I
Wish I'd known it back then
That everything comes to an end
And at the end I wouldn't be there
Life sure ain't fair

Tabasco sauce in your coffee
You didn't like it, then you punched me
I made you laugh and made you cry
You taught me how to live and die
It's cliché to say "I'd give
Anything so you can live"
But I will never forget

The life we had an' the times we spent
But I
Wish I'd known it back then
When everything would come to an end
And how at the end I wouldn't be there
This life sure ain't fair

Where have you gone? Can I come, too?
I can't imagine life without you
But the tears I cry are there for me
I feel your loss, selfishly
We'll travel onward and slow
'Cause life goes on, "So it goes."

Whether hope in God or in man
I hope you found your promised land
And I
Never knew it back then
That everything comes to an end
An' at the end I wouldn't be there
Life sure ain't fair

*

That sequence from *A Certain Kind of Light* ends where it begins. Wil drives home and gets back to his house in the country. He talks to his little dog, takes a soak with his eyes closed in the hot tub in the yard. In the dark sky, the lights of the city twinkle in the distance.

On the drive home, Wil continues to ruminate over the question of whether he gave the patient false hope. Did he do the right thing? One of the attendings seemed to think he did ("Denial is a natural coping mechanism and it has a place and a time … we know that people who have hope usually do clinically better"). Another didn't seem so sure.

In the end, Wil decides it wasn't false hope he offered. "No," he clarifies. "I was buttressing the hope he brought with him." Raising a finger from the steering wheel, he half turns to the camera while still keeping his sharp eyes on the road.

He says, "The last thing that dies is hope!"

Chapter 9

I'm roused from my mid-afternoon sermon in the garden by a sudden quiet. Sometime during my reverie, I closed my eyes. When I open them, I see the woman talking on her phone is gone and I'm alone again.

It's nearly three-thirty. Time to walk back to the office. I have a meeting scheduled at 3:45 p.m. with Sofia, the director of the spiritual care department. She wants to go over my annual report with me.

I make my way up to the seventh floor of the administrative building, which is right next to the hospital. Sofia's office is one floor above the CPE classroom and the space where I have my desk. She first came to this hospital in the 1980s. For a long time, she was the only chaplain. She's built the entire spiritual-care department from just herself to the network of staff chaplains, educators, and students it is now.

I respect her a lot. I wonder how she's handling the thought of retirement. My experience of the baby boomer generation is they do not go out easily—for good reason. If they're like Sofia, they probably feel more than a little uneasy about entrusting what they've built so carefully to younger colleagues who have no idea how fragile everything was in the beginning and how much they had to fight for it. They're also often facing an enormous transition not just in their working life but at home, as their children leave the house. It's a challenge I'll have to face myself at some point. I try to glean as much as I can about work and life from leaders like Sofia.

I knock on the door. I hear a small rustling inside before Sofia opens it. She is a tall Black woman, almost as tall as me. She wears her long silver hair in a bun on the top of her head and has bright brown eyes with specks of gold.

"Come on in," she says. "I was just getting this thing here, this piece of technology, figured out."

"You mean the computer?"

"Is that what they're calling them now?" She winks at me. Sofia's lack of tech-savvy is a running joke in the department. She still shows videos on VHS. But she has a good sense of humor about it; and no matter what medium they're on, the films and documentaries she chooses are powerful, moving, and impactful on chaplaincy training.

We go over my annual report. I'm glad to hear Sofia supports my goals: specifically, my plan to integrate more pieces of art—poems, songs, paintings, films—into my next unit of CPE.

"So," she says when we're done, reclining and resting her elbows on the arms of the chair, "how are you feeling about tonight's shift?"

"I'm feeling okay—even though that's not a feeling." We both smile. "I do have a question for you," I say. "Something I've been thinking about. You know how some patients request you to see them, but then when you get there, they don't exactly know why they want you there?"

"Yes." Sofia nods deeply.

"How direct are you with them?"

"Do you mean when the patient gives you this 'stay with me, I want to be alone' vibe?"

"'Stay with me, I want to be alone,'" I repeat.

"Yeah, well—sometimes people want both. Or they don't know what they want."

"And sometimes," I say slowly, "I think they want me to stay with them *so* they can be alone. Something about me being there—not necessarily *doing* anything or even saying anything—allows them to feel more at ease with that 'aloneness.'"

"Right. I hadn't thought of it exactly in those terms, but that's true, too. That captures chaplaincy as a whole, doesn't it? We have to figure out how to find the right balance between being there for a patient and giving them space."

"And I suppose we have to figure out the right punctuation: 'Stay with me. I want to be alone.' 'Stay with me, I want to be alone.' 'Stay with me! I want to be alone!'"

"Anyone ever tell you that you think too damn much?"

I think that's what my ex-wife said on our wedding night, I think. Aloud, I say, "Not since last week when you told me."

As I'm leaving, Sofia says, "Well, I hope tonight is exactly what it needs to be for you."

"Superstitions aside, I hope it's quiet."

Sofia smirks. "You brought it on yourself, then."

We laugh and I thank her for her leadership before heading back downstairs to check in with the other chaplains. Between four and five o'clock, my colleagues hand off calls and referrals they couldn't get to or that came in near the end of the day. One of the resident chaplains tells me he couldn't get to a call because—he "didn't want to go."

While I appreciate his honesty, I tell him, "Talk with your educator about this reason. I think he'll find it rather curious."

This resident is a married man in his forties. He has six or seven children and is from a conservative Christian denomination. For much of his year-long residency, he's struggled to see any views of God that are different from his own. He wears a clerical collar even though it's not part of his tradition and I suspect it's because he likes to feel powerful and create confusion.

"Are you Catholic?" patients often ask him, to which he responds, "No, I'm not," without so much as a word of explanation.

At 5:00, most of the staff leave and the building gets quiet. It's a time of transition I've come to notice and appreciate more since I started this line of work. I stand in the classroom adjacent to my desk and watch the sky: the clouds changing color, the sun dropping to the horizon.

> *So soft upon the Scene*
> *The Act of evening fell*
> *We felt how neighborly a Thing*
> *Was the Invisible.*[26]

My eyes alight on the phở restaurant across the street. Suddenly, I want a bowl of phở with a coconut smoothie and maybe even a bánh mì for later—one never knows what kind of night this will be.

I call in my order, make sure I have all my pagers on my belt, and walk over. These moments are infused with tension. If I get paged, I'll have to forsake the food and tend to the call. Of course, I know this is the right thing to do. Of course. I also know I won't be able to avoid arriving at the call with some disappointment, even bitterness, in my heart.

I acknowledge the selfish, petty feelings. This gives me the best chance of seeing them dissipate.

I walk fast. The heat of the day has eased just a shade. I can feel the cooler air against my beard. In the restaurant, the owners, a sweet Vietnamese couple about my age, recognize me. They wave and hurry over with the food.

"You on call tonight?" the wife asks in her thick accent. I tell her I am. The husband rushes ahead of me to open the door. "You do good work. Thank you for what you do."

Either they're trying to get rid of me or they can sense I'm uneasy I'll get paged and want to enjoy my food while it's still hot. I'd make a bet it's the latter. They are kind and considerate people. They know a lot about what it's like to work at the hospital just from their proximity to it. I thank them profusely while they wave and get back to work. They've got at least twenty other customers inside.

Dark orange is spreading across the horizon when I settle back at my desk. I open the containers and breathe in the scent of this excellent broth: the perfect balance of fish sauce and salt, ginger and onion. The oil from the beef bone makes this the best phở I've had in the United States.

Many Seventh-day Adventists are vegetarians. I'm not one of them. I want to be healthy and I also want to enjoy the things I enjoy. As the comedian Chris Porter says, "Yeah, I wanna live, but the last thing I want to wish for on my deathbed is a chalupa."[27] An important part of identifying with a particular religious denomination is figuring out which aspects of that denomination are salvation issues for me—does this affect whether or not I'm going to heaven?—and which are merely traditions or lifestyle choices. It's an interesting theological distinction that I think a lot of religious people struggle with.

In any case: I'm tipping the bowl of beautiful not-plant-based broth, just about to witness its glorious, fragrant splash over the vermicelli noodles, when my trauma pager beeps.

That was close; I almost ruined it. I snap the lids back on the styrofoam containers and hope my dinner will still taste good when I get back.

As I walk to the emergency department, I start worrying about the styrofoam. *Can I put that in the microwave? I'm not sure there are any ceramic bowls in the kitchen. Maybe this call won't take too long and I can go to the cafeteria afterwards and get a paper bowl. It's open until 1 a.m. Even a big cup might work. I hope the guy I know in the cafeteria is working. I don't know many of the others. I've worked in this hospital for a while now and I still don't know the names of most of the people I see multiple times each week. I'm not good at getting close to people. Why is that?*

Before I get swallowed in self-deprecation, I realize I'm at the back door by the ambulance bay and badge my way in. I greet the charge nurse for the night, Craig, the same nurse who left me a message Saturday night about the urgent call. In his mid-thirties, he has a few days of stubble on his cheeks and a mustache that's only slightly longer. The shape or placement of his eyes makes him look as if he's constantly startled.

He gives me a "what's up" nod. "Hey, man. Uh, patient is in seven. Still can't find his family."

He's shifting papers around on the desk and talking to three people at once: me, the nurse standing next to him, and whoever is at the other end of his earpiece.

"I'll check with social work to see if they've located family yet," I say. "Who's on tonight?"

"I think it's Abby. Not sure. Hey, man, you catch the game last night?"

I peer at him. He's gazing not quite at me, but into the air over my shoulder, still looking surprised, as if the invisible someone on the other end of the line has just given him a shocking response to his casual query.

I give him a "what's up" nod in lieu of a goodbye and head to the room. Inside, there's a nurse, a lot of debris on the floor, and the unmoving body of a man. I catch up with an attending physician a few feet down the hallway to get some information: such as, is the man alive.

The man is dead. I find Abby from social work at the unit station: a bank of workstations in the center of a wide hallway. This long desk is filled with computers and phones. Facing both of its longest sides are patient rooms. Abby is on one of the phones trying to contact a family member; she has the patient's wallet and ID in front of her.

"Any luck?" I ask.

"No." She hangs up and looks at me. She has long blond hair today, but sometimes it's brown. She wears checkerboard low-top Vans and is snarky like me. I'm certain if I'd known her in high school, I would have wanted to stand outside her window playing a Peter Gabriel song on a boombox I held aloft in the rain.

"Oh, hey," she says. "Hey, I'm glad it's you tonight. Y'all have some interesting students in this unit, you know that?"

"'Interesting' is an interesting word." I smile.

"Nope." Abby gives me a playful shake of her head. "Nice try. But I'm not one of your students."

*

"Hey, Keith, I think maybe I am called to be a chaplain."

I hear these words rather frequently. They come from students in courses I've taught and from aspirants for CPE programs. I hear them in CPE applicant interviews. Sometimes, it's just random people I meet who share this news as soon as they find out I'm a chaplain.

I'd be lying if I said I've ever understood what someone means when they talk about being "called" to chaplaincy—or anything else. This phrase has never landed with me and yet I can't seem to escape it. When talking amongst themselves, my fellow seminarians would always ask one another if they had received "a call": a lofty term cloaked in the overtones of holiness, when what we're really talking about is a job.

When I was teaching at another seminary, one of my students approached me in the hallway right before class. He said eagerly, "Chaplain—Pastor—Wakefield, I believe God is calling me to be a children's hospital chaplain."

My rich internal dialogue contrasted sharply with my external response. Internally, I was thinking, *I want to be envious for having such certainty about one's call. But I think "dubiousness" is a more accurate description of what I'm feeling right now. I also want to ask, "How do you know that? What do you mean by 'a call'? Do you have any idea what chaplaincy actually is?"*

All I said out loud was, "Oh."

"Yeah! I really like kids. And to be quite honest," he added, with less sheepishness than I would have liked, "I don't know if I'll be able to get a call to a church."

Damn! I should trust my instincts more. In this case, letting the internal become the external would have been perfectly appropriate. This student made me angry. The whole idea of chaplaincy being the "B-team" of ministry—the presumption being that people go into it only because they can't cut it in a parish or synagogue or mosque—is extremely annoying. Particularly in American Christendom, many people accept that there is an established hierarchy in religious service. This hierarchy esteems religious leaders at designated houses of worship over those who serve in the community and are based at hospitals, police stations, college campuses, or the military.

To be fair, this impression hasn't come out of nowhere. Historically, parish pastors who made a mess of the churches they tried to lead—hapless but often nice guys (yes, usually guys)—were given grace and received invitations to go pray with sick people in the hospitals. Thankfully, at some point, we decided sick people in hospitals deserve better than parish leftovers. Particularly in the last fifteen to twenty years, there's been a trend towards professionalism and training in chaplaincy and heightened requirements for employment. The culture in most seminaries, however, has not quite caught up with this shift.

Of course, in many rural or small-town communities, pastors and other community faith leaders continue to step into hospital chaplaincy as volunteers, offering spiritual care without the benefit of formalized training or structured programs. While the professionalization of chaplaincy has raised the bar in many contexts, the presence these volunteers provide remains deeply valuable, often meeting critical needs where no formal chaplaincy exists—for them, I am grateful.

I looked back into my student's sincere eyes. He had a wife and four kids and was nearing graduation. He didn't have any prospective "calls" lined up.

"I think it's wonderful to be exploring that area of ministry," I said. "I suggest you do some research on it first. If you like what you see, then apply to do a unit of CPE. If you get in, you'll get a better idea of whether chaplaincy is a good fit for you."

He smiled. But when he walked away, he was hanging his head a little. I suspect he thought his supernatural certainty about a "call" would serve as a surefire ticket to simply fall into chaplaincy. Even if students are accepted into a unit, they must commit to working hard on themselves to stay there.

*

And there are many reasons aspirants might not be accepted. For example, some people are simply "too wounded" to do well in CPE as they are.

Louis, an aspirant in his mid-thirties, applied for a unit of CPE. He was open and vulnerable on his application materials about the many traumas in his past.

He remembered waking up at least twice to find someone had overdosed at his kitchen table. He couldn't remember anything that happened before he was eight. His parents were drug dealers; they "did what they could to make ends meet."

At thirteen, Louis was orphaned and entered the foster care system. He bounced from house to house for the next five years until he aged out. Then he was homeless. He had his own stint with addiction as well as run-ins with the police for robbery and theft.

Somehow, after time in prison and achieving sobriety, Louis met his wife and had two children. Now, he was pursuing a degree in religion. He said it was in "finding that higher power" that he found the strength and conviction not to turn back to his old way of living.

When I talked to him during his interview, I liked him. I admired him for getting to where he was, especially after all he'd been through.

But I had concerns about how his background might "show up" in the hospital setting. He answered questions with brutal honesty but demonstrated little to no self-awareness. I saw almost no reflection on how these significant moments had affected and shaped him.

In the interview, I quickly found out he hadn't had any help getting to the point of being able to self-reflect. When I asked him, "How have you processed all this trauma?", he squirmed a little in his seat.

Flicking his eyes around the room, he said nervously, "I've never really talked to anybody. Gotta just keep looking up and out."

After the interview, I knew accepting him into the cohort would not be good for him, me, or, most importantly, the patients. But I wanted to help him. I wanted him to understand that me telling him "no" meant I cared for him.

The only way to start was to reject his application. I did so the standard way, via email. Within thirty minutes, he wrote back. He was very gracious. He asked if I would mind talking with him again to help him better understand what he was lacking.

My educator had told me, "It's not our practice to offer feedback about why a decision has been made." I thought about it, then talked with my educator. I asked him if we could make an exception in this case as long as I kept the feedback general. I wanted to reach out to Louis not as an interviewer, but as an educator and a chaplain.

My educator agreed. I wrote Louis back to impart the information about our policy. Then I added, "Happy to discuss our practice if you would like."

We talked on the phone later that afternoon. I told him I couldn't give specific details about any individual.

"However," I said, "I'm hesitant to accept any student with significant past trauma who doesn't have the support of professionals around them. A counselor, a therapist, a spiritual director … I think it would be wise for anyone who has experienced a tremendous amount of pain to seek out someone to help them process it before and during their time in a hospital. In a hospital, they'll be coming face-to-face with people whose experiences can easily trigger those memories."

Louis responded enthusiastically, gratefully. "Yeah," he said, "I know it. It's about time I started processing all the shit I've lived through. I'm gonna find someone. Thank you!" Whether he did or not, I don't know. But he was one of the most authentic people I've ever met. I choose to believe he did.

*

Unprocessed, unresolved pain or trauma casts a heavy shadow. It affects every relationship in your life and reverberates out into the world. Nowhere have I seen this more poignantly in my personal and family history than in my Grandpa Joe's story.

Grandpa Joe served in the Korean War as an air force mechanic. Once, he fixed a plane and watched it take off. Then it crashed due to a mechanical error. All of the men on board were killed.

After that, Grandpa Joe lived with a deep regret, a feeling that he didn't do enough. He also felt he was incompetent and a failure. He passed his insecurities on to my mom, who passed them on to me.

I don't know if Grandpa Joe ever worked through his guilt. I never saw it happen. He was mean and bad-tempered as long as I knew him.

But at the end of his life, when he was dying of brain cancer, his interactions with his hospice nurse, who was Japanese, seemed to shake his deep-seated racism at least a little. His wife, my Grandma Marv, said he was very kind to the nurse.

"She's been wonderful and he's so grateful to her," Grandma Marv said. I hope this is a sign he found some healing before he died.

*

I have visited some people whose pain was too much for me to bear. I've had to exit the room because of it. Sometimes it's simple, like the person is the same age as me. Or they remind me of someone close to me. I find it easier to deal with the patients who remind me of others than those whose pain offers a sharp reflection of mine.

This is the awareness I was trained to have. Now, I train my students to have it. I'll explain why.

Being in the middle of another person's pain demands an ability to tolerate our own. The intensity of emotions, and the unpredictable ebb and flow of those emotions, that occurs when, as Jim Coons once said to me, "people's lives are being dismantled before their very eyes," is not natural for most people. You must learn how to handle it.

When a patient's emotion touches on a part of my story and I feel overwhelmed by it, it's usually because I haven't adequately worked through my own pain. Fortunately, I have the support of my colleagues to help me do that. Most people don't have the luxury of a wise and professionally trained set of emotionally intelligent colleagues around them. And sometimes they don't have the resources to seek professional support; or they face cultural stigmas or other barriers.

I feel lucky that way. With the help of the people around me, I can work through an emotion or issue that's blocking my ability to reach and help my patients. Then I'm better equipped the next time someone's sorrow speaks to mine.

*

In 2016, I visited a patient who had come to the United States from Australia because she was in a relationship with an American. They got married and had a few good years together. He was very wealthy and took care of her. Until, one day, he didn't. He kicked her out and wanted nothing more to do with her.

I try to stay aware that most often I have only one side of a story. That's another reason it's wise for chaplains not to get too sucked into the content details but instead to listen effectively and name the emotional side of the story.

This woman started listing the friends she'd lost because her husband had introduced her to everyone she knew in the U.S. Now, they were all on her husband's side. And all her family members in Australia were dead or she was not on speaking terms with them.

"Dead or estranged," she said. "There isn't really a difference."

"That must be incredibly lonely," I said to her—and to myself.

*

At the time I was visiting that patient, I had just moved to the Los Angeles area—alone. I'd left my marriage and was living on my own for the first time in fifteen years.

The bathroom doubled as the kitchen in my minuscule one-bedroom apartment. It screamed "divorcee cliché." My whole situation screamed "divorcee cliché." I've never felt more isolated and lonely in my life.

As soon as I named this patient's loneliness, I connected to it like lightning to a tree. All of a sudden I was on fire, and I wanted out.

*

Once I was in a committee meeting during my CPE process when one of my mentors told me I struck him as someone afflicted with the condition of "mental assent without confession."

I nodded and wrote it down. I acknowledged the depth of the individual words and assumed my mentor was saying something deep and personal to me, even though I couldn't for the life of me figure out what that was.

I said to him, "I'm not familiar with that phrase."

He gave me an unmistakably condescending look. "You haven't heard that term before now? I'm surprised."

"No, I haven't. Could you expand on it a little?"

He wouldn't. His response was basically along the lines of, *You want me to do your work for you?*

It didn't feel like a very educational moment. It felt more as if he were trying to wield power against me and make me feel small. This was not only annoying, but disappointing; I suspected there was something educational in what he was trying to express to me.

Later, I did some digging. I found out "mental assent without confession" is a phrase used in some Christian circles to distinguish between "true faith" of the heart and a "lesser than" hope or belief that does not go beyond the intellectual. The idea is that faith requires action rather than just agreement. Based on passages like James 2:26 ("For just as the body without the spirit is dead, so faith without works is also dead"[28]), some zealots use even stronger language to describe it:

> *Faith without a corresponding action is dead, ineffective and useless.*

*It is like a corpse, which has no life and does nothing but rot. This is
why some Christians are saved but have a life that is rotten.*[29]

Other writers and thinkers who use the phrase are less judgmental;
they seem more interested in helping others develop a richer and more
meaningful spiritual life. Due to my mentor's arrogant tone and the fact
that he wouldn't elaborate, however, I had to assume he was in the former
camp. I found myself wishing I could tell him to fuck off.

This was during a time in my life I call my "wilderness period." I was
going through a time of unbelief. I believed God existed, but I wouldn't
have paid with my life for that conviction. As Jack Nicholson once said,
"I may be godless, I may be faithless; I still pray that they can hear me."[30]

And, from Christian Wiman in *My Bright Abyss, Meditation of a
Modern Believer*: "Sometimes God calls a person to unbelief in order that
faith may take new forms."[31]

I was asking myself questions like: *What do I do with the message that
Jesus died for others, ultimately rescuing humanity from eternal damnation?*

I began to think of myself—and still do—as a "Christian in recovery."
I believe in Jesus as a rescuer. I also ask myself, *But how does that work?
What does that actually mean?*

I don't think these kinds of questions trouble my relationship
with God. When someone speaks of a person "kicking the bucket,"
I don't think the person who died literally kicked a bucket. However, I
don't go so far as to say that buckets don't exist.

But these kinds of questions can cause trouble with other people who
are in relationship with God. I don't think my mentor would have said
that to me if I were Buddhist, Hindu, Muslim, or anything other than
Christian. For some reason, us Christians feel we can tell other Christians
how to believe, as if any of us have the cornerstone on what "good" belief and faith look like. Some of us even seem to feel we're clairvoyant and

can see into other Christians' minds and hearts.

To be fair, I'm sure this isn't true only of Christians. What is it about being within a faith community or other type of shared belief system—certainly activists in political movements do it—that makes us weaponize the very doctrines that supposedly unite us and judge one another on how we actualize our faith?

How's this for confession: adultery took me further away from many people, including friends, family, and people in the church. But strangely, it brought me closer to God.

*

Coming closer to God after breaking a commandment: I don't imagine that's a conversation most church leaders would be eager to have.

I can understand why. But when we look at the biblical stories of David and Bathsheba, the woman at the well, Mary Magdalene, and "the woman caught in adultery," I invite any preacher to revisit their sermon notes if they believe these people should have been shamed, cast out, fired, or shunned forever. That's contrary to what Jesus said to them.

Of course, Jesus said nothing to David or Bathsheba because their Hebrew Bible story occurred many years before he walked the earth. But their blood did run through his; he is of their lineage.

*

In my mind, the judgmental and generic comment from my mentor stands out in stark contrast to other criticism I received during this time: namely, the emails I got from my friend Brandon.

Brandon wrote me an email with the subject line "your mid-life crisis." It was five pages long. It included a lot of detailed commentary and proscriptive advice about what I should and shouldn't do, as well as the apt description, "You basically took the life you were building and drove it into a brick wall at seventy miles an hour."

It was personal, passionate, and meaningful. He knew me and my situation so well and he cared not just about me, but about everyone involved.

This made his feedback incredibly valuable. The thing that made it priceless, and shows how close a friend Brandon is, is how he responded when I called to tell him how much I appreciated everything he'd taken the time to say.

I paused before adding, "But I'm probably not going to do any of that."

I heard him sigh, heard his characteristic nasal chuckle. Quickly, he pivoted. He'd be there with me in the world I'd chosen whether he agreed with me for having chosen it or not.

"Okay, fine," he said. "Then now what? How are we gonna get through this?"

Chapter 10

In his book *Love's Executioner*, Irvin Yalom writes about a "great paradox of life," which is that

> *... self-awareness breeds anxiety. Fusion eradicates anxiety in a radical fashion—by eliminating self-awareness. The person who has fallen in love, and entered a blissful state of merger, is not self-reflective because the questioning lonely I (and the attendant anxiety of isolation) dissolves into the we. Thus one sheds anxiety but loses oneself. This is precisely why therapists do not like to treat a patient who has fallen in love. Therapy and a state of love-merger are incompatible because therapeutic work requires a questioning self-awareness and an anxiety that will ultimately serve as guide to internal conflicts.*[32]

Perhaps in 2001, when I was merging with my first wife in the Øye hamlet, I experienced a lack of questioning self-awareness. The same could not be said in 2015, when Marianne and I had journeyed across the country so she could change jobs for the third time in three years.

I wasn't feeling good about it. These days, my mind kept returning to a fascination with the thought of detangling myself from the "we" and becoming a "questioning lonely I."

Since 2013, I'd wanted to pursue the training to become a Certified Educator for chaplaincy. But in 2015, a university a Minnesota built a position—director of the newly forming University Health & Wellness Center—with Marianne in mind. They wanted her to lead a wellness initiative on campus. In a flashback to our move to Alabama, the university wanted to give me an incentive to come as well. The dean of the seminary at the same university let me know they were looking for someone to fulfill the duties of the seminary chaplain, who had retired. He told me they had already offered the position to someone else, a chaplain on the east coast, and were awaiting his answer. But he did promise I could teach some graduate and undergraduate classes.

I agreed to go. After we moved to Minnesota, I started teaching not only Intro to Chaplaincy and Pastoral Counseling, but also, ironically enough, Marriage and Family, even as my own marriage was beginning to unravel.

When Marianne and I got together, neither of us had much experience with relationships. We didn't have a handle on basic skills like communication. Often, we hid our real feelings because we were afraid the other couldn't take it.

Based on our personalities, we also fell into patterns we didn't know weren't sustainable. I was passive and didn't want to make decisions. Marianne was organized and decisive and glad to take control. I wanted her to—but I also reserved my right to silently resent her for it. That wasn't fair to her.

While I was teaching in Minnesota, I led the charge to create a chaplaincy concentration for the Master of Divinity program. I worked with professors in the Christian Ministry department to develop it. I chose courses I thought would be most pertinent and did the administrative work necessary for seeking approval for the concentration.

Then the east-coast chaplain declined the position the dean had told me about. In January of 2016, I was encouraged to apply. I did so and got an interview in February. Almost all the seminary professors were there in person or by phone, as well as the dean and the assistant dean. At the meeting, the chair for the Christian Ministry department also pitched the idea of the chaplaincy concentration. They were all enthusiastic about the idea and approved it.

The chair concluded by saying, "Now, I want you all to know that Keith did the majority of the work on this. I only helped him."

That was nice. I continued to feel good as my interview got underway. Almost no one else in the room knew what CPE was and I felt knowledgeable and confident.

Not long after the interview, I found myself being "wined and dined" by the dean.

Except, not really—he took me to lunch at a sandwich shop. In the car on the way there, the dean told me everyone had voted. They all agreed they wanted to offer me the position.

However, he hedged, since I didn't have a doctorate, they couldn't hire me as a faculty member. I'd be a "lecturer." I'd get paid for the courses I would teach on contract, plus a modest bursary in exchange for being:

> 1. *the leader of the concentration in chaplaincy for the M.Div program;*
> 2. *the chaplain of the seminary;*
> 3. *the sponsor of the chaplaincy club;*
> 4. *an advisor for all chaplaincy students; and*
> 5. *the head of an internship/field placement program (which I was also charged with creating), in which I would place*

students as chaplains in police and fire departments, hospitals, corporations, etc.

Meanwhile, I would also work on completing a doctorate, which the university would pay for.

To say the least, it seemed like a lot. Developing the field placement program alone would require establishing contacts at numerous institutions and developing a system for how to place students and monitor their progress out in the field—not to mention figuring out administration, insurance … just this one part of the job would require the hours of a full-time position.

In the car, the dean leaned across the gear shift to offer me a congratulatory handshake. He was a short, kind man with a strong Eastern European accent. When he smiled at me, I struggled to smile back. He looked surprised when I hesitated and said, "Can I have a few days to process this?"

My noncommittal response made for a very awkward lunch. Internally, I was thinking this seemed less like a grand and generous offer meriting congratulations than a gesture towards "hire him, we need to keep her." Someone who envisioned their future solely in the academic world might have viewed the offer differently. But I had a nagging worry. Was I that person? I liked teaching college classes. But I preferred the intimate, experience-based learning that happens in CPE.

On the way home, I thought about how I could make as much money as the university was offering working part-time as a chaplain at a local hospital. I wondered if I should consider applying there.

There was also a deeper issue at play. Did it make sense for me to keep teaching a class on "Marriage and Family" when it was becoming clearer all the time where my own marriage was headed?

I went home, looking to be consoled. I wanted to just sit in the emotion, process it—but not fix it. Marianne's boss at the time was the university president and I knew she would be tempted to go to him about this. I explained that I didn't want her to. I begged her not to. I was already working there because of her. I was only being thrown a bone because each move we'd made over the last few years had been to advance her career. Now, she had a great deal of authority over the entire health and wellness initiative on campus.

In every new place we went, however, I was starting over.

"Don't try to fix this," I said. "I need to think."

I didn't tell her—and maybe I wasn't even admitting it to myself—that maybe some small part of me was glad about the nature of the offer. This could be my impetus to action, my opportunity, my way out.

Marianne agreed. She promised. But the next day after work, she told me she had talked to her boss.

She said eagerly, "He says, 'It's the right job, but the wrong offer.'"

I was so angry. I felt she had stabbed me in the back. Marianne couldn't understand why and I didn't have the emotional bandwidth to show her any compassion, to realize that she was incapable of understanding. I couldn't see her side, see that this was her way of showing love.

*

I wasn't great at explaining what I wanted. I was also bitter that she never asked.

Marianne might not have wanted to know the answer. She didn't want me to pursue CPE educator certification or even to be a hospital chaplain. If we both worked at a university, we could have the summers off and spend them traveling together.

I got my revenge. That evening, mostly out of spite, I looked up openings at hospitals in California. There was a residency position in CPE open in the LA area. I applied and interviewed a few days later. Within ten days, I had received an offer.

I knew as soon as I got it that I was going to take it. Then I realized I had to tell Marianne—and figure out what in the world my life was going to look like. This position didn't exactly entail a daily or weekend commute.

I told Marianne I needed to find meaningful work to do. I had to go to California. Her reaction was much like the dean's in the car: utter surprise.

"No," she said. "It's impossible. It's unthinkable."

Then some of our friends got involved. They heard me when I explained I needed my career to go in a different direction. They all knew Marianne's drive and passion. I think Paul, the Adventist youth pastor we'd met a few years before we got married, was the one who sealed the deal for her.

He said, "I think Keith needs to be out from under your shadow for a time to find himself and his own voice. This is a good opportunity for him to do that."

Marianne agreed. But I wasn't being fully honest with her or my friends. In fact, my reasons for moving back to California were three-fold. I wanted to:

1) pursue the career I was passionate about;
2) leave my marriage; and
3) be near a woman I knew who lived in the Los Angeles area

One day in July 2016, I packed my car full of books, clothes, and, weirdly enough, some childhood keepsakes. Or maybe it wasn't weird. As excited as I was, I was already feeling vulnerable and in need of comfort. Into one of my suitcases I tucked a music box shaped like a drum. It spins as it plays "The Little Drummer Boy," my favorite Christmas song.

It's topped with a little wooden horse and has "Great Grandma Leeds, 1982" marked on the bottom in pencil.

As I drove away, I felt like the biggest badass on the planet. I turned my music up as far as it would go and belted out songs in the car with an abandon I hadn't felt since I was sixteen and got behind the wheel by myself for the first time.

Talk about clichés—I listened to Tom Waits. I slept in my car at a highway rest stop in Des Moines with the seat back and my feet up on the dashboard. I stopped at a Denny's on I-80 and paid in cash. In Cheyenne, I read Bukowski's *Factotum*: "I was a man who thrived on solitude; without it I was like another man without food or water. Each day without solitude weakened me. I took no pride in my solitude; but I was dependent on it. The darkness of the room was like sunlight to me."[33]

It was amazing. I love to drive, especially when I'm alone in the car. I always have. Even now, I'm not a good passenger. I get restless and I never quite trust the person who's driving.

I wasn't divorced yet. Marianne and I had agreed to do marriage counseling over Zoom, but I never had any actual intention of working things out. We only participated in a couple of sessions and I came back to Minnesota just once to see her. I flew there one evening after work, spent the next day there, and flew back that night. I took only one day off.

The visit didn't resolve anything. I didn't even know what I was doing there. I couldn't clarify what I wanted, which was divorce. I didn't have the courage, the know-how, the ability to engage. I was non-confrontational and passive and instead I put it all on Marianne to figure out. I can't imagine what it was like for her to have things drag out like that, to live in a constant state of uncertainty.

I'm not sorry I left my marriage. I wouldn't be the person I am today, and have the life I have, if I hadn't. But I regret the miserable way I did it.

Marianne deserved better. I wish I had been a stronger person.

*

As I drove into the night, I had no concept yet of what freedom would be like. So I drove full speed into my "wilderness period." "Rock-bottom" is another good word for it.

The fourth ultimate concern of life, as described by Yalom, is "isolation." There are three different types: *interpersonal, intrapersonal,* and *existential. Interpersonal* isolation is more commonly known as loneliness. It's isolation from other individuals. We experience *intrapersonal* isolation when we partition parts of ourselves from our own consciousness. We stifle our feelings and desires. We accept oughts or shoulds and distrust our wishes and judgments. We don't know ourselves at all.

*

In times of personal crisis and upheaval, I think there's often a big gulf between how we see ourselves and how others see us.

When I left my marriage to come back to California, many of my friends and family members were shocked. And most of them didn't even know my biggest secret: the woman I'd come to California for was a student doing internships at several sites around the greater LA area. One of her intern sites was near my apartment. So she stayed with me for seven or eight weeks.

I created a terrible gulf between myself and many of the people I loved by keeping this from them. For a while, that isolation was buffered by the fog, the fantasy, the dream I was living in.

But people who had known me a long time—my parents, for instance—saw through that. They didn't know exactly what was going on, but they could see how broken and lost I was. A dam broke for them, too.

Maybe when I was younger, they had thought I was aloof and independent and didn't need them. This is probably what Jim Coons was getting at when he told me they were giving me space.

Now, they could see how much I *did* need them. They didn't come at me with any "I told you so's" about working in the family business or anything else. They just supported me.

I couldn't afford the plan I had hatched. When I went to them, my dad said, "We'll help you every month. We didn't help you at all with school the first time."

They also got me a bed, furniture, pots and pans. Their generosity was crucial in my success. And after I finished my training, I was able to pay them back.

My sister Lisa was there for me, too. She gave me a lot of emotional support. Since she was also in contact with Marianne, and felt both of our pain, she was in a difficult position. A few months after Marianne and I split up for good, Marianne sent Lisa a "goodbye" letter; she wanted to cut off communication. I'm sure she wanted to start fresh, clear her life of any ties and reminders of me and the bitter way our relationship ended.

That was hard for Lisa. She lost a family member. The pain caused by my decisions was reverberating all around me.

*

One person in my life who wasn't shocked to find me on my own in California was my childhood friend Chris. When I met up with him and told him about the problems I was having with Marianne, he said, "She's an intense person. I'm actually surprised you guys made it as long as you did."

"Really?" I was taken aback at first. Then, after thinking about it, I wasn't. I thought about the brief time Marianne and I had lived with Chris when I was an associate pastor in the Sacramento Valley. Chris had seen the differences in our personalities and could sense even then that those differences were causing conflicts between us. While he wasn't surprised about our separation, it made him sad. He always got along with Marianne and enjoyed the times when we were all together. He's a great friend. To hold no animosity or judgment toward either of us is a real gift.

*

I was so cut off even from myself that I wasn't real with the woman I had come to California for any more than I was real with Marianne.

At the end of her internship, the relationship ended, too. When I lost her—one of the forces that had drawn me to this new life—the dreamy, hazy stupor I had been floating around in ended abruptly. The rosy colors of the fantasy dissolved. Around the same time, Marianne let me know she was done, too. She was filing for divorce and I'd receive the papers soon.

It was then that I found myself curled up on my bathroom floor. I took a shower and cried under the hot water until the hot water ran out. I got out and fell to my knees with my hands on the back of my head. I looked at the dark brown linoleum with a faded tan pattern on it. In some places, it was starting to peel.

And there was still another blow to come.

*

During the first few months after I left Minnesota, the only thing that kept me grounded was my CPE residency. Despite the mess I'd made of my personal relationships, I knew I was in the right place when it came to this foundational part of my life.

The residency included four units of CPE and eight or nine on-call shifts a month. I covered about a hundred beds in six or seven different units. There were four of us in residence. I embraced my peers and got close to them, especially a guy named Isaac. At this point, I'd lied to everyone important in my life. With my peers, I could start fresh.

A week or two after I collapsed in despair on my bathroom floor, a confidential patient was admitted to the medical unit of the hospital. She was on my unit, she was my patient, but I didn't visit her. I did see her husband once in the hallway, though I didn't know who he was at the time.

The hospital put in extra security measures because of this patient and the activity of staff members was strictly monitored, primarily because of privacy concerns. We were all aware there had been cases like this at other hospitals around the country in which staff members were investigated and even fired for accessing a confidential patient's record when they had no reason to do so.

Our hospital had added an extra layer of security to its medical record system for certain patients; it was called the "break the glass" feature. Any staff member who accessed the record system could see the patient's room number. But they could see the patient's name—or their alias if one was being used, as they are for psych patients, high-profile patients, and trauma patients —only if they clicked on the chart. Once they clicked on the chart, a message popped up: "You are trying to view confidential information. Do you want to break the glass?" To proceed, an employee needed to input their ID number as well as a reason they were accessing the chart, such as "patient care" or "direct patient care."

I didn't "break the glass." But one day when I was in the records system, I was just staring at one of the hospital computers and moving the mouse around without thinking about it much. My mind, unsurprisingly, was on other things. I clicked the confidential patient's room number and discovered that she had been given the alias of a historical figure associated with the Adventist church.

Huh, I thought. *That's weird.*

Two days later, the name changed, this time to *another* historical figure associated with the Adventist church. For a while, my mind became absorbed in the strange mystery of why this confidential patient had been given two pseudonyms closely associated with Adventism. This small, stupid thing gave me a distraction from the mess of my life.

Eventually, I lost interest. I had forgotten about it when I was summoned into the office of my educator. He showed me an email he had received from the Chief Compliance Officer at the hospital. I was to report to a committee meeting the next day on the eighth floor, the highest level of the hospital.

Sitting across from my educator in his office, I felt the bottom of my world, the ground beneath my feet, begin to tilt and slide.

*

I was so angry with myself. What had I been thinking? That was the problem. I hadn't been.

I knew how seriously hospitals take patient confidentiality. They have to. When they don't, they put patients and staff in danger.

Case in point: once early in my career, a trauma patient was admitted with gunshot wounds into the hospital where I was working. She had no ID on her and staff didn't know who she was.

Around 7:00 a.m. the next morning, a man and a woman identifying themselves as the patient's brother and sister came to the hospital. Their description fit the patient, so security sent them to the emergency department. The bedside nurse led them into the patient's room. There, they started to cry, almost uncontrollably.

She left to get them a box of tissues. When she returned, the two visitors were gone and the patient had been stabbed to death. The people responsible for the botched hit had found out where their target was taken and had showed up to finish the job.

*

The day after I found out about my disciplinary issue, I attended a meeting with the head of Human Resources; the Chief Compliance Officer; someone from cybersecurity; and a member of the hospital's legal team. They showed me a print-out of all my computer activity, line-by-line, every click of the mouse.

"Explain this touch on the account," someone would say and point to the day and time. "Now, explain this one ...."

I didn't think I had done anything wrong—though I wasn't certain. "I didn't open the chart," I said, over and over again. "Yes, but I didn't open the chart ...."

They were just trying to scare me. They succeeded. Worse yet, I froze up when I was trying to explain myself and couldn't remember the pseudonyms associated with Adventism that had piqued my interest in the first place.

As I left the meeting, my mind was scrambling. If I were fired, I didn't know if I would recover. I couldn't lose my job along with everything else. If I did, where was I? Who was I? I felt as if I'd break into pieces, collapse into dust.

I'd never get another residency. I'd never get another unit of CPE. I had thrown away my marriage and an academic position. I'd lost my mistress and if I lost this, I'd have done it all for nothing.

What was going to happen to me? I had a vision of returning to my parents' glass shop back home. I was going to end up doing the kind of manual-labor job I had run away from.

I was jolted by the realization that this wasn't even an option anymore. My dad had retired and sold the building. I had nothing to fall back on.

In *Reflections on the Art of Living*, Joseph Campbell describes "the dark night of the soul"[34] that one must pass through on their way to the light of revelation. The path descends into the abyss, where no one wants to go.

That day after the meeting, I found my friend Isaac and confided in him what had just happened. I was in the abyss. It had been thirty years since I had cried in front of another human being. That day, I wept in front of him. I was completely broken.

But my tears were also telling me a story. They were a call for me to grow up. I needed to take responsibility for what I'd done and how I'd done it. I needed to see that this moment was the culmination of all the choices I'd made. I wasn't quite ready to embark on this part of the journey, but I was starting to acknowledge that I'd have to.

For the first time, I was also grieving the loss of my old self, the loss of the life I'd left behind.

I wasn't fired. There was nothing left to do now but to come back to work the next day and keep going.

Chapter 11

"Here, help me find this guy's family," says Abby from social work.

We're in the unit station looking for someone connected to the patient who died alone in room seven. Abby hands me his driver's license. I sit at a computer behind her and start searching. I find someone on Facebook with the same name. Scrolling through pictures of this person walking on the beach with a golden retriever, standing in front of a Christmas tree, sitting on a couch eating a piece of pie, I study his features and decide he looks like this patient. I find a few phone numbers and give those to Abby.

It doesn't make sense for me to call because chaplains aren't allowed to give out medical information. I can repeat it, but I can't say it first. I've sometimes found myself in the position in which I'm the first contact with the family of a patient who has died but I have to talk around this vital piece of information until the physician comes to officially inform them. Inevitably, the visitor looks at me and says, "*What?*" as if I betrayed them or led them on.

Only then can I say, "Yes, I'm sorry. She's dead." It's a rather rough situation for everyone involved, so I encourage Abby to call.

At the first number, they don't know him. On the second or third, she finds someone who can identify him. They are surprised but not shocked. They live five hours away and I later learn this patient was flight-lifted here.

Since the patient's family won't be coming to the hospital tonight, there's nothing more for me to do here. Plus, my phở is getting cold. I tell Abby I'm sure I'll see her later.

*

Let me rephrase something. I said, of the patient in room seven, that he died "alone"— to indicate that no one who loved him was there. But perhaps I should have said that instead. After all, someone might have been in there with him at the time of his death: a physician, a nurse, an environmental services worker.

More importantly, the fact is, at least according to Yalom, we all die alone.

The third type of isolation in Yalom's classification—and the most relevant in the CPE context—is *existential*. This is separation from the world. Someone experiencing existential isolation isn't just lonely and in need of the company of others. They feel an "unbridgeable gulf between oneself and any other being."[35] This feeling of separation is related to a certainty that one is alone in how they experience the world. No one can understand the way they feel or perceive things.

The knowledge that we will die can be cause for tremendous existential isolation. No one can take away the inevitability of death from anyone else.

Most patients in the hospital are dealing with some form of existential isolation. It's very gripping to be in the room with it. No matter how much I want to help a patient bear their fear and suffering, the patient knows they are ultimately alone in it. The closest I can get to that pain is to listen to what the patient says about it and watch how they react to it.

Patients also feel a separation from themselves. Their bodies are diseased and out of control. They have no power to stop it.

*

ULTIMATE CONCERNS: THE PLAYLIST
Ultimate Concern #4: Isolation
Top Ten:
    1. Isolation—Joy Division
    2. Running Away—Bob Marley
    3. 911/Mr. Lonely—Tyler, The Creator
    4. The Fool on the Hill—The Beatles
    5. I Just Wasn't Made for These Times—The Beach Boys
    6. Wearing the Inside Out—Pink Floyd
    7. Where the Streets Have No Name—U2
    8. Super Rich Kids—Frank Ocean
    9. Hope There's Someone—Antony & The Johnsons
    10. Who Are You—Tom Waits

Bob Marley wrote "Running Away" when he went into exile in England from Jamaica. He was experiencing interpersonal isolation from his wife, who stayed behind. But the lines that get repeated most are about a disconnect he feels within his own consciousness and his inability to escape from himself.

*

The resolution to existential isolation is relationship. When we "are able to acknowledge our isolated situations in existence and to confront them with resoluteness, we will be able to turn lovingly toward others," says Yalom. Relationships don't eliminate isolation; we each exist alone and always will. But we can choose to exist with others in such a way that "love compensates for the pain of isolation."[36]

*

My student Ernie was in his second unit of CPE. He identified as "spiritually independent" and found solace in the isolation of his chosen belief system. But he also liked relationships. He was sweet-natured and got along well with staff, educators, and his peers.

It's my job to assess students' primary areas for growth. I thought Ernie could grow by finding room for others within his "spiritually independent" framework. He focused on applying my advice to his relationships with his adult children. He had a tenuous relationship with them and they had tenuous relationships with each other. When his son came out as gay, his daughter—a fundamentalist Christian—did not approve and shut him out of her life.

Ernie supported his son, lived in the same house as his son and his husband, and acted as the rather unsuccessful mediator between his two children. He had a negative history with fundamentalism; both of his ex-wives were devout conservative Christians and he associated many of the negative feelings he had about them with their religious beliefs. This prevented him from finding empathy for his daughter and from being as compassionate and kind to her as he was with most people.

Then his daughter had a child. Ernie's heart softened. He wanted to be in his grandson's life. Through CPE, Ernie met many people who were estranged from family and friends. They held petty things against each other for a long time. Then at the end, they often longed to reunite, but sometimes, it was too late.

Ernie didn't want that. Exploring his issues with fundamentalism led him to a greater gentleness with his daughter. She was naturally more drawn to him, and in turn, she opened her heart as well. She invited Ernie's son and his husband to her son's birthday party. When he told me about it, Ernie sat in my office and cried.

Martin Buber wrote, "A great relationship breaches the barriers of a lofty solitude, subdues its strict law, and throws a bridge from self-being to self-being across the abyss of dread of the universe."[37]

*

I see a lot of strained relationships in my work. Sometimes, I see a great one, too.

One December, the day before Christmas Eve, I was paged to the emergency department to meet with a woman named Rhonda. When I came into the waiting room reserved for the families of critically ill patients, the first thing I noticed was that she was much too calm.

On my way over, I had passed her husband, Kyle, in one of the trauma rooms. Many people were in there working on him and a LUCAS machine had been placed on his chest. The LUCAS (Lund University Cardiopulmonary Assist System) is a mechanical chest compression system used when patients are in cardiac arrest.

Usually, family members are pacing the floor. If they're sitting, they often can't keep their hands or legs still. Rhonda was reclining in her chair engrossed in a magazine, one leg crossed casually over the other.

She was in her mid-fifties, with long straight hair, a mix of brown and gray, and curled bangs. She wore a thin zip-up jacket but big snow boots. When she saw my badge, she gave me a sweet, peaceful smile.

"Kyle and I are Christians," she said, "so I'm glad you've come to keep me company. Thank you!"

As we started to talk, I watched her carefully. She seemed to have been beamed straight out of a 1980s news interview with a woman utterly nonplussed about the fact that her trailer smack in the middle of tornado alley had just been sucked up by a storm.

Why did she seem so unworried? Was she in denial? Or did she and her husband have an acrimonious or distant relationship? I soon found out the opposite was true. They had been married for thirty-five years. They had never had any children because, as Rhonda said, they were "too selfish to share each other with anyone else."

That evening, Rhonda had prepared a chicken dinner just the way Kyle liked it: pressure-cooked, then battered and pan-fried. While she cooked, she looked out the window and watched Kyle putter around the property in the light snow that had fallen that afternoon. He adjusted a light here, a plastic reindeer or Santa there, on their double-wide trailer. They both loved Christmas.

At dinner, they dropped cheeky hints about the presents they'd put under the tree. They found it difficult to keep secrets from one another.

Just before he finished eating, Kyle grimaced. He held his side.

"Are you okay?" Rhonda said.

"Just a tight muscle." A few minutes later, it happened again. Kyle confessed that after coming inside, he'd also felt a tightness in his chest. He'd chalked it up to the shoveling and yard work he'd done.

Rhonda wondered if they should call an ambulance. Kyle was fifteen years older than she was and she wanted to make sure it was nothing serious. Kyle insisted he was fine. But an hour later, when they were watching a Hallmark Christmas movie on TV, the pain grew more intense.

"You can be mad at me if you want. I'm calling 911," Rhonda said.

Despite Kyle's assurances, the emergency responders felt uncomfortable leaving him at home. Still, Kyle was awake and talking as Rhonda and her husband blew kisses to one another and exchanged "I love you's" through the back window of the ambulance. After wrapping up the food on the table, Rhonda drove to the hospital in her car.

Even now, her biggest worry seemed to be that Kyle would be irritated with her. "I hope I did the right thing. He just looked like he might be in a lot of pain."

It was then that I knew I had to go find a physician to talk to her. The fact that no one had come already was most likely an ominous sign. Physicians are human beings like everybody else. They don't like to deliver bad news and in my experience, the families of dying or dead patients often wait longer for information than other families do.

*

Empathy can be a tricky thing for physicians to navigate. They don't want to lose empathy, but they can't let it distract them, either. I realized this once when I was having a big mole dug out of my scalp. The surgeon asked me how my day was going, so I answered. When I realized he wasn't listening to my response, I got annoyed.

Then I shook myself out of it (not literally; there was a man standing above me with a sharp instrument in his hand). I reminded myself that the most pressing issue at the moment was the large hole in my head that needed to be sewn up. The doctor didn't need to see me right now. He needed to see a scalp. I needed a dangerous growth removed and he needed to do his job smoothly and successfully and not worry about any mistakes he might have made when it was time to go home and enjoy his time with his kids that evening.

*

When I told Rhonda I was going to find someone from Kyle's medical team to give her an update, a ripple of worry disturbed the calm in her eyes for the first time. Just for a second, and very faintly, like a leaf falling on the surface of still water.

I could see her searching my eyes for a clue. "Okay," she said. "I'll just be here."

"I'll be right back," I said.

The attending physician on Kyle's team came. He told her that Kyle had had a heart attack. Then he said gently, "So we've been doing compressions, because his heart stopped …."

A switch was flipped. Rhonda exploded. "You mean he's *dead*? No wonder I got the chaplain sitting with me for fifteen minutes! Take me to him—*now*!"

In the doorway of the trauma room, Rhonda saw the LUCAS machine on Kyle's chest and immediately pressed her hands together in prayer. "We are Christians and we believe in doing everything possible to save life," she declared to the room. "So everyone, keep working." She went straight to Kyle's head and held it in her hands.

The attending physician said, "He's been without a pulse for forty-five minutes."

Rhonda pursed her lips and shook her head. "That doesn't matter. I've got the chaplain here and he's going to pray."

The entire team—no fewer than twenty-five people—turned to look at me. I was standing in the doorway. I forced a smile and went to Rhonda, feeling as if I were onstage.

"What should we pray for?" I asked her.

"That God brings him back. I can't live without this man. Pray that he gets a heartbeat again and comes back to me," said Rhonda.

I looked up at the attending, who raised his eyebrows. I exhaled.

"Okay. Let's pray for that," I said.

After I said "Amen," Rhonda and I both looked at the monitor. The attending was looking at it, too.

At first, his mouth was clenched. Then it fell open. He didn't take his eyes from the monitor as he said, astonished, "Huh. We have a pulse."

Rhonda didn't look surprised at all. She nodded affirmatively.

"Hi, honey," she said. "Here you are. And here I am."

I looked around the room at the team. Everyone's eyes were on me. We were all shocked and time seemed to slow down for a minute. Gradually, everyone returned to their duties. After another forty-five minutes or so, they got him stabilized enough to be moved to the MICU. Rhonda wouldn't budge from Kyle's side and she didn't want me to go anywhere, either. Together, we followed Kyle's bed upstairs.

By the time we got there, it was about 10:30 p.m. Rhonda stayed with him all night. I left when I got paged to other calls, but in-between each visit, I'd check back in with her.

Around 3:00 a.m., Rhonda wanted to have a serious conversation with me. She was wondering if she should complete a DNR form. She didn't want to. She didn't want to let go.

"But I'm afraid he's in pain," she said.

Kyle hadn't opened his eyes. Rhonda told me she thought God might have sent Kyle back to her so she could say goodbye. Now, she wondered, was she being selfish by trying to keep him here as long as she could? It wasn't easy for her to reconcile this feeling with her religious belief that life should be sustained at all costs.

I talked through everything with her as she processed her grief and the decision she had to make. I gently affirmed that a DNR is neither right nor wrong.

In the end, she did it. At 6:30 a.m., Kyle died for good. Rhonda and I gathered up his belongings and I walked her to the parking lot. It was filled with fresh snow. There were no tire marks anywhere.

Rhonda and I talked near the doorway, feeling a blast of warm forced air every time one of us got too close to the censor and the doors slid open. "You know," Rhonda said, "since we got married, we've never spent a night apart. Can you believe that? Tonight's the first night we won't be together. And it's Christmas Eve."

She started weeping and collapsed into my arms. With the help of a security guard, I got her to a chair inside where she sat for about twenty minutes. Finally, she got up the strength to go out to her car and drive home.

In the meantime, it had started to snow again. I hoped it wouldn't delay my flight. I was flying home that night to be with my parents and my sister. I was so excited when I bought the ticket. Now more than ever, I didn't want to be alone on Christmas.

*

If we don't seek out great relationships to help us bear existential dread and our own mortality, we sometimes attempt less productive and even destructive ways to assert some kind of power over isolation and death.

In the last couple of months of 1988, when I was in the fifth grade, I went through a period of having terrible nightmares that made me dread going to sleep. In the dreams, my arms would get torn apart like a character from *Scrooged*, which I saw in the theater around Thanksgiving. As the days got darker, so did my thoughts and feelings. Things only got worse when I stayed up late watching *Tales from the Crypt*. I did everything I could think of to put off going to bed. Once, I bribed my parents.

"I'll clean the living room if I can stay up," I said.

I don't know what they made of my behavior or what they were thinking by indulging it, but they let me do it.

I had a fish tank in my room that my dad had made for me. I demanded that the light on the tank be left on all night. I wasn't afraid of the dark; I just wanted the light to keep me awake. But almost every night, I fell asleep for a short period of time. When some disturbing dream woke me up, I'd crawl to my parents' room (the floors were creaky, and crawling reduced the racket I made) and watch the clock on my dad's side of the bed.

When it's 3:46 a.m., then I'll wake him up, I'd think.

The time would come and go. If I woke him, he'd pick me up and carry me back to bed, and I didn't want to go. Eventually, staring at the clock made my eyes tired and I fell asleep on the floor.

Other ways I'd occupy myself at night: sneaking out of the house and walking around the block in the dark. And scooping my live, wriggling goldfish, neon tetras, and harlequin rasboras out of my fish tank and flushing them down the toilet.

*

My parents were distracted: my mom by a boundless grief, my dad by attending to her. My Grandma Honey had died that summer. In my own anxious way, I was now fascinated with death, even as I could not quite grasp the concept of it.

Grandma Honey—her real name was Helen—was my mom's mother. She divorced her first husband, my Grandpa Joe, when my mom was still in high school. He cheated on her, but for years before that, he was also abusive to both Grandma Honey and my mom.

Grandma Honey married her second husband, my Grandpa Ellwood, when I was two or three. I always associated the two of them with one another. Grandpa Ellwood had once been a pharmacist and had a lot of money. But at some point, he went bankrupt. Then he found Grandma Honey and married her and they moved into a mobile home. He never seemed bitter about the material things he had lost. In fact, he was one of the most sweet-natured people I've ever known. He had a nice laugh that started out high and wound down to a mellower note at the end.

Throughout my childhood, Grandma Honey was a very kind and loving presence in my life as well. Much of that might have been down to the deep and enduring love of Grandpa Ellwood; she wasn't always like that when my mom was growing up. At that time, Grandma Honey struggled with alcoholism and didn't do much to protect my mom from Grandpa Joe.

Ellwood adored my grandmother. After she died, people asked him if he would marry again. He'd always shrug and say, "I've already had the best. Anything else would be second-rate."

*

When I was little, Grandma Honey often baby-sat Lisa and me in her mobile home. Lisa was much more social than I was and spent her time there chatting happily with Grandma and following her around. I often wanted to be alone, so Grandma Honey would make me frozen pizza and set me up in the back bedroom, which had a television and a canopy bed without a canopy. I'd shut the door and jump on the bed and climb up the wooden posts and swing around on them.

The Dukes of Hazzard was my favorite show to watch in there. I loved seeing the cars jump and I loved how no one who lived in Hazzard County was bad, not even Boss Hogg. The bad people all came from out of town.

Before she opened the door, Grandma Honey always knocked first. "Keith, can I come in?"

"Just a minute!" I'd scramble to make the bed, then sit nicely on the smooth comforter with an angelic smile.

My mom told me that once when she came to pick me up, Grandma Honey went to the door and whispered, "Watch this. I always do this. You hear him jumping around in there? When I say his name, listen to him in there cleaning up."

On other days, I'd watch *Care Bears* with Lisa, pretending to hate it but secretly digging the fact that cool things shot out of the bears' stomachs. Or I'd make a time-traveling fort out of the orange cushions from the ottoman in Grandma Honey's living room. Grandma would crouch in it with me and say, "Okay, where are we going?"

The answer was always Albuquerque. One of my uncles had lived there and I'd heard it on *Bugs Bunny*. I'd never seen Albuquerque, but I liked the way the word sounded. It was fun to say.

Grandma Honey was sweet, but she wouldn't be disrespected, either. Once I must have been really naughty. I can't remember what I did, but it pushed her buttons. She marched me down to the glass shop, handed me off to my mom, and said, "Betty, I love you. But I can't—anymore—with him today."

She wore tight-fitting beige or brown polyester slacks and her hair was arranged into a halo of short gray curls, very neat and even. The hairstyle was too perfect and it always looked the same. I was suspicious.

I liked to point at it and say, "Grandma, that's not your real hair!"

My mom never joined in on the teasing. And once when she brought Lisa and me to the mobile home, I found out why. The front door was open, so I ran in, Lisa right on my heels. Then we burst into Grandma Honey and Grandpa Ellwood's bedroom.

I heard exclamations of surprise. Grandpa Ellwood was running stark naked into the bathroom. Grandma Honey was nude as well. But I barely noticed any of that; all I saw was a gray poofy wig sitting on the vanity.

I crowed, "Ha! I knew it! I knew you wore a wig!"

My mom was yanking us back out of the room while Grandma shouted, "Get out of here! We'll be right there!"

Was I scarred and traumatized for the rest of my life by finding out that my grandparents were having sex? Not at all. I think it's pretty cool.

*

Grandma Honey smoked for over forty-five years. When she was sixty-seven, she started to feel unwell in the mid-summer and doctors discovered she had cancer. It had metastasized to so many organs, they could only speculate on where it may have started. Maybe in her lungs, but it could have been her liver or her pancreas.

It didn't matter much. She died less than three weeks after she was diagnosed. My whole world changed so irrevocably, with such horrific force, in such a short period of time, that my family is still feeling the reverberations even today.

We went to see her in the hospital. I was filled with dread the whole way there. Less than a year had passed since my traumatic visit to my dad's friend Tweed.

It was a shock to see her lying there. She had always looked so strong and healthy. Now, Grandma Honey had lost all her vitality. The same woman who had crouched in my fort with me just weeks before had to use all her energy just to lift her hand. And I was seeing her with her wig off for only the second time. She looked more like an alien than a person.

The room was dark, the curtains drawn. That helped a little to shadow her startling appearance, but it also made the space gloomy. Grandma Honey was on the ground floor in the corner room, right next to the door leading to the street. Hospitals weren't yet as closed and inaccessible as they became after the arrival of Covid-19.

As I had done when I visited Tweed, I stayed far away from the bed. But this time, I was feeling more than fear. I was old enough to know about death, though too young to understand it. I knew my grandmother was dying. At the same time, it never crossed my mind that I'd never see her again.

I was afraid to come near Grandma and afraid to leave.

"Mom," I said, "can you come outside? I have to tell you something."

"In a minute," Mom said.

I knew the reality would be much longer than that. I kept pushing.

"No, Mom, I *really* have to tell you something now." My shoulders drooped and I found a spot to stare at on the floor. I began shifting from one foot to the other—I still do this when I'm antsy.

My mother took Lisa and me outside and we stood on the steps. The hot sunlight was blinding after the dim, cool room.

"What is it?" she said.

I buried my face—my nose beginning to run, my eyes beginning to blur—in her chest and started crying. I felt as if my tears were a river of pain rising and nearing its banks. Once it reached them, it might be unstoppable. Who knew what would happen then?

Out of the corner of my eye, I saw two people walking toward us from the parking lot. They were laughing. How could they be laughing? What could possibly be funny at a time like this? Just past this door right behind me, my grandma lay dying.

"They're laughing at me," I said.

My mom was the emotional one in our family. What my dad, sister, and I lacked when it came to showing emotion, my mom made up for and then some. She would often cry at sentimental television commercials. She'd try to hide her tears until she couldn't. Then she'd look back at us and smile.

My father would always—always!—laugh at her. For me, the message was clear: crying was a laughable thing to do. If I cried, I'd get the same reaction.

"They aren't laughing at you," my mom said.

But I couldn't hear her. It would be over thirty years before I let this happen again. I wiped my cheeks with my wrist, sniffled, and pushed myself away from my mom.

"Are you ready to see Grandma?" she asked me.

I glanced at Lisa, who was squinting and shading her face with her hands. Her cheeks were already turning pink. Though her hair was brown while mine was blond, our complexions were equally unsuited to a California summer. Our skin went from pale straight to sunburn then back to pale again, with lots of painful peeling in-between.

I looked back at my mother and nodded—but I was lying.

"Okay." She took my hand. "Let's go back in."

We walked through the door again. My legs were heavy, my arms tingling. I wanted to flee somewhere, anywhere, else. My mind went dizzy as it tried to wrap itself around the concept of death.

I thought about how when I woke up in the morning in my room and saw one of my fish floating on the surface of the water in my tank, I flushed it down the toilet. But Grandma couldn't be flushed down the toilet, could she? Were there bigger toilets?

On and on my mind raced. Inevitably, out of everything and nothing, the dreaded question arrived, the one I'd been blissfully ignorant of until this point: "When will I die?"

I didn't even know I'd muttered it out loud until my mom stopped walking and knelt down. She had heard me. But there are so many questions parents can't answer.

She placed a hand on each of my shoulders. "Listen to me," she began, looking directly into my eyes. When she told me to listen to her, most often it meant I was in trouble. Somehow, I knew that wasn't the case now. Still, the moment was even more fraught and serious than usual. I listened attentively. She opened her mouth to speak. I could tell she was being careful. I appreciated that she was taking the time to be with me.

She looked deep into my eyes and lied: "You don't have to worry about that. You're not going to die."

*

There are so many answers children can't question.

I wanted to believe my mom, but the comment never sat well with me. While I wasn't capable of knowing she was lying, exactly, I knew something was off.

But I *had* always believed I was special. My mom had often told me so. She and my father tried for five or six years to get pregnant before I arrived.

"I remember holding you in my arms a few days after we got home from the hospital," she would say, "and I told God how precious and special you are. I gave you to God right there."

At just a few days old, my mom gave me away. I had never understood what that meant, either. As children, we all gradually grow into a better understanding of the world. I was growing.

When my sister arrived four years later, my mom instilled that sense of specialness in her as well. My mother had had a late-term miscarriage a couple of years after I was born, so Lisa was a miracle baby.

I was slowly becoming aware of causality: *this* happened because *this* happened. Grandma Honey died because she had cancer. She had cancer probably because she smoked for so long. My living fish died because I flushed them down the toilet.

But what about those that just floated to the surface one day for no apparent reason? Did they have cancer? They didn't smoke. I began to understand the law of nature that everything dies. No matter what I wanted or what I did, death was universal and impersonal.

At the same time, I had two defenses against my fear of death that helped me get through this cataclysmic period of my childhood:

> *1) I am special and will never die*
> *2) A personal and ultimate rescuer exists to protect me*

Believing my mom when she told me I was special, and believing my teachers at church when they told me Jesus was an "ultimate rescuer," served me well. Jim Coons was particularly vital in this process. He gave me not only the second lesson but also the first (or the first part of the first).

I'm thankful for the lessons. And in some ways, their relation to reality doesn't matter. As it is for many children, my "ultimate rescuer" was Jesus, but I think the term can be taken more broadly. I'm always curious to hear what people believed about death as children, as far back as they can remember. I think that those who grow up with personal beliefs like these—whether those beliefs are instilled in them directly by others, or they arise simply out of being greatly loved, cared for, and protected—are better able to build the foundational structures that shore us up in the face of the shocking realization about the universality of death, both as children and for the rest of our lives.

Years later, I found this articulated by Irvin Yalom:

> *Though these beliefs are abetted by explicit parental and religious instruction in afterlife myths, in an all-protecting God, and in the efficacy of personal prayer, they are also grounded in the infant's early life experience.*[38]

The idea of an "ultimate rescuer" also combats the fear that we might just be floating around isolated in a meaningless world—because this rescuer connects us to one another.

*

The day Grandma Honey died, my mom was at her bedside with Grandma Honey's sister Theda.

My mom wanted to be alone with Grandma Honey when she died.

At one point, my Great-Aunt Theda got up to get a cup of coffee. Soon after she left, my mom swears that a strange green glow called to her. She felt compelled to get up off the cot where she was lying and go to the bed.

"Mom?" she said. "Mom?"

Grandma took her last breaths in the few moments that Theda was gone. People often say of a loved one, "She died just as she lived." Honestly, I find this to be true. People with messy lives tend to have messy deaths. Peaceful people with their affairs in order go out in a calm and orderly way.

A similar situation happened at my first visit as a hospice chaplain. I was at a bedside with the daughter of a patient whose biggest fear was that her daughter, an only child, would be alone when her mother died.

The daughter asked me to pray. When I asked her what she wanted me to pray for, her answer was rambling, frantic, all over the place. It took a while to sort it all out and find a coherent, meaningful message. At some point in the middle of the prayer, I looked at the patient and was pretty sure she had died. I stopped in the middle of the prayer and the social worker in the room and the patient's daughter looked at me. I looked back at the daughter, and she turned her gaze to her mother.

"Mom? Mom?" Then she yelled: "*Mom!*"

I got a nurse, who checked the patient's pulse, then called in the med team. They declared her deceased.

The daughter said to me, "You were the first visitor today." Turning back to her mother, she added, "She decided to die while you were here, so I wouldn't be alone."

*

I'm glad my mom got what she wanted from Grandma Honey's death. After the funeral, she started to spin out, psychologically and emotionally. Grandma Honey had been a strong stabilizing force in her life.

When my mom turned sixty-two, her mind started to shut down. She retired from the glass shop and didn't get another job. Today, she has severe dementia that's left her unable to do much on her own. My dad, six years older than her, stays by her side taking care of her every day.

I have a video of my mom reading a book to my son when he was ten months old. Her dementia was progressing rapidly at that time, but she could still read. I love watching it. My son is giggling and loving every minute.

*

My mom saw Grandma Honey cry only once, right at the end of her life.

Grandma Honey was out shopping for material to make Lisa's Halloween costume the day she was taken to the hospital and never left. She fell as she was getting out of the car in a store parking lot.

When my mom brought Lisa and me back into her hospital room after I cried out on the steps, she told us to hug Grandma Honey and tell her we loved her. Lisa was only six at the time and didn't understand most of what was happening. She went up to Grandma Honey and told her she loved her for the last time in her sunny and innocent way.

Saying goodbye felt impossible, but I followed my sister's lead. I was crying as I told Grandma Honey goodbye. As Lisa and I left the room, Grandma Honey began to cry, too. I think it broke her that she was too weak to help me get through this. And she knew she'd never see either of us again.

After she died, my dad made a beautiful urn out of plexiglass for her ashes. Lisa and I lowered it into the hole in front of her gravestone at the cemetery in Paradise, California.

*

When I think of Grandma Honey's illness and death, I often think of a day I went to her house not long before she got sick. I had an ear infection. I fell asleep while I was there, and when I woke up, there was a bowl of ice cream and Cocoa Puffs on the tray in front of me. My mother didn't let me have sugary cereal so this was a big treat for me.

I took a bite, but the crunch of the cereal was so loud in my clogged ear that I started crying from the pain. Grandma Honey came over and scratched my back with her long fingernails until I fell back asleep.

Chapter 12

6:15 p.m., Monday, August 22, 2022

I'm heading back to my desk when Craig the charge nurse grabs me. He asks if I'll visit a patient who came in tonight. She's currently under psychiatric evaluation.

The patient is, according to Craig's report, "seeing things." She believes there's a satanic cult who meets on the back patio at her apartment complex.

"She asked to speak with you. Well—we sort of offered," Craig says with a big grin.

The patient looks to be in her mid-40s. Or she could be in her 30s, with years of intensity and worry written on her face. She tells me almost verbatim what Craig just said. Then she shows me pictures of rocks in various arrangements on the lawn outside her sliding-glass door.

"Tell me I'm not crazy," she says.

This isn't for me to determine and this may be exactly why people under psychiatric evaluation request my presence: they want someone there who will simply let them talk, hold space for them, and accept them at the deepest level of their humanity.

"I can tell you that sounds incredibly scary," I say instead.

"I'm so scared."

Just looking at the pictures and validating the emotional impact they've had on her seems to give her comfort—so much so that all of a sudden, out of nowhere, she falls asleep. She looks peaceful, cuddled under a few blankets, her long black frayed hair spread across the pillow. I look at the security guard by the door and we shrug. I wait a moment. Then I tip-toe away from the room and return to my desk, where my now-chilled phở awaits me.

*

I once did a residency in an adult psychiatric unit. Listening to the interpretations psych patients had of what was going on around them made me see the world differently. Who's to say the "sane" always have the clearest concept of reality? The content that psych patients contribute to conversations doesn't always make sense. But their emotions are very real and they are more aware of them than many sane people are.

And regarding the patient who was worried about cults—it's not as if I don't worry about evil.

My perception of evil arises from my view of existentialism, which is a philosophical belief that we are each in charge of ourselves. We are free to make choices that determine our development as people and our paths in life.

Where those choices lead us depends on what parts of ourselves we choose to express and actualize. As Aleksandr Solzhenitsyn says in *The Gulag Archipelago 1918-1956*, for which he attempted to record all the prisons and labor camps that arose in Russia after the Bolsheviks came to power, "The line separating good and evil passes not through states, nor between classes, nor between political parties either—but right through every human heart—and through all human hearts."[39] Like Solzhenitsyn, I believe the capacity for evil is in all of us, just as we all have the capacity for good.

This sentiment is echoed in many literary and sacred texts. In Mark 10:18, Jesus responds to a young man who calls him "Good Teacher" by saying, "Why do you call me good? No one is good but God alone."

Carl Jung writes in *The Red Book* about the common dream of entering a cave. The cave is a symbol of the darkest parts of ourselves. The trip is a descent into hell, but it's also an important part of self-realization and self-actualization. Only when we confront the darkest things we are capable of can we come out on the other side and see the lightest parts of ourselves and the good we can do if we choose it.

Of course, some people don't choose it. Instead, they exploit and exert power over others in a malevolent way; and in my experience, that combination of tragedy and malevolent exploitation often leads to trauma. Such an event forces us to face not just *what* happened, but *how it could* happen. It rattles our very understanding of what the world and humanity are like.

"How could I have done such a thing?" a patient who had fought in the Vietnam War once said to me. "I can't believe the things I've done."

I talk to my students about the importance of being able to articulate what they believe in. Many other people have the luxury of keeping their beliefs private. Not us. It's a requirement of the job to "dream out loud" what we believe. It's also helpful to have a philosophy of evil. You never know what you might have to confront when you go in to visit a patient. You don't want to have to face the darkest parts of the human soul without some preparation.

*

I visited a patient once who was confronting the reality that her husband was having an affair. "How could he do such a thing?" she said.

That "could" asks a deeper question than "why." It also implies that she could never imagine herself—or maybe any other decent person—being capable of it.

When Marianne found out I was having an affair, the information called into question everything she believed about herself and the fifteen years we had spent together.

"Everything about our relationship was a lie," she wrote to me.

That's not true. But I understand what she was saying. My actions called everything into question. They changed her whole world—our whole world.

I said to the patient, "It seems like you're saying: *I thought I knew him, and knowing he's capable of doing this is incredibly scary.*"

She said, "Yes. Yes! If he could do this, then what else could he do? What else is he capable of?"

A far more extreme example: a prisoner I met who had murdered and raped at least four people, with the details unclear as to which act came first. I had always envisioned evil as being embodied in a person who looked and acted the part—Satan incarnate, foaming at the mouth and all the rest. But the patient was quite charming. I liked him. Only afterwards did I find out what had landed him in prison.

*

The mark evil leaves can also be unmistakably present—in fact, impossible to miss.

I was once asked to visit a woman who had "aged out" of sex slavery and somehow ended up at the hospital. For years, she had been kept as a prisoner and sex worker. Now, presumably, she had been discarded.

It was the worst and most uncomfortable visit of my life.

I was nervous to enter the room. What sort of a person would I encounter? Was she still a "person" or just a shell—a body that had been used, abused, and thrown away when it no longer served its purpose? What did that kind of confinement and abuse do to someone?

She had requested to see a chaplain. I couldn't find the charge nurse and for a while I paced back and forth in front of her room. Occasionally, I tried to peek through the blinds. I saw her sitting on the bed, facing away from the door. She had long black hair down to her elbows and wore a gown that was gaping in the back. I couldn't see anyone else in there, but I knew there must be: a nurse or a CNA (certified nursing assistant)—because the patient had expressed suicidal ideation. That was one piece of information I knew: she had told someone at the hospital that since she was "too old" to be of service anymore, she had wondered if she'd be better off dead.

Finally, I found the charge nurse. I wanted as much information as I could before going into the patient's room. Unfortunately, the nurse was not very helpful.

"Any idea why she made the request?"

"No, I don't."

"Anything I should be aware of in there?"

"Not that I know of."

"Do we know her name? I see she's listed as a 'Doe' in the chart."

"Yeah, no. We don't know who she is."

My final question—"Am I the right person to go in there?"—was met with a shrug. The charge nurse walked away.

*

Information before a visit is invaluable. It helps me wrap my head around the situation I'll be walking into. Then I can anticipate some possible outcomes and remind myself of the best practices for responding to them. I always end up having to wing it to some extent. But my improvisations are most effective when they're based on the principles and techniques I've learned in my training.

Early in my training, I got a call saying that a patient was preparing to be discharged. The patient's wife wanted a chaplain to meet with the patient first, but I didn't know exactly why.

The two women were sitting side-by-side with their arms around each other. The patient was already in street clothes. Though it was mid-summer and over ninety degrees outside, both women wore striped wool beanies and long-sleeved flannel shirts. The patient's wife stared at the patient the entire time, only glancing at me a once in a while.

After we introduced ourselves, the patient said abruptly, "Sometimes I think it would be better for everyone if I wasn't alive anymore."

"Oh," I mumbled and felt my blood pressure rise.

I had had no idea she was expressing thoughts about suicide. I had learned how to respond to this. There were specific things I was supposed to ask. But learning about what to do is one thing; being faced with the pressure of the conversation in real life is another. I could remember only dimly what I was supposed to say and all the words were scrambled in my head.

I was supposed to ask, "Are you thinking of taking your life?" I imagine she would have said she was. The correct follow-up was, "Do you have a plan?"

Instead, I froze. The patient stared at me for a moment. Then she said, "I want to go home and just take a bottle of pills and never wake up."

"Do you have a bottle of pills?" I asked.

"I have a lot of pills. They're about to give me more."

"Okay ... have you talked with anyone about this?"

"I'm talking to you about it. But I don't think you're being very helpful."

It was hard to argue with that logic. I tensed up even more. I desperately hoped she would ask me to leave. Then I felt horrible for hoping that.

About thirty minutes later, I met with my educator—my first educator, the formidable Dr. Müller. I explained what had happened and what hadn't happened.

"I was just so uncomfortable," I said.

Over the black thick-rimmed eyeglasses resting on the tip of his nose, he looked straight at me and asked, "What was the source of your discomfort?"

"That's a good question ...." His stare was unflinching. "I don't know," I said. "I suppose how ill-prepared I was."

His eyebrows went up and his mouth took on the shape of someone saying "Oh" for a long time.

"You're surprised by that," I said.

That visit was ten years ago. I want to know what happened to that patient, and I'm terrified to know. (I do know, at least, that I followed up with the nursing staff. They made sure the patient talked to more experienced staff at the hospital and she was discharged only after much consultation.)

After the visit, I went home and studied the subject of suicide. I read two very helpful books on it by Edwin Shneidman. Less than four months later, I led a didactic (an oral presentation on a given topic that's relevant to clinical work and care) titled "How to Recognize a Suicidal Patient" for the hospice company where I was doing my second unit of CPE.

In CPE, we call this process the "Clinical Model of Learning." It often involves learning a lesson by fumbling an interaction with real people rather than in an essay or on a test. It's painful but effective; you never forget it.

*

Outside the room of the patient who had been a victim of human trafficking, I hesitated another few minutes. My breathing was getting more labored and intense. I wondered if I should reach out to a female chaplain.

But I didn't care much for the female chaplain who was available. I am not immune to getting caught up in the mindset I chastise my students for: convincing myself that a patient needs not just a chaplain but *me*, and no one else but me. As nervous as I was, I was also curious. And arrogant. I think part of me believed I would walk in there and model a different behavior than she was used to—and thereby begin to "correct" and change her idea of men.

Needless to say, that's not what happened. The blinds were drawn and the room was dark. A CNA was sitting on a small sofa tucked into a shadowed corner across from the bed, facing the patient. I knocked on the door and introduced myself as I normally do.

"Hello, my name is Keith. I'm one of the chaplains in the hospital and I'm coming by to see how you're doing," I said.

The patient didn't seem to hear me at first. So I knocked softly again on the wall by the bathroom. She looked up. When she saw me standing in front of her, as far from the foot of the bed as the small room would allow, she jolted upright.

"Oh—oh—oh!" she cried.

Her wide face grew flushed. She began smoothing her hair and pulling it back behind her ears. She stood and began walking in a tight one-square-foot pattern, her hospital-issue socks with non-slip feet occasionally gripping on the floor. "I'm sorry," she said. "Forgive me. Okay. Okay. Let me just ... I want to ... I need to ...."

The sitter and I exchanged a quick heartbroken look. I already wanted to leave. But should I? The patient had asked for a chaplain.

Then, as quickly as she had stood, the patient went back to the bed. She kneeled in the middle of it, facing me, her legs folded beneath her. I was already far away from the bed, but I took another step back. The heel of my shoe hit the wall behind me.

The patient sat on her heels, her knees together, and leaned forward. "I just," she said, "I just want to make sure … I need to … I must honor you … and show you … that I respect you …."

I felt sick. It was as if a tape were playing in her head. It sounded so rehearsed. She used those exact words: "You are a man and I must show you respect. Forgive me for not doing that immediately."

I raised my eyes at the sitter before turning back to her. "My name is Keith," I said again. "I'm a chaplain. Do you know what that is?"

"No. No—please, can you tell me?"

"I'm just here to say hello. And to say, if you need anything, I'll be here to help you."

"Oh, thank you. No—yes—You are a man. I must honor you," she said for what might have been the tenth or eleventh time.

I couldn't take it anymore. I was starting to feel the weight of the Hippocratic Oath. As a chaplain, I'm not required to take this oath, but it still feels relevant every time I step into a patient's room. I certainly wasn't helping her any and she was considerably more agitated than she'd been before I arrived. I kneeled so I could look her in the eyes.

"I'm going to leave now," I said.

"Okay." Her eyes widened. Then the reel kept playing. I nodded to the sitter and walked out. I went straight to the bathroom on the unit and threw up.

*

After that visit, I had trouble getting the details out of my head, especially at night. I couldn't fall asleep. I sought out a clinical psychologist who specialized in trauma and was certified in EMDR (eye movement desensitization and reprocessing) therapy, an evidence-based mental health treatment that can involve moving your eyes in certain patterns while you process traumatic memories or distressing events in your life. It's based on research showing that our bodies hold on to stressful experiences. Our brains respond by storing memories of the traumatic event in the limbic system—our "emotional brain," the part of the brain that can keep us in the "fight or flight" survival mode—rather than processing it through the prefrontal cortex. This is the more logical part of the brain. It helps us make sense of our experiences and helps our bodies understand that a stressful event is over. Triggering events—a sight, a sound, a smell that reminds you of that event—can cause you to feel as if you are reliving it over and over, the way passing by the man who wore Tweed's cologne sent me back into my frightened ten-year-old self.

Trauma can also show up as avoidance. We might run away, like my student responding to patients who mentioned using alcohol with some level of rejection rather than facing her own experiences, or Grandpa Joe adopting a blanket hatred of Japanese people after his involvement in the war.

The pain of trauma always feels fresh. Without intervention, it never fades away.

In a successful EMDR processing session, those triggering memories can be accessed and reprocessed. You don't forget the event, but it gets processed in a different way. After treatment, I felt a shift in my body. I was able to sleep again. My brain stopped relentlessly running over the details of the event and remembering it didn't provoke such an intense emotional response.

I also started reading, for my devotional time in the mornings, works that helped me understand and face the malevolence people are capable of: *Last Witnesses: An Oral History of the Children of World War II* and *The Unwomanly Face of War: An Oral History of Women in World War II*. I read *The Rape of Nanking* by Iris Chang, watched *The Flowers of War*, and read Christopher R. Browning's *Ordinary Men: Reserve Police Battalion 101 and the Final Solution in Poland*.

I came to recognize that I, too, am capable of malevolence. I haven't done anything so extreme as the acts that left that patient traumatized, without an identity, on the precipice. But I've acted repulsively, disgracefully. When I look back at some of the things I've done, I'm utterly surprised at myself. I've hurt people simply because I could and because I knew the way to make it hurt the most. I too have caused trauma.

*

I don't know what happened to the patient who was a victim of human trafficking and aged out of it. That's almost always the way it is with patients, unless we run into them out in the world somewhere. As soon as they leave the hospital, we no longer have access to them. We never know if they healed physically or psychologically or if what we said or did made any lasting difference in their lives.

We don't know and we have to live with not knowing. Knowing could make it much worse and the patient is no longer within our own story.

I don't believe I reached that woman. I never talked to her not really. I witnessed her survival: what she had to become to survive her horrific experiences and all the men who had hurt her. Our brief interaction made me uncomfortable and I didn't know how to respond.

Looking back, I recognize that wanting to get as much information as possible before entering her room was my brain, with its propensity to overthink, already trying to make sense of an uncomfortable situation. As I said earlier, information is valuable; but at some point, I was just stalling. My prefrontal cortex was trying to regulate my limbic system—meaning, my thinking brain was trying to pull me away from unpleasant emotions.

When I met her, I was overwhelmed and left. My nervous system couldn't handle what was happening, what I was witnessing: what me showing up as a man triggered in her. I threw up because my body wanted to get rid of it all.

I'm sure that wasn't the first time she felt so agitated—she had expressed a desire to die, after all—and I doubt it was the last. I wonder if she did end her life after she left the hospital. It's hard for me to sit and think about, so I try not to. If our brief interaction was so difficult for me to bear, I can appreciate, given that she *lived* through the horrors that brought us both to that moment, why she sought ways to avoid facing them, too.

I think my decision to leave prioritized me over her. I wanted to escape my discomfort. Maybe it was the right decision at the time; maybe not. In any case, my body felt the dissonance of it all—it wouldn't let me rest. That told me I had more to do, more to learn.

Chapter 13

I find a bowl in the cupboard, wash it out, and dump my congealed dinner into it. With some sadness, I put the bowl in the microwave. I'm aware I'm feeling the loss of my phở's fresh warmth more than I'm feeling the loss of the man in room seven—the man in the photos with the dog and the Christmas decorations. I'm disconnected from that sadness. I have to be.

I sit back at my desk while I eat and try to zone out on YouTube reaction videos, a strange phenomenon I'm fully addicted to. I particularly like watching people listen to songs I know but they've never heard before. Witnessing their reaction to it in real time is satisfying. Maybe I like how I can foresee the future. I know when a particularly rapturous moment of the song or video is coming. I anticipate it will cause a reaction in this listener because that's what happened to me when I first heard or saw it. I stare at their faces, full of anticipation.

I suspect this is why some reactions get more views than others.

The most popular "reactors" know how to play into the "Oh, wow!" or "Holy shit, this is amazing" response that viewers like me are looking for. It's a measure of how lonely I get, particularly when I'm on call at night, that I find comfort in the "company" these videos provide.

I don't care for hearing the reactors' opinions on the songs. Nothing against them, but I tend to scroll forward once they start doing any analysis.

I finish my phở and melted coconut smoothie and take my things down to the bank of sleep rooms. There's generally a gap in calls between 6:45 p.m. and 7:30 p.m. due to the shift change. If anyone pages me during that time, it's usually an emergency.

Many of the staff members on call overnight have access to a small individual room dedicated to sleeping. When you open the door all the way, it hits the footboard of the twin bed inside. There's also a locker, a desk, a chair, and a table with a television I've never switched on. It's a big, clunky hand-me-down that's not hooked up to cable or the internet. I think maybe it gets a few local channels, but I spend any entertainment time I have in here with my virtual friends on YouTube. On the desk is a computer with a monitor I've been told not to turn off by someone who obviously doesn't have to sleep here.

Surprisingly, though the room doesn't have any windows, it's quite well-ventilated and isn't musty or smelly.

I set my bag on the chair and decide to call my wife and son to see what trouble he's causing her—so I know what I'll be facing tomorrow. Shuang rejects my call and sends a message: "Talking to my parents. Will call you later."

In life and in marriage, it's always helpful to know where one stands in the pecking order.

*

By February of 2017, my marriage was over and so was my affair. I joined a dating app.

It was a weird new world. When I met Marianne, I didn't even have an email address. And quickly I realized I'd been living a very insulated life in the Adventist community.

For a while, I just chatted with a lot of people. Eventually, I went on a few dates. Once a woman said, "What are you doing right now?"

Unsurprisingly, I wasn't doing anything. The woman was a stand-up comic. She took me to The Comedy Store in West Hollywood, where I met a lot of other comedians and artists.

When I responded to the inevitable "So what do you do?" with "I'm a chaplain at a hospital," at least fifty percent of them responded, "Oh— you have a *real* job."

I had never heard this before. At first, I didn't know how to take it. Soon, I realized it wasn't meant to be belittling. Many of them were scrapping together bits of employment here and there while they pursued their artistic dreams. Since most of the people I talked to were no longer nineteen, but around my age, they weren't always sure they were still on the right path.

They often told me personal stories. Honestly, I get this a lot. When people find out what I do for a living, I sometimes see their eyes light up: *Oh, great, a free therapist!* I've gotten accustomed to quickly hearing very intimate things from people I just met. I wouldn't say I'm comfortable with it, but it doesn't surprise me anymore.

One woman at the comedy club told me about the death of her grandfather. She couldn't make sense of it. "Sometimes I wonder if that's why I'm still chasing this dream. Do you think that's wrong?" she said.

But I got something out of it, too. I was meeting people in an authentic way and they felt my job was honorable and meaningful.

It was also nice to talk about creative things with people in the arts community. At that time, I was figuring out a few important things about how being a chaplain functions in my life. Much of the work involves short-term relationships that do not have a clear resolution. In many ways, this is a liberating part of the work.

At the same time, it was leaving me feeling I wanted a project I could start and work on all the way to a satisfying conclusion. Chaplaincy is an abstract field and I wanted a practical, concrete task to focus on.

When I was thinking about what my creative activity would be, making films seemed like the most difficult but still achievable one. Producing the film about Wil with Brandon had been satisfying. I thought maybe I'd try to make one myself this time. I didn't know much about the theory behind putting a film together, much less how to run a camera or edit raw footage. But I was curious about it. And I liked the idea of a big challenge that would keep me busy: a long and interesting project.

I learned quickly, though. My second film was a short-form documentary about a pedicab driver in Chico, California, named Mike "G-Ride" Griffith. Mike's story is about overcoming addiction and homelessness to become a beloved fixture in his community.[40] *G-Ride: The Mike Griffith Story* won an award for "Best Editing" at the Front Range Film Festival in Colorado. It was a great feeling to see I could accomplish the work and then start on another film.

*

I thoroughly enjoyed my ventures into the dating pool. But chatting with Shuang felt different right away.

She seemed very spiritual, though a little on guard about it. We communicated for two weeks before we decided to meet in person. I was more excited than I'd been before any of my other dates.

Then, on the day we were going to meet, Shuang acted funny. She didn't want to meet anymore. She wrote that she was concerned about me being religious. She was afraid I was going to try to convert her.

Fair enough. This is what a lot of Christians are known for.

I wrote to Shuang, "I don't have any intention of converting you. I can't even convert myself."

And then: "And I don't believe everyone is or needs to be religious. But I think everyone is spiritual."

Shuang wrote back, "Completely agree." She agreed to meet. But now it would have to wait; she was going to China for two weeks.

Shuang was from Beijing. A talented landscape architect, she had earned her MA in architecture in China but needed to pass a final test to get her license there so she would be a licensed architect in China. She was already licensed as a landscape architect in the United States and had successfully designed the landscape portion of a cruise-ship terminal in China. Eventually, she would successfully pitch a design in a posh conference room to representatives of the King of Dubai for a project there.

I appreciated that she let me know exactly where she stood emotionally. CPE had brought out this appreciation in me. In CPE, we were always saying, "Can we be more raw and real with each other?"

When I was still in a relationship with Marianne, my growing taste for the raw expression of emotions had rocked the balance of our relationship. Neither of us had the foundational understanding of relationships to try to find a new type of equilibrium.

With Shuang, it was a relief to not have to guess or anticipate but to *know*. That's not to say I'm not scared when Shuang gets angry with me: like, lashing-out-and-ripping-the-bedcovers-off-me-at-2:30-in-the-morning angry.

But I like that she's upfront with me. And we work through whatever provoked the fight and learn more about one another. I could tell early on Shuang wanted a strong partner, an equal, someone she could count on to spar with her when she challenged him. And her behavior gave me the permission to model it.

I've always connected to the perspective of Ellen White, one of the founders of the Adventist Church, on the story in the Hebrew Bible about the creation of Adam and Eve. I know this passage has been used to justify everything from an argument against women's ordination, to a belief that women were created primarily to serve men, to an argument *for* women's ordination—much of which is based on various translations of terms in ancient Hebrew. It's much too complicated to get into here, so I won't. I'll just say that regarding the creation of Eve, White notes the significance of God taking a bone not from the top of Adam's body, nor the bottom, but the middle. Eve is not to grovel at Adam's feet, nor to rule him, but to stand beside him as an equal. I'm like Adam. I always wanted an equal, too.

While Shuang was in China, I started looking for open positions. My residency in California would be ending at the end of August. The only pertinent opening for the career path I was now on was at a hospital in Colorado: a Certified Educator Training position. I applied, interviewed, and received an offer.

These positions are hard to get if no one at the program knows you. I felt honored that they saw potential in me.

I knew it was a long commitment. It can take up to six years to finish the process. I decided not to say anything to Shuang—yet. We were still communicating, though not as much; she was often busy studying for exams.

After she came back from China, we made plans to meet on a Sunday in May. My divorce was going to be finalized in court the next day. I still didn't tell Shuang about Colorado. I was afraid that if I told her, she wouldn't want to meet, and I selfishly wanted to meet her.

We went to a Japanese barbeque restaurant. I got there first and backed into a parking space so I could see the other cars pull up. Shuang arrived a few minutes later in a silver Volkswagen Beetle. When she got out of the car, I noticed her long dark brown hair against her dark blue blouse.

We sat at a table near the door. Before we even ordered, I told her I was moving to Colorado. She started crying. That moved me immensely: she was feeling what I was feeling and she wasn't afraid to show me.

We kept talking and getting together. I loved her curiosity and the way she was unafraid to express not only her dark emotions, but her light ones. I loved her playfulness. When she was teasing or being silly, she'd turn her head to the side and look back and forth between me and the wall, pursing her lips as if she were sipping a drink from a straw.

My lease was up at the end of July and I spent my last month at her place before moving to Colorado. During that time, I fell in love. I also traveled to Beijing to meet Shuang's parents, who were incredibly supportive of our relationship.

Later, her mother joked, "You're the only person I've ever known who can calm Shuang down." When she met me, that's how she knew I was a good person and would be good for her daughter.

Shuang wanted children. This had been another issue Marianne and I struggled with: she didn't want children. The older I got, the more I thought I might. After I started chaplaincy, I met a lot of lonely elderly people who regretted not having kids. I wasn't sure anymore that I wanted to miss out on this experience simply because I'd adamantly pro-claimed I didn't want kids when I was in my twenties.

Since Shuang and I were both in our late thirties, time was of the essence. Shuang drove to Colorado with me in September and flew back. Later, she told me that after our first date, she went home and wrote in her journal, "I could move to Colorado." She moved there in March 2018. We were married in June.

7:35 p.m., Monday, August 22, 2022

I head down the hallway to the communal bathroom. It's generally quiet at this time, since most people who sleep here don't come in until late at night. As soon as I brush my teeth and wash my face, my code pager starts beeping. This pager doesn't give a number, just a message: "ADULT CODE BLUE, 75 yr, F, CICU, 397. FAMILY PRESENT."

I take my toiletries back to the room and start walking to the hospital. About halfway there, my phone vibrates. Shuang is requesting a FaceTime call. I keep walking while I answer.

"Hey!" I watch my son's pixelated face appear. Then it comes into focus.

"Hi, Bàba-poop." He laughs hysterically.

"Buddy, you know you gotta stop saying that." Unfortunately, I can't repress my own laughter.

"Bàba, guess what? I ate all my dinner and then I showed Chase and Rubble to Grandpa and Grandma." Shuang and her parents call each other on WeChat almost every night when we're getting our son ready for bed.

"Oh, wow, that's exciting. Were Grandma and Grandpa nice to Chase and Rubble?"

"Um, yeah," he says softly before dropping the phone on the table.

"He ran away," Shuang says.

"You guys doing okay?"

"Yeah, he's fine. Lots of energy. It's nice that he can go potty on his own. What's not as nice is that he pees on his pants while sitting on the toilet. So we cleaned the rug and changed clothes. Twice."

"He needs to learn to sit farther back on the seat. Then he's gotta pull his pants down far enough that he can open his legs. Then he can push down and pee in the toilet."

"Okay. I think that's a lesson you can teach him."

"Sure. Okay, I'm about to respond to a call. Probably gonna take a while. Will say goodnight and I love you now."

"Okay. You, too. Oh, he's back. Say goodbye to Bàba," my wife says.

My son grabs the phone, looks directly at the screen, and says, "Bye-bye, Bàba-poop." His hysterics are cut off abruptly when he stabs at the button to end the call.

With that, he's gone. Reluctantly, I put my phone back in my pocket.

In the cardiac intensive care unit (CICU), I find the husband of a patient sitting on a chair, his elbows on his knees, his chin in his palms. He's staring into the ICU room. At least twenty people surround the bed. In machine-like order, they're calling out numbers, barking instructions, demanding more supplies. Every once in a while, one of them glances out to briefly meet the spouse's unwavering stare. It's a very stoic look. I have difficulty discerning if I'm seeing shock, disbelief, grief, anger—perhaps all those and more.

The attending physician has a thick gray beard and is wearing a yamaka. He's also sporting green crocs and a tie with Disney characters on it. He has a commanding, yet controlled presence; he never raises his voice louder than necessary. He looks at the clock above the head of the bed. A timer that starts at 00:00 marks the time that's passed since chest compressions began. It currently reads 31:15.

There comes a point, especially near the end of one's life, when providing care crosses the line from "helping" to "harming." We call it futility of care.

I roll a chair next to the man and introduce myself. He glances up and smiles. Then he goes back to staring into the room.

"Is it okay if I sit near you?" I ask.

He nods. I sit down at his left, just slightly behind him. I want him to sense I'm there, but not feel overcrowded.

Chest compressions continue as the timer keeps clicking. 42:30.

When the clock hits 54:05, the attending looks up at it again. Then he exits the room and comes toward us. He kneels next to the patient's husband and looks up at him, sighing deeply before he speaks.

"Sir," he says, "you see the efforts my team has put in for the last fifty-five minutes. At this point, even if we were to get a pulse back, her brain has been without oxygen for so long that there's no way she wouldn't have significant brain damage. The efforts we're putting in now I fear are only causing her harm. If she can feel anything at this point, I believe it's only pain. Is it okay if I ask my team to stop?"

I see a tear drop from the man's eye. He nods again, but this one is shaky, like a stutter.

The attending raises his arm. At the signal, the team stops. Time of death is called.

No matter how many times I witness it, this moment is always a profound one. The space goes from cacophonous to very quiet. The anxiety of activity is over. Another feeling settles over us that's hard to name. It's not quite just shock or grief—but a mix of these. Also an awareness of the gravity, the beauty, the fragility of life. That awareness feels sharply poignant in the wake of these moments when so many people were trying to keep life here and intact. It's as if, even though we haven't gone anywhere, we've all entered into a sacred space.

The patient's husband can feel it, too. The feeling is as palpable on him as if it's a cloak thrown over his back. Together we listen to the shuffling of twenty people's feet on the floor. The team members are walking out, most of them in single file, their heads down.

Then something happens I've never seen before. The man stands up from his chair; I see now he's at least eighty. He extends his hand to every person walking out of the room.

With each handshake, he mutters, "Thank you for trying to save my wife."

He never misses a word or a hand. Some of the team members start to cry and run for the break room. When the last person is gone, the man, the husband, now a widower, turns to me.

"I'm a man of few words," he says, "so I thank God he sent your silence to comfort me."

I nod and shake his hand.

"If you don't mind, I'd like a few moments with my wife. Then maybe you can come in and say a prayer." He shuffles into the room and puts his hand on the shoulder of the nurse who is cleaning up his wife.

I go back to the break room. Staff care is a priority during a code call. I pay attention to how, say, a nurse who just did chest compressions for the first time is handling the experience—particularly if the patient didn't make it. If a patient dies on a code call, and there are no family members present, I go into the room to check on the nurses. Then I'll talk to the social worker to see if they've found the family yet. If they haven't, I'll leave my name and pager number with the charge nurse. Then I'll leave; there's nothing more for me to do. I don't want to pray over a deceased person I know nothing about. They might have had strong feelings against God or religion and praying over them would be disrespectful. I err on the side of doing nothing religious until I know there's something I can do that will honor this person's memory and not offend.

The care team of the seventy-five-year-old patient is doing as well as they can be. Most of them are eating. Others have gone to tend to other patients.

I wait outside the room until the patient's husband beckons me in. Then I ask him how he and his wife met. Who chased who? I also use the question I stole from the late, great Wil Alexander.

"What's she famous for?" I say.

Before I ask this question, I'm always listening for verb tense. If a family member or friend is still using present tense, I reflect that back to them. I'll use past tense only if they've moved on to using it themselves. Listening to not just what they say but how they say it lets me gauge where they are emotionally, spiritually, and practically when it comes to accepting death. It helps me determine what they need.

Almost always, this question prompts a laugh or a smile. Then a little joke, before a sigh and a deeply personal memory.

"She was never a great cook," this man says. "But I never let her know, because it was better than having to cook." He smiles as he runs his fingers through her long gray hair. "She knew it, too. That's what I always loved about her. She saw right through me and kept on loving me in spite of it."

The man's children arrive. They are shocked. I can feel their grief intensify as they look at their mother in the bed.

"This is my son and my daughter," he says to me. To them, he says, "Kids, this is my chaplain. He's been with me for a while now and I'm grateful for it."

My chaplain. I feel overwhelmed—in a good way. I rarely get feedback beyond, "Thanks for being with me." That's also nice. But to be claimed by the possessive lets me know I've made a difference on a day when this man lost a great love, a day that has to be one of the worst of his life.

Chapter 14

9:07 p.m., Monday, August 22, 2022

I walk up to the MICU to see how the night staff are doing. The police are still on the unit. The bedside nurse expresses some anxiety and the overall mood is still tense. But he says he is "doing okay."

I stroll around and greet a few people I know, introduce myself to some I don't. I do what I can to not appear bored. I like to be paged, but not too much. On-call shifts are weird and by nature unpredictable. We can generate visits on our regular units if we want to when we're on-call, but it's not required. Sometimes I like to, just to stay occupied. I also sometimes feel I should save my energy in case things get crazy.

I get a call telling me that after a man was discharged from the emergency department earlier this evening, he had a heart attack in the parking lot, right in front of a car where a mother and her two children were waiting for their father to get out of surgery. The two little girls watched for forty-minutes as the fire department performed CPR on the patient before taking him back into the hospital. The mother wants to meet with me to see if I can provide some closure for the kids.

I find out the patient's status before going to see them. Status: dead.

I meet with them in a small room outside the pre-op area, about an hour and a half after their ordeal. One girl is about six, the other maybe eight. They want me to tell them that "the man got into the hospital and took his medicine so now he's all better."

I take a deep breath and try to figure out a way not to share patient information. Oh, the stress of applying written policies to practical situations ....

I look at the mom and back at the girls. I open my mouth and wait for words to come to me.

"They gave him some medicine," I mutter and hold my breath.

Some of the tension on their faces releases. "That's good," the younger girl says. "My daddy is getting some medicine right now, too. Right, Mama?"

Then they want to know if I'd like to see some pictures they drew while waiting for their dad to come out of surgery.

"That's one of the best things I can think of seeing today." While they're scrambling to pull them out, I glance at the mom, who mouths an inaudible, "Thank you."

As it turns out, it *is* a nice moment of my day. The pictures are a riot of color. The older girl has drawn faces and stick figures, but the younger girl's bold abstractions are even more appealing to me right now.

They remind me not only of my son's scribbles, but of a good memory I have from a spiritual reflection group I led in the adult psych unit where I was in residency. Each patient was given a blank sheet of paper and asked to draw while listening to four different pieces of music. The lesson was about processing the emotions prompted by external stimuli.

One day, a patient came up at the end of the session to hand me a drawing that was quite good. It turned out he was a professional artist.

"Art is never done until you give it away," he said. He signed it, "Thank you for helping me find me."

*

It's nearly 9:30 p.m. I decide to make my way back to the sleep room. "Do you need anything while you wait?" I ask the mom and girls.

"We're fine now. Thank you," Mom says and the girls chime in: "Yeah—thank you for looking at our drawings."

I start down the hallway, cross the bridge, and am halfway back to the sleep room when my pager beeps. This time, I end up in the chapel. The nurse who helped facilitate the discharge of the man who just died of a heart attack in front of the little girls is having a minor crisis.

"It's my fault he's dead," she says.

She's only a year out of nursing school. Between the four of us— the nurse herself; a pharmacist sitting in the chapel with her; Craig, the charge nurse in the emergency department; and me—we decide it's best she go home for the rest of her shift. At first she puts up some passive resistance—"No, no, I can do it"—but I can see the relief on her face when she realizes she can leave.

Craig is fantastic. "We've already got your patients covered. Go home, take care of yourself. Let us know how we can support you."

Before she leaves, I ask her if she feels as if she can drive. She says she can. I ask her what she'll do when she gets home.

She thinks about it, taking the question seriously.

"I have two dogs. I'll take them for a walk and process this," she says.

*

Second-guessing yourself is part of the job. You have to get used to it.

Once in the middle of the night, I was called to the bedside of a patient who had been dead for four hours. His wife refused to leave him.

If she left, she would have to face the reality of life without him.

I was there for an hour. Someone called the woman's nephew, who walked in looking flustered and tired. His shirt was untucked and buttoned wrong. He was more direct than I was.

"We have to go. We can't stay here anymore," he said.

She started to hear him; I could see it on her face. But still, she didn't follow.

The nephew and I got her inching toward the door. She went back to the bed multiple times to hug her husband and kiss him. The last time, she gave me a desperate look and said, "I don't want to leave him. What if he wakes up and I'm not here?"

She heard herself say it. Her shoulders shrunk and her brow relaxed a little. She was a small, slender Ethiopian woman with a thin face and only a few lines around her eyes, though she was in her sixties or seventies, like her husband.

"I'm being crazy, aren't I?" she said. "I am. He's not going to wake up again, is he?"

I looked back at her, my jaw clenched. When she moved closer to me, I put my arm around her. Her shoulder came up to my armpit and I tucked her into me there.

"No, he's not." Then I added, "Not yet."

Then I regretted it. Was it wrong to express my hope in Christianity—is it just wishful thinking? Is it just my own coping mechanism? What is that?

But if it made her feel better—? I don't know. How can I know what the right or wrong thing to do was? How can I possibly know?

*

I'm heading back to the sleep room again when I get another page around 10:30 p.m. I turn around and head back across the bridge and into the burn unit, the closest place with a phone. I dial the number.

"MICU, this is Karen," she says in only three syllables.

"Hi, Karen. Keith. Chaplain." Her efficiency is catching. Who needs complete sentences?

"Hey, Chaplain," Karen says.

When I first started in chaplaincy, I noticed that many people in the hospital follow the practice of using the title instead of my name, even when they know it, even when they've just heard it—the same way staff will call one another "Doctor" and "Nurse." It's funny how this doesn't carry over into every role. Even though chaplains often get lumped in with social workers—we both often function as a liaison between families and the medical team—no one ever says, "Hey, Social Worker."

Early in my training, being called "Chaplain" made me uncomfortable. I had imposter syndrome. *Don't call me "Chaplain,"* I would think. *I don't know enough to be one. I'm just a student or a resident.* Now, though, I feel okay with it.

"I have the family of a patient who just died asking if you would come and say a few words," Karen says.

"Sure. I'll be there in about five, ten minutes."

"Sweet!"

I always wonder what words to say on these calls, and if the ones I choose are close to the ones they want.

The family members are grouped around the bed of the deceased man: three people I'm guessing are the patient's wife and his two adult children, probably in their early twenties. The daughter is wearing a death-metal t-shirt, a nose ring, and a row of earrings running all the way up each earlobe. Her brother is dressed similarly with a backpack he never takes off. Their mother is in a white t-shirt with holes in it to reveal the dark bra underneath. I ask them to introduce me to the patient.

"What's he famous for?" I ask.

"He is," the patient's wife begins. Then she pauses. "Well, he *was* an eternal optimist."

"Doesn't look too optimistic now," mumbles the daughter.

"Not now, Mia, you selfish little c—."

Mia clinches her lips and turns her body away from the others. She shakes her head at the floor.

"Sorry … Anyway, would you say a prayer, Chaplain?" the wife asks.

"Sure … What would you like me to pray for?"

"Just whatever you usually say in these situations."

I have a working principle I teach my students: do not work harder than the family. My role is to invite them into the work they need to do. But I cannot, nor should I attempt to, do their work for them.

"You-all don't strike me as a 'usual' kind of family."

"Damn right!" Mia exclaims, still looking at the ground.

The wife smiles at me, showing her yellow cigarette-stained teeth. "Are you married, Chaplain?" She leaves no time for me to shake my head, let alone answer. "This one here is still single. Big surprise, given the mouth on her."

I smile awkwardly at Mia, who walks to the couch beneath the window and stares outside, her arms folded across her chest. This room has a view of the children's hospital with its blue, red, and yellow panes of glass. A life-flight helicopter is landing on the roof. Mia focuses on that rather than acknowledge what's happening in the room. The other two step farther away from the bed as well, for a reason I can't ascertain. People respond to grief in so many ways.

"I mean, come on, Mia. Look at him. Obviously a normie—but he's got a job, he's making his way through life with some stability and meaningful work. What do you think?"

"Mom, quit trying to pimp out Mia," says the son.

Mom smiles at me again and I smile back. Then she sighs. "Can we pray?"

"Okay. How about this: I'll open a prayer and then I'll pause to give you all space to say what you would like to Adrian, each other, God, the universe, or whatever you connect with beyond. How's that sound?"

Mom and son come back toward the bed and wait. After a moment, Mom walks to the window, puts her arms around her daughter, and subtly rocks her. I hear a sniffle. Mia wipes her eyes before they turn and hold each other. They whisper together for a minute before returning to the bed.

Mia gives me a sheepish look. "Sorry."

"No sorrys. It's hard to lose someone you love." I feel a little jolt of anxiety. I shouldn't have said that. I don't know if she loved him or not.

"Yeah, it is." Her voice is soft and tearful.

"Let's pray?" This is intended and received as a real question. "Here we are, joined in a circle around a loved one …"

The rest is their space. I won't divulge what they graciously share in my presence.

Regardless of anyone's beliefs, these moments are meant to create a memory. A ritual or experience can honor the moment and offer meaning. Not everyone wants this, which is why I tread lightly after a death. When a family asks me to be present, I suggest a little more—a prayer, a poem, a sacred reading, a song—than I would otherwise. When I'm paged by a nurse or a physician who says a family needs support, I try to get as much information as possible before introducing myself to the family. And I get ready to back off if they send me a signal that they don't want me in their space.

When they've all had a chance to speak, I say, "Amen." Then I wait.

The patient's wife breaks the silence. "Thank you. What happens now?"

"There's nothing else you need to do here that can't be done over the phone."

"I mean—what happens now to him."

I wait, hoping she'll clarify. Is this a question about the body or the soul? *When someone asks about the soul—What happens now—I mean, to my father—now that he's dead? Where is he?*, I begin with, *All I can say is I am in awe of the person who can confront such a question; and I'm skeptical of anyone who answers it.*

I watch this patient's wife carefully. I don't think she's going to give me more information.

"Do you mean, what's the process with his body?"

She affirms with a nod.

Thank goodness—that's always easier. "So after you leave," I say, "he'll go down to the morgue. He'll stay there until you let us know which funeral home you choose. Then they'll come get him."

"We don't know which one yet …."

"That's okay. I imagine there are a lot of things you don't know yet. I recommend you remember to breathe. Take care of yourselves and each other. I have a sheet of paper I can give you that will help explain the process that needs to happen once you leave. For now, maybe you'd all like to spend some time alone with him?"

They say they would.

"I'll step out. When you're ready, let me know. I'll get you the form and take you to the exit." I turn to leave. Then I remember there's one more thing. It's important, but awkward. I hate talking about it. But this whole visit has been awkward, so hopefully one more awkward thing won't make much of a difference. "Oh, and make sure you take all his personal belongings with you. If he has any jewelry, a wedding ring, anything you want to keep. Once he goes to the morgue, you won't be able to see him again until he's at the funeral home."

"Oh, good. Thanks for that," says Mia. "We'll get everything."

Immediately, she and her brother begin putting things into a paper bag. Tasks can be helpful to distract us when we're grieving.

I turn again and head toward the door, sliding the curtain closed behind me. I grab the form and wait for them to come out of the room. There are exceptions, of course, but it doesn't take the family very long at this point. On average, they come out after five or ten minutes. Sure enough, within five minutes, the door opens. I talk them through the form with its overwhelming amount of information and circle the number of the department that will follow up with them tomorrow or the next day.

*

Working in a hospital, you learn not only that physical care is often intertwined with spiritual and emotional care, but that paying attention to the smallest practical and logistical details can have a profound effect on the experience of both patients and families. You also learn that no matter what your official job is, and what your expectations are going in about what that job will entail, at some point you'll find yourself performing a task you never expected and you might not feel all that qualified to do.

On my way back to the sleep room—will I get there this time?— I pass by the burn unit again. This is a place where hospital chaplains typically spend a lot of time, particularly in the most intense section of the unit, the Burn ICU.

During the Covid-19 pandemic, I spent even more time than usual there. We were doing the best we could to help families maintain contact with their loved ones when hospitals were closed to visitors or visits were severely limited.

The pandemic was an incredibly difficult time for healthcare workers, not only because of the sheer volume of patients, the suffering we saw them go through, the horrors of an unknown disease, and the logistical difficulty of safety protocols. We also knew that separating ill and dying patients from their families would negatively impact the health of patients and magnify the pain and the shock of loss in communities around the world. That was hard to take emotionally.

And of course, we were terrified of infecting our families. At that time, I had both an infant son and two people over seventy in the house; Shuang's parents were staying with us, having travelled from Beijing to be there to help with the baby. They meant to stay until May, but they got stuck in the United States when flights were cancelled. They ended up staying until September. When they got back to China, they had to quarantine in a hotel outside of Beijing for two weeks, getting their groceries delivered, before being allowed to return home.

When lockdowns began in the United States, I moved into the basement of our townhouse while my wife, in-laws, and son stayed upstairs. Three weeks into the lockdown, I celebrated my birthday by ordering pizza and eating it alone. That's when my isolation hit me.

Every workday ended with a shower at the hospital before bagging up my clothes, putting new ones on, and heading home to immediately throw my clothes into the washing machine. I've never done so much laundry in my life. At some point in the evening, I'd video chat with my wife and son. This was more frustrating than anything else. The connection wasn't great because everyone was using the wifi.

One night about three months in, Shuang was holding my son for me in front of the camera while I made goofy sounds, trying to engage him.

At one point I stopped and said, "This is stupid. I want to hold him."

So I did. I started going into the common areas again. I still distanced from Shuang's parents, but I needed to hug my wife and son. Being at the hospital was actually quite safe. I wasn't assigned to the Covid unit and when I went there on call, I didn't go into patients' rooms but looked in through the window on the door. In general, I avoided the emergency department. If I did go there, I wore not only a mask but gloves, scrubs, and goggles.

Being a frontline worker had its trade-offs. I got social interaction at work and never felt the full impact of the "stay at home" order; I was pretty oblivious to the toll it took on so many people who were locked up in their houses. On the other hand, at home, Shuang strung up tape between the fridge and the door leading down to the basement to create an invisible barrier. It was kind of funny. But interacting with my in-laws started to feel similar to visiting a Covid patient in the hospital: from a distance and through glass.

*

At the hospital I worked in during the worst of the pandemic, a request came in to set up a virtual visit for a family in the Burn ICU. The patient was at the end of his life and many of his family members were coming together to say goodbye. They needed someone to make technical arrangements so they could do so. I took an iPad from the department office into the unit.

Burn ICU is a rough place. Always a little warmer than the rest of the hospital, it has a smoky, charred smell that grows more intense when a new patient arrives. It's the scent of not only burning flesh, but fabric. When a patient comes in, their clothes must be peeled off. Often, the flesh comes with them. The smell always reminds me of living in the house with Brandon. In the evenings, we'd sit on the porch and Brandon would flick his lighter and burn the pants of his pizza delivery uniform. Never to the point of flames—but a few times he'd singe his leg hair. Both of us would scrunch up our noses against the stench.

"It was unlike anything I've ever experienced," I've heard many burn patients say about the experiences that land them there. "I was so afraid."

Some units, like surgical trauma, are loud, but Burn ICU is very quiet—except when patients are in acute pain, such as when they're taking a shower, or "wash-out," as they call it. Then gut-wrenching screams fill the unit. They express not just physical pain, but anger and fear. The water disrupts the skin so it can heal, but the process is incredibly painful.

To get through this kind of darkness, both the patients and the staff often develop a dark sense of humor. Once when I was on the unit, I was checking a chart on the computer when I heard a horn fanfare echo off the walls of the shower room.

I swiveled my chair in that direction. I found myself staring at the back of the head of a nurse who was also looking in that direction.

"Is that—is that Johnny Cash's 'Ring of Fire'?" I said.

"Yeah," she said. "Yeah, I think it is."

The patient had requested the song be played to help him bear the pain of his wash-out and the nurses had obliged. Why not?

Burns heal slowly. Patients are often there for months, creating a strong sense of camaraderie and kinship on the burn unit. One patient, Antonio, was in the unit for two and a half years. He had doused himself with gasoline and lit himself on fire on the lawn outside a government building. He made it very clear it was an act of political protest.

"I was *not trying to kill myself*," he said.

When he was discharged, he became homeless. After a while, he fell into suicidal despair and lit himself on fire again. When he ended up back on the burn unit, he told me he was grateful to be back around people who cared about him.

His family was so pissed off. It wasn't easy to help them develop some kind of understanding and compassion for him.

*

The virtual "goodbye visit" on Burn ICU was strange and difficult. I'm not a voyeur, but I felt like one. I was seeing into the homes of people I didn't know, looking at the intimate details of their lives. Distraught about what was happening, they weren't exactly preparing for company. Cats tried to climb into their laps. I saw dirty dishes, clothes hanging on the furniture.

Plus, I couldn't step out of the room when they wanted to say deeply personal things. Someone had to hold the iPad in the air so the family had a steady image of the patient; he certainly couldn't hold it himself. The patient, Vincent, had burns on over eighty-five percent of his body. This percentage is on the border of hope for survival. It's a grim prognosis, though. I'm not easily disgusted or disturbed, but I struggled to look at him. Only his nostrils and mouth were visible through the gauze. The rest of his body was covered. Tubes ran down his mouth and nose. He had been unresponsive since he'd arrived on the unit a few months prior. He'd been caught in an explosion on a construction site.

I called the contact person from the family and was able to connect the iPad for a video call. Working the iPad was no easy feat; I was wearing latex gloves to protect the patients from germs.

Before I turned the camera on Vincent, I talked to the family about what they could expect to see. "None of his skin is exposed and you won't be able to see his eyes. His eyes are closed and there's gauze over them. You'll see a little dried blood around his nose. That's from putting the tube in."

In several squares on the iPad, wide eyes looked back at me. I could feel their anxiety. "Is everyone ready?" I asked.

One "square" said, "Hang on. I need a minute."

We all waited calmly, silently acknowledging that none of them would ever be ready. Eventually, the relative nodded and told me to go ahead. I said, "Okay. Here he is." When I turned the camera on Vincent, his mother, despite the fact that she had been spending as much time as she could in the hospital with her son before Covid-19 protocols were enacted, covered her mouth with her hand.

Still, she and the other women on the call had a lot to say. "I love you, honey. We're here for you. We're praying for you. Never forget that we love you and always will!" The men struggled a little more; their words were often a miss. "Hey, Vincent. Vinny? Hey Vin—how are you doing, bud?"

The hardest part was when someone begged Vincent to respond. "Do you hear us, Vinny? Just turn your head a little. Please, Vinny—please!"

His head didn't twitch. I felt a tear run down my cheek.

As moved as I was, I was also silently willing them to move this along. My arms were getting tired. I couldn't rest them on anything except the IV pole and there were so many drip lines connected that I didn't dare start fiddling with it.

My arms started to droop. I was getting hot in my gloves and gown. Sweat started trickling down my arms. But how could I tactfully interrupt? *This is all very sweet, but I don't work out enough and my arms are giving out. Can we take a break for a second?*

I couldn't. I toughed it out. Soon, I couldn't even hear what they were saying anymore.

That is, until one voice got through: "Hey, Chaplain, thanks! We're done now. You can turn it off."

"Okay. Yeah. No problem." I lowered my arms and tried not to let the pain and stiffness show when I turned the camera around. They were wiping their eyes. Several of them had gotten up from their chairs and were pacing the rooms they were in like sharks.

*

On another video call, this one in the Covid-19 unit, a woman couldn't figure out her iPad. I tried not to get frustrated with her.

"No, I don't see you," I said, over and over. "No, sorry, still can't …"

She got frustrated too and was mad I couldn't help her. *I'm sorry, lady,* I thought but didn't say. *I'm not IT. I don't know what else to tell you.*

Finally, she called to her son: "Hey, can you help me figure this damn thing out?"

The son figured out how to turn on the camera. When it came on, he was sitting there completely naked.

"Okay," I said, quickly looking away. "I can see you now."

"Okay, now go away, Mom," the son said. "I'm doing something."

*

As the Covid-19 pandemic progressed, hospitals started to open up to visitors again, but there were still limits. In a way, things got even more complicated for visitors and hospital employees.

At the hospital where I was working at the time, each patient was allowed four visitors in a twenty-four-hour time period. I was requested by the family of a Mexican-American woman in her forties or fifties who had been an alcoholic for a long time. Her two daughters and her sister were with her. The patient was dying from cirrhosis of the liver and her medical team thought she might not last through the night.

The daughters came to me and said they wanted their younger brother to come in to say goodbye to his mother. He was only seventeen and he hadn't seen her since he was seven or eight, when his parents got divorced.

"Okay," I said, a question in my voice.

"But our dad was here this morning," the younger daughter said. "That makes four. We don't want to cause any trouble …"

"Does he want to come in?" I asked her. "Your brother?"

The daughters exchanged a look. "Yes. He's willing."

I talked to the charge nurse. She didn't want to say no but she also didn't want the breach of protocol to happen on her authority.

"I'm just going by what the command center says," she said.

"Okay," I said slowly. "What if I brought him in here without asking permission? Would you report me?"

She smiled. "Of course not."

I met the patient's son Gideon downstairs. He was tall and skinny, wearing a t-shirt and sweatpants and carrying a baseball cap. His eyes were terrified. The security guard was asking him questions. "What's your name? Who are you here to see?"

"It's okay," I said. "He's with me."

We went upstairs but as we were nearing the unit, Gideon's steps started to slow. Then he stopped.

"Are you ready?" I asked him. A mix of emotions was on his face—sadness and fear, but maybe hostility, too; there must have been a reason he hadn't seen his mother in nine or ten years.

"No."

"Okay. That's fine. There's no rush." His sisters came out to be with us. It was an hour before we got Gideon onto the unit and another fifteen minutes before he stepped into his mother's room. At that point, he looked out the window rather than at the bed. I stayed in the room and asked again what I could do to help.

One of the daughters, the older one, said, "A prayer?"

I went to the bed. "Gideon, do you want to come over here and pray?"

Gideon walked over. Then, even more amazing, slowly with the speed of a cat stalking a bird, he reached out and took his mother's hand.

The older daughter drew in a sharp breath. She said in a high voice, "Mom—Mom? Do you feel that? That's Gideon's hand. That's Gideon's hand in your hand."

The patient had been unresponsive for a long time. Now, she shook her head slightly and her eyes got wet.

It was too much for me. It was so beautiful. I knew I was going to cry and I made some bullshit excuse and left. The patient died that night, and her son was there. Once he got there, he stayed the whole night.

I'm still so proud of that: that I had the strength to take on that authority and make a decision that gave a seventeen-year-old boy closure. I'm proud of Gideon for showing up and following through. I'm proud of his sisters for facilitating it.

*

At the end of life, verbal communication often breaks down for both physical and emotional reasons. Sometimes, physical touch is all you've got. You have to be comfortable with that to be a chaplain. I once held the hand of a woman for forty-five minutes as she summoned the strength to sign a DNR (Do Not Resuscitate) form.

I felt a little bitter at the beginning of that visit, and ashamed about it. It was a Friday afternoon. I had been contemplating using the start of the Sabbath as an excuse to pass the visit on to someone else while I waited for the last minute to tick by on my shift. Instead, I went. Very quickly, the patient pulled me into a handshake and wouldn't let go.

Her hand was thin but strong. It was calloused and I could feel her bones. The room was filled with family members whose mood became heightened, uneasy, desperate, when I came in. They knew I was from hospice. I was there to facilitate her death.

I found myself in an awkward position, both figuratively and literally. For my initial handshake, I had reached out my left hand to her rather than my right because a table was in the way and I was on her left side. Now, my arm was crossed over my body and I was in a contorted position; I didn't want to turn my back on either the patient or her husband, who was beside the bed. I started to pull away after a minute, if only to shift positions, but her grip tightened. So I gave up.

"Squeeze once for yes, twice for no," I said. "Make sense?"

She squeezed twice, laughed, and coughed. Fog filled her CPAP (Continuous Positive Airway Pressure) mask and for a moment obscured her expression. I was getting the sense from her family that this was a woman who loved jokes and laughed a lot.

Kierkegaard: "What if everything in life was a misunderstanding—what if laughter was really tears?"[41]

Enjoying life that much can make it difficult to leave it. She was scared, she was sad, she didn't want to let go.

The paper and pen were already in front of her. The hospice company was getting impatient. It was the end of the day on a Friday and they wanted to get this done so they could facilitate the business of death over the weekend. Knowing that the family and patient were aware of this pressure made me feel even more shame.

Eventually, she did it. She let go of my hand for just the amount of time it took her to sign. Then quickly she reached for me again.

I knew the administrative staff in the office downtown were waiting for my call. Once they knew I had the signature, they could initiate the transfer to hospice next morning. There, she would be taken off the breathing machine and die.

Instead of rushing out, I took the patient's hand again. I made sure to give her my right one this time so I could settle in comfortably for another little while. I wanted her to understand this wasn't just a transaction. No. Not for her and not for me. For me, it was a beautiful way to start the Sabbath.

Chapter 15

11:37 p.m., Monday, August 22, 2022

I've made it to the sleep room. I hang my badge on the doorknob so I don't forget it when I leave the room (I've been locked out of the room in my pajamas before). Then I change into pajamas; find fresh sheets in the locker to replace the rumpled ones one of my colleagues slept in the night before; drape two towels over the glowing computer monitor and prop a pillow against it for good measure; and get into bed.

When I was a resident, I would play pranks on my peers when they were on call in the sleep room: set the alarm clock to go off in the middle of the night, page them at random times. Fun stuff like that.

I send Shuang a message that I'm going to sleep, then flick off the lamp. Light from the hallway still beams into the room through a crack around the door.

*

I'm woken up by my pager vibrating on the nightstand. I've been doing this long enough that I can sleep with my pager on vibrate without worrying that I'll miss a call.

The clock says it's 1:30 a.m. I was sound asleep. I turn on the lamp, read the number on the pager, and pick up the phone next to the bed.

"NICU, this is Holly," Holly says in a hurry.

"Hi, Holly. This is Keith, the chaplain for the night. I got a page." I'm mumbling and it's hard to open my eyes. Neonatal intensive care unit—this isn't going to be good. I do not want to go where Holly is about to send me.

"Hey, Keith. We've got a mom and dad here who are about to remove life-support on their twenty-day-old boy. They'd like you to come and say something." (*What am I gonna say?*) "Also, they're Seventh-day Adventists and they're asking for a chaplain from their faith tradition if possible." That request is like meeting someone named Ganesh from India and asking him if he knows Chintan "who is also from India." The chances are nearly impossible that I could find someone from a specific denomination at 1:30 in the morning when there is no "religious" reason to call someone, such as bringing in a priest to administer the Sacrament of the Sick.

I sigh. "Well, tonight's their night. I'm an Adventist."

"Oh, great," Holly says, without any proper sense of awe. "I'll tell them I got one for them."

I can only laugh and say to myself: *Yeah, you do that; good work.*

*

Being a Seventh-day Adventist doesn't usually mean I'm the hero of the night. More often, it means having to perform linguistic gymnastics so I can be true to my beliefs while still meeting a family where they are.

Many times, I've found myself at the bedside of a family member who has died and heard a family member say, "He's with Grandma now," or the like. Many people, Christian and otherwise, believe in the immediate ascension to heaven after death. This conflicts with the Seventh-day Adventist doctrine of the "rest period" after death that ends with a resurrection.

When I'm asked to pray that a loved one is in heaven, I try to find words that speak to this spirit without compromising my theology. Ultimately, no one knows for sure what happens after death, so I'm perfectly willing and prepared to be wrong. But not knowing shouldn't stop me from believing something.

"We look to a time when there are no more tears," I might say, or "Grant us hope that one day we will be reunited again."

Baptisms for a dead or dying infant can be painfully tricky. Seventh-day Adventists don't believe in infant baptism and I'm not authorized to perform one. When families request a baptism—and I'm the chaplain on call so I'm the chaplain they get—I try to look at the situation as, *This family is looking for a ritual that will help them grieve.*

I might perform what I call a blessing. But I don't perform the baptism. I don't say, "I baptize you in the name of …."

Instead, I sometimes involve the family directly. I might say, "Mom, would you like to sprinkle the water? Dad, will you say the words?" Then I'll hand them a card with the words on it so they can keep it with them.

*

"I'm on my way," I say to Holly in the NICU. "Be there in twenty minutes."

"Awesome! That's fast. I didn't realize you guys were on site."

Damn it. I could have said an hour and gotten a few more minutes of sleep. I wouldn't normally be *so* whiny and insensitive… but I've been to so many deaths tonight, more than the average. I'm exhausted.

"Yup. We're here all the time. See you soon."

I hang up and set an alarm for ten minutes. I'm so tired. I have the feeling I'm going to fall back asleep while I lie here.

But I don't. My mind is racing, trying to sort out the unknowns I'll be walking into with this family. The alarm goes off. Begrudgingly, I get out of bed.

There are many ways chaplains mentally prepare to enter a situation like this. Most new CPE students rationalize that "These parents are having a much more difficult time than I am. I'm being selfish for not wanting to go and be with them." This is not helpful. Dismissing my internal state of fear, disdain, anger, or frustration only means I let those feelings stew under the surface. Potentially, they'll bubble up during the visit and muddle my ability to be present for the family.

And being present for the family is the crucial part of the service—not forcing myself to feel what I'm "supposed" to feel or getting down on myself when I don't. I've found it's better to acknowledge, honor, and air out those feelings so I can move through them and focus on the work. Also, the parents' life and mine are on completely different trajectories. Comparison is of little use. Where would I even start?

I am the chaplain on call for the night. I have to go, no matter what I want or how I'm feeling. So I choose to honor what I'm feeling on the walk there, taking the long way to the unit so I have more time to get myself together.

Tonight, I mutter, *This is stupid. I don't want to be here. My wife and son are asleep at home. I miss them. I didn't want to sign up for this shift in the first place … I knew this would happen! I knew I wouldn't sleep tonight. My whole night is ruined. And I'm not going to have time or space to nap tomorrow, because I have housework to do when I get home. I'm not looking forward to this at all …*

I'm still talking under my breath when I get to the unit. I have to shake myself to get ready. But I'm glad I've released all my petty shit.

Now, hopefully, I'm freed from carrying it into our encounter. I need the capacity to be with others in an emotional place I would never want to be myself.

Before I go into the unit, I take one more moment: close my eyes, take a deep breath, and let it out.

The NICU: soft ambient lighting and very protective personnel. The nurses have a heightened awareness of whoever comes and goes. They are suspicious of outsiders. Security is tight, as it is on any unit with babies or children, because of the threat of abductions.

It's largely a woman-centered space. We deal mostly with mothers and generally female chaplains are assigned to those units. As a man, I always feel invasive there, so I never go unless I'm called.

Even female chaplains are more careful than on other units not to intrude unless they're specifically requested. We try to be overly sensitive to the possibility that family members are wrestling with questions about why God is allowing this to happen. We never know what we represent to others. Our presence as spiritual advisors might provoke even more anger, confusion, and pain.

I feel uncomfortable as I move around the unit because I know I'm being watched. I always ask a member of the staff to take me everywhere and to guide me to where I'm supposed to go. The feeling doesn't go away until I'm at bedside.

Tonight, a nurse sees me and asks, "Are you Keith?"

"Are you Holly?"

"Thanks for coming. So, Mom is in here." She points to a sectioned area in a small pod encircled by a cloth curtain on sliding rings. "I think Grandma and Aunt are in there, too. I'm not sure where Dad went. Anything you need from me?"

"I don't think so." She seems rushed so I don't want to keep her. At the same time, one of her patients is about to die, so I want to know:

"How are you doing?"

"Me? I'm great." This is almost certainly a lie. "Oh, I almost forgot: they're Spanish-speaking only."

Crap!

The work we do to connect with people emotionally and spiritually is not easy even when we're speaking the same language. If only I had paid attention in tenth-grade Spanish class, instead of writing out the lyrics to Guns N' Roses songs ....

Now I'll have to add a third-party, a medical interpreter, into the equation, and I never know what to expect. I'll be calling someone on the iPad at 2 a.m. and hoping to get video. Audio-only leaves us all staring at the floor while the interpreter translates through the tiny speakers.

"Oh—that's helpful to know." I smile.

"Yeah. Sorry I didn't tell you earlier ..."

"It's okay. Is there an iPad set up?"

"Yes. It's in there with them."

I stand outside the curtain to give myself another moment. Once when I was talking with a patient through an interpreter, everything was going great—I felt a tremendous connection with the patient even through the translation. Then she asked if I could pray. I said the first line of my prayer and heard from the translator—silence.

I repeated it. Again, nothing. "Can you hear me?" I asked the translator.

"Yeah. I can hear you," he said.

"Great. Then why aren't you translating?"

"Oh ... I'm not religious."

"I see." I tried to keep my tone under control. "Well, then, this is your lucky day. Because I'm not trying to get you to believe the words I say. I just want you to translate them into French. Because I don't speak French. You've done great up to this point. Do you think you can continue?"

There was a brief silence. Then a hesitant, "Yeah."

"Fantastic. Now, do you want to explain to the patient what you do and do not believe, or simply let her know you were having 'technical issues?'" I let the translator know I had written down his translator ID number. He chose the latter option and continued.

I know there's not a high likelihood that I'll get this same translator tonight, since that was French and this is Spanish and there's a large pool of translators who are on-call all over the world. But you never know. Many of the interpreters are multilingual.

I gently open the curtain to establish a connection with Mom. Dad is back in the room as well. They both look very young—nineteen or twenty, maybe. Or maybe I'm just old. Mom's thick, dark hair is wound into a braid on the top of her head and Dad wears a small gold earring and a gold cross around his neck.

They are hovering over their tiny baby, who lies beneath the plexiglass of an incubator that protects him from temperature changes. Mom's sister and mother have stepped away for the moment. I give the couple an awkward smile and subtle wave and locate the iPad. With a series of motions, I try to relate to them that I'm going to take the iPad out of the space and connect with a translator before I come back in to introduce myself. I think they know what I'm communicating; I'm sure I'm not the first to do this pantomime since their baby's been on the unit.

I tap around to find a Spanish interpreter. I'm relieved when I see a face on the screen different from that of the middle-aged French interpreter. This is a young man in his late twenties with big ears and a flat-top haircut. He's wearing a white collared shirt and a headset and he's as professional as he looks. When I give him a brief synopsis of the end-of-life situation I'm bringing him into, he says calmly, "Thank you very much. I'm glad to have that information ahead of time."

"I'll probably pray. I'll keep my sentences short," I go on. "I'm very comfortable with silence, so there may be lots of it. Quite frankly, what words am I going to offer that will make a huge difference?"

"Okay, Chaplain. I'm ready to introduce myself to Mom and Dad when you are," he says.

I feel relieved. He's already personifying them: *Mom and Dad* instead of *the parents* or *them*. I'm feeling a little better. I have a partner in this. I'm not alone.

"Okay, let's go," I say.

In the room, I position the iPad so the translator can see both the baby and the parents. I introduce myself and they welcome me.

"Thanks for coming, Pastor," Dad says quietly. Some Spanish speakers have told me there is no word for chaplain in Spanish. Others have said there is, but it's closer to "military chaplain" and doesn't quite fit in the context of the hospital. Whatever the word is, it's not common. Sometimes I'll say, "I'm like a priest for the hospital—but I'm not Catholic." This gets some confused nods and we just move on. Most often, I'm called "Pastor" or "Father."

"Not a place either of us wants to be, huh?"

Dad breathes in sharply through his nose. "No. That's true. But I'm glad you're here."

Mom is still hunched over the incubator. Her hand is stretched through the opening on the side and she's softly stroking her son's tiny fingers.

"Full head of hair on this little guy," I say.

She clenches her lips and begins sobbing. Dad wraps his arm around Mom.

"What's his name?" I ask and they tell me. "Beautiful. Is he named after anyone?"

"My great-grandfather," says Mom. "He died a few weeks after I was born. So when we found out our son wasn't going to survive more than a few weeks, it just seemed fitting." She pauses and laughs, tears still running down her cheeks. "Is that weird? It's weird, right?"

"That's really special and meaningful."

"Thank you," she whispers.

Dad's head is hanging. Sometimes he looks up from the floor to glance at his wife. Often, fathers minimize the importance of their grief. They say, "I just need to support her" or "It's more painful for her." Fathers grieve too and I often find myself drawn to the father in these scenarios.

I tell them I'm a Seventh-day Adventist and they nod and smile softly. They don't know about the mystery of why I'm the one on-call tonight. I'm thinking about it, though. I like thinking about a mysterious force working behind the scenes. I think intuition—following your instinct that you're on the right path without fully understanding why—can sometimes collide with meaning-making. Searching for an answer as to "why" is pretty useless. But I still like to ask the question and send it into the ether. It's a way of acknowledging something beyond myself while keeping myself intact. I call this mysterious force "God."

Mom requests that I say a prayer with them and give the baby a blessing. Could there be a more difficult moment in a mother's life? The prayer will initiate the disconnection of the life-sustaining interventions. It's the bridge between the parents who want as much time as they can get and the medical team, who is often getting antsy. They're afraid "helping" has become "harming" and the baby is suffering.

*

I've heard the protestation many times, concerning the removal of life-sustaining interventions, that it's "not God's will." But I rarely hear from the same people who say this that *placing* someone on life-sustaining interventions is "not God's will." "Life at all costs" seems to be the mantra of many Christians, who also sing about how they long for a place beyond this world.

I'm not mocking them. I'm simply trying to name the inconsistencies that are often a part of grief.

A euphemism commonly used when life-saving interventions are removed can reinforce the idea that we are failing these patients—giving up on them, going against God by throwing them to the wolves. Often, a nurse or respiratory therapist will request my presence when they "withdraw care."

In the beginning of my career, I was hesitant to call people out on language like this. Now, I take more risks.

"Well," I say, "*we'll* still be there. We'll still be caring for them. So it's just the machines we're withdrawing, right?"

More often than not, they recognize the value of the observation. "Right," they say. "You're right."

*

As I get older, and go through more experiences, I feel myself gaining knowledge that gives me more to offer in situations like the heartbreaking one of the couple in the NICU.

I once met with another young couple in the middle of the night. They were the new parents of premature twins, a boy and a girl, born three days apart. Both babies developed an infection and were treated with steroids to increase their strength. The boy responded well; the girl didn't. Their care team told the parents to "prepare for the worst and get ready to make a decision" if she didn't improve.

Both parents were exhausted. The babies were in two different hospitals because the girl required a higher level of care. The father had been traveling between the two. Since we were in a big city that wasn't easy to navigate, the trip often took up to two hours.

The mother said to me, "I feel like I want to do everything I can, and I'm not doing enough."

"You are doing everything you can," I told her. "I know it doesn't feel like much. And as a parent, that feeling never goes away."

*

In the NICU, we move from "Amen" to a moment of silence. I make it a practice not to be the first one to break the silence after a prayer. In these cases, however, I almost always have to. The parents never break it. They just can't. And they shouldn't have to. That's what I'm here for.

Chaplains can hold silence for what is considered an uncomfortable amount of time—and sometimes I like to see if I can go beyond that time. Even in a situation like this one, game-theory helps me get through it.

The only sounds are the hum of ventilation, the random two-tone beep from a monitor, and a couple of shoe squeaks on the floor.

After a few minutes, I ask, "Shall I have the team come in now and begin the process?"

Their heads sink. Mom wipes a tear. "Yeah. And I want to hold him as soon as I can."

I say, "I'll make sure you do."

Chapter 16

In February of 2022, I officially became a certified educator for chaplaincy. Most hospitals that have CPE programs want a Certified Educator to be the director of the department as it's the highest level of education you can get in chaplaincy. It's like a professional doctorate in an academic field.

To get there, you need at least four units of CPE and then a year or two of work experience as a chaplain. After I did my four units and some PRN work, I did a second residency and got four more units of CPE before I started my Certified Educator Training. CET is made up of several phases, including periods of observing a CPE educator and leading CPE units under supervision.

There's also a lot of writing and feedback. Candidates write three substantial theory papers that show their work is grounded in fundamental theory and research; my theorists were Ellen White and Kierkegaard for spirituality/theology; Jean Piaget and Irvin Yalom for personality; and Patricia Cranton and Jack Mezirow for education. We also write about sixty "competencies" that demonstrate (or don't) a candidate's readiness for the training. Competencies are text prompts that invite the candidate to show with examples, illustrations, and videos how they have attained competency in the areas outlined in the prompt. Some example prompts: "engages in broader context to understand and safeguard the welfare of others" and "articulates a well-formed theory of supervised education for the teaching/learning of pastoral/spiritual care in individuals and groups."

Certification is dependent on the approval of two committees at different points in the process, which can take a few years to complete. At the same time as the candidate is writing and reflecting, they're also training students and using practical implementation to make sure the theories they're writing about work off the page.

*

Later that year, I began working at a Stanford Health Care in Palo Alto, California. There, I met the Venerable Dr. Longyun Shi. She introduced herself, then added, her eyes revealing a smile beneath her yellow surgical mask, "You can call me Yun." She is the only person I've ever met who has slept under a tree for a month as a part of her intense dharma training. (In my life, I have "slept" under only one tree and not intentionally; as a kid, I was climbing a tree in our yard when I let go of a branch to wipe dust out of my eye. The next thing I remember, I was waking up on the couch inside.)

Yun takes small steps but is always in a hurry. She is a monastic nun: in her own words, "a woman who vows to dedicate her life to serving all sentient beings in need with contemplation and compassion."[42] She practices Vinaya (the doctrines and disciplines regarding the daily life of monks and nuns as they are described in Buddhist canonical texts), meditation, and wisdom to attain the ultimate Buddhist goal of Nirvana. The length of her hair doubles every two weeks. Twice a month, on the first and fifteenth days of the lunar calendar, she shaves it.

"I don't even need a mirror anymore," she says proudly.

Yun was the first Buddhist nun to become a board-certified chaplain in the United States. She holds a PhD in religious studies and teaches courses at Stanford. She sees her work as a professor as an opportunity to "[assist] people to live a life with wisdom." As for being a chaplain, she says that "The quality interfaith chaplaincy training is an excellent way to practice Bodhicitta [awakening or enlightenment]." During clinical service, Yun doesn't see people as Buddhist, Catholic, Jewish, or any other specific denomination: "I only see future Buddhas, since everyone has a Buddha nature, according to my Buddhist perspective."[43]

Yun is also a co-founder of "China CPE" an organization bringing clinical chaplaincy training to mainland China. It's just three people and maybe a handful of additional volunteers. "We have many applicants and only a hundred students!" she told me. I marveled that she could say such a thing without the least bit of nervousness in her voice.

"So many applications," I said, "and only six of you to go through them all?"

"Yes. We work very hard."

*

Even when I began working at UCLA Health as the Manager for CPE programs, I kept in touch with Yun. Her work, and the connections she helped me to make, led to my own involvement in the fledgling chaplaincy movement in China.

I found myself in Beijing about to do a presentation about hospital chaplaincy in the United States. I had been invited by the deputy director of the volunteer committee within the Chinese Association for Life Care and by a palliative care physician at Beijing Tsinghua Changgeng Hospital.

The day was sweltering and I was also sweating from nervousness. I got out of the taxi and stared up at the Chinese characters on the side of the building. I looked at my feet and saw I was standing on a dusty sheet of plywood. The entire area was a construction zone.

"Is this the Beijing Tsinghua Changgung Hospital?" I asked.

My cab driver pointed at the fare, shook the money in his hand, and gave me an "OK" sign with his other hand. Then he signaled for me to close the door. Reluctantly, I obliged.

I found my way to the fourth-floor conference room, still unclear if I was in the right place. I was discovered looking lost by Zhu Choi—she also went by Jasmine—the person I'd been working with for the past few months in preparation for this presentation.

For thirty minutes, I met with the directors, Jasmine, and seven volunteer chaplains so we could get to know each other. The conversation revealed to me that currently, there are no chaplains employed at hospitals in China, only a few volunteers. As American doctors and members of the clergy did in the late nineteenth and early twentieth century on the East Coast, the Chinese Association for Life Care is working to integrate chaplaincy into the structure of hospitals in China. They're starting with Beijing Tsinghua Changgeng, the first hospital affiliated with Tsinghua University.

My presentation was supposed to last ninety minutes. After nearly three hours, Jasmine had to end it. I was the first hospital chaplain any of the physicians, nurses, social workers, pharmacists, or volunteer spiritual caregivers had ever met. I was honored and thrilled that they all gathered to listen to what I had to share. I was also a little surprised. I still struggle with feeling like an imposter. I doubted whether my experiences in hospital chaplaincy in America had any relevancy to people in mainland China.

They asked so many good questions. And when I showed footage Brandon had shot while we were making *A Certain Kind of Light*, I could feel everyone in the room feeling the beauty, that heart-stopping, pain-stopping beauty, that Wil could pull out of the direst situations. It's the kind of beauty that can lift us out of ourselves and connect us for a moment to every other beautiful thing in the world and beyond the world.

I knew why they couldn't stop listening. Because those moments fill the kinds of encounters I was describing. Not every time—it's hit or miss. Sometimes they're awkward or even ugly instead of beautiful. You never know if you're going to make things better or worse. But you keep going in, anyway. And you have to believe that's beautiful too.

*

While I was in China, I met people who expressed a wish that there were more accounts about chaplaincy available to the public—films, books, articles—texts that share the importance and impact of this ministry through first-person accounts and stories.

I took that sentiment to heart. I decided to do what I could to help fill that gap and started assembling a compilation of my experiences. You've almost finished reading it.

*

2:55 a.m., Tuesday, August 23, 2022

I get back to my room around 3:00 a.m. I try to go back to sleep, but it's impossible. After half an hour of tossing and turning in the twin bed, I give in to my restlessness and go for a walk outside.

The morning is crisp, the air fresh. I don't really want to be awake on an overnight shift, especially knowing I still have several hours to go. But I do like the stillness when most of the city is asleep. And the stars are so nice, a sparkling backdrop for the clouds.

Russian Proverb: "The darker the night, the brighter the stars. The deeper the grief, the closer is God!"[44]

At the entrance to the emergency department—the only entrance open at this time—Willy, a security guard, is rocking back and forth on his feet to boost his blood circulation. He's also wiping the top counter of his two-tiered desk with sanitizer. Willy is tall, thin, in his early sixties. He has dark skin and a gray-white beard to match his white-gray hair. He was born and raised a few blocks from this hospital and knows the area better than anyone I've met.

"Long night, eh?" I say.

"I'll say. How you doing, Chaplain? How's the night?"

"Well, it's turned into morning."

"Ha. Yeah, that happens."

"Can I ask you something, Willy?"

"Shoot."

"What keeps you engaged while you're working this shift?"

"Ah, well. There's always something happening around here."

"That's it?"

"Almost. If there isn't something happening, then I make sure to be doing something. Everyone's replaceable. Hell, right after you give notice at a job, they've already posted the position. So I do what I can to make sure they don't get it in their heads to hire someone else. I got family, kids, grandkids, and oh—I didn't tell you: I'm a great-granddad now." His shoulders square back and he lifts his chin up high.

"Congratulations, Willy!"

A man comes up behind me and nudges his way past. "Where's the doctors at?" he asks, some pain in his voice.

"Right this way, sir." Willy puts his arm around the man's shoulder. "Always good to see you, Chaplain."

"You too, Willy."

I walk back to the sleep room, take out my laptop, and watch You-Tube videos. Now, I wish someone would page me. I'd rather be productive than just sit and waste my time. "Everyone's replaceable." The cafeteria opens at 6:30 a.m., so I set an alarm on my clock for 6:25 a.m.

My alarm wakes me. I must have fallen asleep. Now I'm kicking myself for setting it because I didn't think I'd fall asleep. I only wanted to know when I could walk down for breakfast. I roll over and doze off.

At 7:15 a.m., I wake up again. I'm starving after being up half the night. In the cafeteria, I get a cup of yogurt and fruit with some granola and biscuits and gravy. I suppose if the bad goes down with the good, it's less bad, and perhaps that's good.

I sit in the middle of the cafeteria. The morning light gets brighter and the room fills with people. On a screen on the wall is a constantly changing spreadsheet filled with cells of various colors. The screen provides information about where patients are in surgery ("Patient in Operating Room" or "Patient in Pre-Op"). Most surgeries begin between 7:00 a.m. and 7:30 a.m., so lots of family members are coming in. Most patients are NPO, which stands for "Nothing by Mouth." Did someone who wasn't too sharp in English decide that "NPO" sounded better than "NBM"? I know it's a Latin abbreviation, but it's too early for semantics. In any case, most patients are not supposed to eat for twelve to twenty-four hours before surgery. The people who come with them often don't eat in the morning, either, out of nervousness, commiseration, being in a hurry, whatever. At this time of day, the cafeteria is also busy with workers changing shifts (night nurses work 7:00 p.m. to 7:00 a.m.). All this to say that I was lucky to get a seat.

Near me are two people probably in their mid-seventies. They're looking confused about the spreadsheet. Most people never make any sense of it, and I'm thankful they don't ask me; I have trouble with it myself. I notice a note in the woman's hand. Both she and the man study each line on the screen, then look back down at their note. I get up to throw away my garbage and return my tray.

I don't know what I'll be able to tell them, but they seem to be more at a loss than most. I ask if I can help. They see my badge and sigh with relief.

"Oh, thank you. Our daughter just went back into surgery for a lung transplant," the woman says. I'm reminded of how quickly people open up to me when they find out I'm a chaplain.

"You must be pretty worried …?"

The man responds, "It ain't supposed to be like this."

"No, I suppose it ain't," I say.

"We just need to keep a positive outlook and get some food," says the woman. "But I want to know where to look on this board so I can keep track of where she is."

I study the number they've been given and eventually find it on the screen. I help them figure out where to look for it—the board flickers and changes quite frequently because there are so many operations that happen each day. Often, as soon as you find your number, it disappears before reappearing in another spot. They express their gratitude and I show them how to get into the food-service line.

I go back to the sleep room, pack my suitcase, and roll it up to my desk. It's 8:15 a.m. and everyone else in the spiritual-care department will be in at 8:30 a.m. While I need to stay until 9:00 a.m. to give the department a report about what happened overnight, I am no longer on call starting at 8:30 a.m. At this point, if a request comes in, I'll refer whomever is responsible for the unit it's on, unless it's for one of my units.

I make coffee from a Dripkit single pack and take in the view from my desk—parking lot, trees, in the distance a low line of blue mountains.

I'm feeling grateful to have made it to this point in my shift. I realize I left my Hammarskjöld book at home. I need to read another book for my inspirational time this morning so I dig around until I find my copy of Christian Wiman's *My Bright Abyss* and open to where I left the bookmark:

> *Radical change remains a possibility within us right up until our last breath. The greatest tragedy of human existence is not to live in time, in both senses of that phrase.*[45]

"In time, in both senses of that phrase." Life is short and getting shorter the older I get. The more I see death around me, the more I realize how much time I've wasted and continue to waste.

*

What is "wasted time?" That depends on your perspective.

I once had a patient who spent his entire adult life doing the thing American conventional wisdom tells us is the opposite of wasting time: working hard at his job. He saved up for thirty years, forgoing vacations and time off. His plan was to spend the last third of his life traveling and having fun, taking his just reward.

Six months before his retirement, he was diagnosed with an inoperable brain tumor. At his bedside, I looked into his defeated eyes, which sagged with anguish. His voice was so broken it was painful to listen to.

"I waited and sacrificed for nothing," he said. "All that time planning and getting so close to living it. But I'll never be able to. What does that *mean?*"

He was looking at me. Before I could speak, he answered his own question. "I'll tell you what it means. Do what you love and are passionate about. Don't wait for 'when I can.' That time might never come. If there's any way you can do it now, if there's nothing holding you back except maybe some stupid plan you've got in your head, then enjoy the blink of time we have in the grand scale of things."

*

I don't think I've wasted too much time this past night. That feels good. But I'm exhausted and ready to go home. I've been "in house" for over twenty-four hours. I'm not even thinking clearly anymore.

*

I'm heading into the morning department meeting when my pager beeps. I was so close!

I wonder whether to return the call or simply send it to the on-call chaplain. It's 8:45 a.m. and it came to my personal pager. I'm no longer listed in the system as being "on-call," so this one is most likely for me. After some hesitation, I dial the number.

The nurse who answers is from one of the intensive care units I cover.

"Hey, Keith, glad I caught you," she begins. *Wish I could say the same.* "Listen, you know the family in 28?" I tell her I do. The patient is a woman from Texas named Alyssa.

"Well," the nurse says, "they've made the decision to proceed with donation. So we're putting together an honor walk."

"Lovely. That will mean a lot to them. Such a sad story all around."

"Yeah, it's just unfair."

I think back on my past conversations with the husband and other family members about this patient. She and her husband loved each other; everyone said so. They had a good life for the time they had together. Now she's leaving. It's not fair or unfair. It's what's happening. Many lives are lived without love and that's why some people feel *their* lives are unfair.

"So this will be tomorrow?" I ask hopefully.

"Uh, no." Her pace is like molasses compared with the other quick-talking nurses I've interacted with on this shift. "It'll be in about thirty minutes."

"Oh."

"Yeah. And … her husband is asking if you can walk with him."

Shit. I know right away this is one of those "exception to the rule" situations when it comes to staying after my shift is over: a specific request from a family I've developed a strong relationship with, to attend the most special of special occasions. When I hang up, I poke my head into the department meeting to give Sofia a head's up that I'll be attending the honor walk and then heading home.

My old pal Chandler, one more time, to get me through to the end: "I caught the brass ring and it shocked me to find out it wasn't gold."[46]

*

The bed with Alyssa on it passes through the doors of her room and into the hall. A few dozen hospital employees and other onlookers—including family members visiting other patients and patients themselves if they are well enough to get up and stand in the doorways of their rooms—are lined up on either side of the passageway. They're here to pay their respects and honor this brain-dead woman who is donating her organs so other people can live.

Everyone is unusually available to everybody else. Most people are crying and offering each other tissues. Staff members who I know are not particularly close—and even some who really don't get along—have their arms around each other.

Usually, none of us think much about this hallway, or any hallway in the hospital. For me, it's just a non-room, a place where I stare at my feet or at signs on the walls while I get to where I'm going and resume the business of life.

But this ritual transforms it. We're all aware of our presence in a passageway between a life that was, a death that will soon be, and a rebirth, a new chance, to someone who's been living on borrowed time. *Radical change remains a possibility within us right up until our last breath.*

The walls are a soft yellow with a deep blue stripe on one side and a forest-green stripe on the other. The carpet is made up of blue and green squares with a random one here and there that's purple or yellow—it's a colorful and cheery passage into darkness. The patient's husband, her two teenage children, her parents, and other family members walk behind the nurse who's pushing her bed.

I've locked arms with the patient's husband. He's only about forty, the same age as his wife. He looks just as I'd expect a farmer from Texas to look, wearing dirt-stained Wranglers and a plaid-button up. He has a sharp jaw and deep blue eyes and each of his biceps is twice the size of mine.

But as we walk, he seems as weak as a child. Every now and then, I feel his knees buckle and his big boots drag on the carpet. It takes all the strength I can muster to keep him on his feet. He feels too unstable to raise these children. I'm glad there are so many family members here.

The patient's nurses, surgeons, and social workers are walking behind us now; at some point, they joined the recessional.

A woman yells out, "Thank you, Alyssa! You're saving some lives! Thank you!" The woman begins clapping and everyone joins her.

At the entrance to the hallway leading to the operating room, we stop. I move to the foot of the bed and look at everyone present, then down at Alyssa. I can barely see them. My eyes are blurring with fatigue.

"These rows of strangers, acquaintances, friends, family, and loved ones are here to honor the gift you, Alyssa, are giving," I say. "While we grieve the loss of your life, Alyssa, and we each do so in our own way, we celebrate your willingness to sacrifice the parts of yourself that will bring life to others who need them. May your death be a gift for life. Amen."

*

Soon after the walk, Alyssa's heart began beating in the body of a seventeen-year-old girl who was in a car accident. Her kidneys were sent to two people in different states. A woman in her mid-fifties received Alyssa's pancreas. Her lungs were flown to Arizona and her liver went to Kentucky.

*

I'm overwhelmed—by sleep deprivation, anxiety, emotions, and life. It's impossible to have gone through all of that and not be changed.

But it's time for my own transition. It's time to make my way back to the parking garage and drive home. It's time to park behind my condo complex, let myself in through the gate, and take my shoes off at the door.

It's time to take a shower. Who knows what germs and substances are clinging to my body and my clothes? I also do a lot of processing in the shower. It's a nice place to think. When I was a pastor, I came up with my best sermons in there—though I forgot them as soon as I stepped out. Today, I take a lot of deep breaths under the steamy water.

It's time to hug Shuang. This moment is different for her than it is for me. We're both deeply exhausted, but for different reasons. She's been wrapped up in the tedious and mundane business of running around after a toddler.

I can feel that. There's a lot of grounding in this hug. All right. Now it's okay to come back. To listen to music while I crash on the couch, to be irritated by the toys on the floor and to pick a few of them up.

It's okay to make a sandwich and chew it slowly while staring out the window at the trees in the courtyard. To watch my son run toward me at daycare. To hold him in my arms all the way back to the car.

We'll listen to music again on the way home. Maybe "The Gambler," or another of his favorites, "Ghost Riders in the Sky."

*

By the time I go to pick up my son, I'm still tired. What will I need to get through this evening? I'll need a lot of peace and strength. "Peace and Strength!" That's how I sign every email and letter I write.

I never used to ask people what they wanted me to pray for. One of my educators cured me of that. He told me to "quit making an 'ass' out of 'u' and 'me'" and ask the patient what they really meant when they asked for prayer.

I tried this out for the first time on a woman who had just signed the paperwork to enter hospice. She was waiting to be discharged from the hospital so she could go home under hospice care. We talked about where she was emotionally. Then she asked if I would pray for her.

It *had* always seemed safe to assume that people wanted one or more obvious things: healing, no pain, to be with their families, etc., etc. But when I asked, the patient didn't ask for any of those.

"Peace," she said. She was pensive for a moment and looked away. Then, with a stern and decisive nod, she looked back at me. Her eyes were very dark brown, almost black.

"And strength," she said.

I told her I had never heard those two words together in the same prayer. I asked her what she meant by it.

"Peace for the decision I've just made," she said, "and strength to go through what I'm about to go through."

Her words struck me. I realized that's what I needed, too: an ability to accept my choices. And then the will to act on them.

"That's beautiful," I told her. "Can I steal it from you?"

She gave me a sweet smile.

"You can have it," she said. "It's yours."

**

Author Bio

Keith Wakefield is currently the Manager for CPE (Clinical Pastoral Education) Programs at UCLA Health in Los Angeles, California. An ACPE Certified Educator, he completed his ACPE Certified Educator training at the University of Colorado Hospital in Aurora. He holds a Bachelor of Arts in Theology from Southern Adventist University (2004) and a Master of Divinity from the Seventh-day Adventist Theological Seminary at Andrews University (2013). In 2023, he earned his Post-graduate Certificate in Research Methods in Health Practice from the University of Bath. Prior to coming to UCLA Health, he was a CPE Educator at Johns Hopkins in Baltimore and at Stanford Health Care in Palo Alto. Keith has chaplaincy experience in medical intensive care, burn, surgical-trauma, cardiology, psychiatry, oncology, and other general-medicine units. An Ordained Pastor in the Seventh-day Adventist Church, he's taught classes on chaplaincy and spirituality in health at Loma Linda University and Andrews University.

Also a filmmaker, Wakefield's first film, a 2015 documentary about chaplaincy called *A Certain Kind of Light*, was directed by Brandon Vedder (*Strange Negotiations*, *La Source*, *Pearl Jam: Live at the Garden*), and earned nominations and awards at several film festivals. His most recent film,

G-Ride, focuses on the story of Mike "G-Ride" Griffith. After surviving homelessness, addiction, and isolation, Griffith found his passion and purpose as a pedicab driver and became a beloved community staple in Chico, California. Released in 2019, the film received awards at the Chico Independent Film Festival and the Front Range Film Festival in Colorado.

In his spare time, Keith can be found passed out at home, because he's just too old to be chasing a rambunctious five-year-old boy around.

Acknowledgements

The word "acknowledgements" itself holds more meaning than on first appearance. It spans a range of emotions, from the routine and obligatory to the truly heartfelt. It can cover everything from formalities to deep, lasting gratitude for those whose support has been indispensable—especially in times of personal challenge or limitation. Below are the individuals to whom I owe my thanks.

I want to express my deepest gratitude to my editor, Cheri Johnson, whose insightful feedback, dedication, and expertise helped shape my writing into a book—this book. You caught my vision, polished it, and helped bring it to the page for others to encounter as well.

I'm forever grateful to my family: my parents, my sister, my wife and son. Your unwavering love and support have been the foundation of everything I do.

To Chris Jones, I'm lucky to have had you by my side throughout my life. From childhood through all the years that followed, you've always been my neighbor, and I hope I've been the friend to you that you have been to me.

To Brandon Vedder, you've been a devoted friend and collaborator, always embodying a creative spirit that inspires. And, of course, the unforgettable stench of burnt leg hair permanently etched in my memory and nasal cavities—thank you for that as well.

My heartfelt thanks to Emily Coons for reading this work and allowing me to share Jim's story as I remembered it. While the memories and reflections within these pages were drawn from my own experience with him, your support in giving me the freedom to honor his memory means more than words can express. Jim's legacy lives on in the hearts of those who knew him, and I am grateful to have had the opportunity to share a glimpse of his life so others can have a small portion of what we knew him to be.

To Gina Harvey, your companionship along the "ACPE path" and our continued friendship have meant so much to me. Your support has been constant and present.

To Angela Li, thank you for helping me navigate the "Adventist path" and for your laugh when I said, "I'm an Adventist by persistence"—you understood exactly what I meant, and that meant the world to me.

To Megan Worthman, for the lunches, the friendship, and the chaplaincy journey together. Your presence is always appreciated.

Dustin Frye, you asked me once how I let others get close to me, and that question still resonates with me. It's a continual presence in my life, and I carry it with me in every community I'm part of.

Chitra Rao, for always challenging me to grow.

To Robyn Hacker, your unvarnished opinions and your ability to help me 'sound smarter' than I am have been invaluable. I'm grateful for your honesty and support.

To Joy and Amelia, your help in getting this book into the world has been invaluable. Thank you for everything you've done to make this happen.

To the many of you who read one or more versions of this draft along the way—Sharon Langfeld, Rev. Dr. Colleen Preuninger, Ty Crowe, David Mandel, Emily Linderman, Laurel Braitman, Garrett Starmer, Angela Song, Isaac Mun, Teresa Jordan, and Longyun "Yun" Shi, Vanessa Able and Mary D. Farah—thank you for your time and insights to help fine-tune this book to be even better than I imagined it would become.

Lastly, I express my deepest thanks to all my CPE educators, students, patients, and their families. Your lives, stories, and lessons have shaped both this book and the way I move through the world in ways I will always carry with me.

Notes

[1] Dag Hammarskjöld, *Markings* (New York: Alfred A. Knopf, 1965), 13.

[2] Gerald R. Winslow, "From Loyalty to Advocacy: A New Metaphor for Nursing," *The Hastings Center Report* 14, no. 3 (1984): 32–40. https://doi.org/10.2307/3561187.

[3] American Psychiatric Association, *Diagnostic and Statistical Manual of Mental Disorders: DSM-IV-TR*, 4th ed.,text rev. (Washington, DC: American Psychiatric Association, 2000), 781-783.

[4] American Psychiatric Association, *Diagnostic and Statistical Manual of Mental Disorders: DSM-IV-TR*, 4th ed.,text rev. (Washington, DC: American Psychiatric Association, 2000), 781-783.

[5] American Psychiatric Association, *Diagnostic and Statistical Manual of Mental Disorders: DSM-IV-TR*, 4th ed.,text rev. (Washington, DC: American Psychiatric Association, 2000), 781-783.

[6] Raymond Chandler, *Farewell My Lovely* (New York: Vintage Books, 1988), 10.

[7] Raymond Chandler, *The Long Goodbye* (New York: Vintage Books, 1988), 344.

[8] "Talking Funny," YouTube video, 35:24. Posted by HBO, April 22, 2011. https://youtu.be/OKY6BGcx37k?t=2121.

[9] Hirsh, J. B., Mar, R. A., and Peterson, J. B. "Psychological Entropy: A Framework for Understanding Uncertainty-Related Anxiety." *American Psychological Association* (2012).

[10] Merriam-Webster, s.v. "ambiguous," accessed June 26, 2024, https://www.merri-am-webster.com/dictionary/ambiguous.

[11] Henrik Ibsen, Peer Gynt, trans. R. Farquharson Sharp (Philadelphia: J.B. Lippin-cott Co., 1936), 251.

[12] Tony Duggan, "Mahler's Ninth Symphony: A Critical Analysis," *MusicWeb International*, accessed June 26, 2024, http://www.musicweb-international.com/mahler/mahler9.htm.

[13] "The Unanswered Question: Bernstein on Mahler," YouTube video. Posted by Deutsche Grammophon, May 5, 2011. Accessed June 26, 2024. https://youtu.be/U5I7lYN5adU?t=827.

[14] "The Unanswered Question: Bernstein on Mahler," YouTube video. Posted by Deutsche Grammophon, May 5, 2011. Accessed June 26, 2024. https://youtu.be/U5I7lYN5adU?t=1285.

[15] "Langsam," OnMusic Dictionary, accessed June 26, 2024, https://dictionary.on-music.org/terms/1930-langsam; Mayo Clinic, "Heart rate: What's normal?" accessed June 26, 2024, https://www.mayoclinic.org/healthy-lifestyle/fitness/expert-answers/heart-rate/faq-20057979.

[16] "The Unanswered Question: Bernstein on Mahler," YouTube video. Posted by Deutsche Grammophon, May 5, 2011. Accessed June 26, 2024.https://youtu.be/U5I7lYN5adU?t=784; "The Unanswered Question," The New York Times, May 23, 1976, https://www.nytimes.com/1976/05/23/archives/the-unanswered-question.html; Leonard Bernstein, "The Delights and Dangers of Ambiguity," Leonard Bernstein Office, accessed June 26, 2024, https://leonardbernstein.com/lectures/television-scripts/norton-lectures/the-delights-and-dangers-of-ambiguity.

[17] "The Unanswered Question: Bernstein on Mahler," YouTube video. Posted by Deutsche Grammophon, May 5, 2011. Accessed June 26, 2024. https://youtu.be/U5I7lYN5adU?t=1053.

[18] Irvin D. Yalom, *Existential Psychotherapy* (New York: Basic Books, 1980), 159.

[19] Søren Kierkegaard, *The Concept of Anxiety: A Simple Psychologically Oriented Deliberation in View of the Dogmatic Problem of Hereditary Sin*, trans. Alastair Hannay (London: Penguin Classics, 2014), 75.

[20] Søren Kierkegaard, *Concluding Unscientific Postscript*, trans. David F. Swenson and Walter Lowrie (Princeton: Princeton University Press, 1941), 164.

[21] David A. Steere, ed., *The Supervision of Pastoral Care* (Eugene, OR: Wipf and Stock Publishers, 2002), 15.

[22] David A. Steere, ed., *The Supervision of Pastoral Care* (Eugene, OR: Wipf and Stock Publishers, 2002), 17.

[23] You can watch the film here: https://lasource.vhx.tv/.

[24] St. Martin's University, "Our Patron Saint: Saint Martin Tours," accessed June 26, 2024, https://www.stmartin.edu/news-and-stories/stories/our-patron-saint-saint-martin-tours.

[25] Mary Jean Irion, "Yes, World: A Mosaic of Meditation," in *Yes, World: A Mosaic of Meditation* (New York: Random House, 1993).

[26] Emily Dickinson, "The Mountains Stood in Haze," in T*he Poems of Emily Dickinson: Reading Edition*, ed. R. W. Franklin (Cambridge, MA: The Belknap Press of Harvard University Press, 1999), poem 1278.

[27] "Chris Porter Ugly & Angry," YouTube video, 23:39. Posted by Dry Bar Comedy, February 28, 2018. https://youtu.be/M8mMcdulDHs?t=1419.

[28] *The Holy Bible: New Revised Standard Version* (Nashville: Thomas Nelson Publishers, 1989).

[29] Jim and Janean, "Transforming Faith or Mental Assent," Jim and Janean Blog, July 24, 2020, https://www.jimandjanean.com/home/2020/7/24/transforming-faith-or-mental-assent.

[30] Jack Nicholson, acceptance speech for the AFI Life Achievement Award, 1994, 7:10 of speech, YouTube video, posted by American Film Institute, June 6, 2011, https://youtu.be/LIopcyACbqE?t=430.

[31] Christian Wiman, *My Bright Abyss: Meditation of a Modern Believer* (New York: Farrar, Straus and Giroux, 2013), 51.

[32] Irvin D. Yalom, *Love's Executioner and Other Tales of Psychotherapy* (New York: Basic Books, 2012), xx.

[33] Charles Bukowski, *Factotum* (New York: HarperCollins, 2002).

[34] Joseph Campbell, *Reflections on the Art of Living: A Joseph Campbell Companion* (New York: Harper Perennial, 1995).

[35] Irvin D. Yalom, *Existential Psychotherapy* (New York: Basic Books, 1980), 355.

[36] Irvin D. Yalom, *Existential Psychotherapy* (New York: Basic Books, 1980), 363.

[37] Irvin D. Yalom, *Existential Psychotherapy* (New York: Basic Books, 1980), 363.

[38] Irvin D. Yalom, *Existential Psychotherapy* (New York: Basic Books, 1980), 96.

[39] Aleksandr Solzhenitsyn, *The Gulag Archipelago 1918-1956: An Experiment in Literary Investigation*, trans. Thomas P. Whitney (New York: Harper & Row, 1974).

[40] "G-Ride: The Mike Griffith Story," accessed June 26, 2024, https://www.gridefilm.com/.

[41] Søren Kierkegaard, *Either/Or*, edited and translated by Howard V. Hong and Edna H. Hong (Princeton, NJ: Princeton University Press, 1987).

[42] Venerable Dr. Longyun Shi, email message to author, November 12, 2023.

[43] Venerable Dr. Longyun Shi, email message to author, November 12, 2023.

[44] Russian proverb, "Не говори, что нет спасенья, / Что ты в печалях изнемог: / Чем ночь темней, тем ярче звезды, / Чем глубже скорбь, тем ближе Бог."

[45] Christian Wiman, *My Bright Abyss: Meditation of a Modern Believer* (New York: Farrar, Straus and Giroux, 2013), 8.

[46] Raymond Chandler, *The Long Goodbye*, Project Gutenberg Canada, https://gutenberg.ca/ebooks/chandlerr-longgoodbye/chandlerr-longgoodbye-00-h.html.

Ultimate Concerns Playlists: Scan the QR code to access a curated playlist featuring all the songs referenced in this book—plus additional tracks for reflection on death, freedom/responsibility, isolation, and meaninglessness.

www.keithwakefield.me

www.ingramcontent.com/pod-product-compliance
Lightning Source LLC
Chambersburg PA
CBHW030912120626
46554CB00001B/116